THE HOUR
that changes everything

THE HOUR
that changes everything

America's Role
in Bible Prophecy

RICHARD PEARSON

The Hour that Changes Everything
© 2021 Richard Pearson

ProphecyUSA.org

Published in Brantford, Ont., Canada by Richard Pearson Ministries, Inc.

Published with the assistance of The Wayne Hastings Company, LLC

Titles for this work may be purchased in bulk for educational, business, fundraising, or sales promotional use. For information, please e-mail mail@prophecyusa.org

Unless otherwise noted, Scripture quotations marked KJV are taken from the King James Version of the Bible. Public domain.

Scripture quotations are from The ESV® Bible (The Holy Bible, English Standard Version®), copyright © 2001 by Crossway, a publishing ministry of Good News Publishers. Used by permission. All rights reserved.

Bold emphasis in selected Scripture quotations are the author's.

All web addresses were current as of the writing of this book.

DEDICATION

I want to dedicate this book to the many people who have helped make this ministry a reality.

First, I dedicate this book to my wife, Karen. She has worked laboriously at my side, encouraging me and believing in the revelation that God gave me in 1986 concerning America's role in Bible prophecy.

Second, Rod Hembree, President of Bible Discovery TV, who, under the direction of God's "still small voice," offered to produce Prophecy USA in his studio. He graciously provided staff, equipment, training, and hours of sacrificial work to bring this TV series into being.

Third, this book is dedicated to my technical and production team, Chris Atkins and Chris Held. These two took my vision and communicated it so professionally to our TV and social media audience.

And finally, to Ted Squires and Wayne Hastings, who, together with the BluePrint Agencies team of professionals, helped produce the written literature you are about to read.

Thank you to everyone. This book is not a one-person effort but a team of believers who, through the "unity of our faith," has delivered a "sure word of prophecy" to our generation.

CONTENTS

INTRODUCTION

FOR LACK OF KNOWLEDGE

If I only knew then what I know now.

How many times in life have you thought that? The divorcée whose spouse cheated on them. The stockbroker who lost everything. The businessman who was betrayed by his partners. The investor whose investment went sour. The parents who made a critical mistake in rearing their child. At some time or another, everyone has looked back on their life and wished they could change decisions they've made.

God said in His Word, "my people are destroyed for lack of knowledge" (Hos. 4:6). Whether it's a lack of common sense, spiritual insight, discernment in others, or a lack of careful consideration of the future, a lack of knowledge usually ends in disastrous results. I'm writing this book to help you make certain decisions that you will look back upon in the future and have absolutely no regrets about making. We will go into the past, address the present, and give you insight into what the Bible declares is coming in the future. This knowledge will significantly impact how you look back at your life when you enter eternity.

The Bible is so exact, it states explicitly that it declares "the end from the beginning" (Isa. 46:10). What you refuse to learn on this side of the grave, you will most definitely learn on the other.

WHO IS RICK PEARSON?

Before we go any further, let me tell you who I am and how this book came to be. I was raised in a fundamental Baptist church with a pastor (who held a PhD in theology) who taught that Jesus Christ was God's Son and died for the world's sins. Eternal salvation, he said, came from merely asking God to forgive you of your sins and then following Him in His ways. And if you would acknowledge those tenets and confess them with your mouth, you would experience a radical change in your life and be "born again." Old things would become new, and you would walk in the "light of the knowledge of the glory of God in the face of Jesus Christ" (2 Cor. 4:6). Even at seven years old, I understood this simple Gospel message and swallowed it with childlike faith—hook, line, and sinker.

One evening, upon hearing our church's customary invitation to come forward, I went to the altar and "got saved." My sins were forgiven. I was saved from being a nonbeliever. I would not suffer eternal hell where there would be weeping, wailing, and gnashing of teeth. Instead, because of the sacrificed blood that Jesus shed, my soul was washed of sin and guaranteed to go to heaven, not because of anything I deserved, but as a gift from God. From that point on, all I had to do was stay away from the Baptist church's five cardinal sins: don't drink, don't smoke, don't swear, don't chew, and don't date a girl that do. Of course, those are pretty high standards, so I thought if I could keep three out of five, I should be OK. I won't tell you which ones I failed to follow.

Our little church taught "cessation theology." That is a traditional theology that accepts all the miracles Jesus performed in the Bible "then and there," but teaches that they are no longer available in the "here and now." This theology also refers to the *cessation* of the miraculous gifts the apostle Paul outlined in 1 Corinthians: tongues, interpretation of tongues, miracles, healings, and prophecies (1 Cor. 12:28). Apparently, after the disciples died, God removed His power from its intervention in our present-day lives. Now we're left with the oldest story ever told, and like Ripley's motto, you can either "believe it or not."

By the time I was eighteen, that theology didn't make sense to me. One day, by divine providence, I saw an evangelist on television who was building a university and preaching that God still healed. I thought, "Wow! What a concept. God is the same yesterday, today, and forever."

I was quite impressed when I visited Oral Roberts University (ORU) as a potential student. The buildings and grounds were like nothing I had ever seen. But there was something more than just buildings. The founder, Oral Roberts, claimed that God had told him to "build Me a University" and "raise up your students to hear My voice."[1]

Wait a minute. This university will teach you how to hear God's voice? You mean God actually talks to people? The Bible is not the only way God communicates? You're telling me He still does miracles? What a mind boggler. Was this stuff real or was it a con job? I wasn't sure, but I knew the ministry was doing well financially—you cannot build buildings and grounds like that without substantial finances.

LIKE A MIGHTY RUSHING WIND

I wondered if God actually performed miracles and if He spoke to people as He did in the Bible. If that were the case, then I wanted to know. I wanted to be like the disciples in the Bible. I wanted to see and experience what they had experienced. One week later, I decided to make a solemn vow.

I was in an apartment in Florida vacationing with my cousin Bill, and I told him I wanted to pray. He agreed, as he was also searching for guidance in his life. In that prayer, we got on our knees, and I made a vow to God. I told him I would go into any jungle, any nation, any place he would send me, and do whatever He told me to do if He would show me that He was real. I was tired of fairy tales and theology that didn't make sense. I deeply desired the genuine thing. I wanted to *know*.

Upon releasing that vow, the apartment's front door blew open, and a wind entered the room and circled us like a whirlwind. I looked at my cousin. He looked at me. And then both of us buried our faces into the carpet. I confessed every sin I could think of, as this presence surrounded us.

As I confessed my sins to God, my words became slurred, and I started speaking in another language. What on earth was happening to me? Speaking this new language went on for about ten minutes. Finally, I put my hand up and said, "God I don't know what's going on but please stop the wind. I can't handle any more of this. I'm yours. But please stop the wind." Immediately, the wind went out of the door, and the door slammed shut behind it. I felt as light as a feather. What on earth had just happened?

According to *Harpers Bible Dictionary*, whirlwinds and storms usually accompanied a theophany, such as God's appearance to Job (Job 38:1; 40:6) and Ezekiel's vision of God (Ezek. 1:4; cf. Nah. 1:3; Zech. 9:14). According to 2 Kings 2:1–12, the prophet Elijah did not die, but a whirlwind, accompanied by chariots and horses of fire, carried him up to heaven.[2]

In 650 BC, God told Jeremiah:

> *For who hath stood in the counsel of the LORD, and hath*
> *perceived and heard his word? who hath marked his word, and*
> *heard it? Behold, a whirlwind of the LORD is gone forth in fury,*
> *even a grievous whirlwind: it shall fall grievously upon the head*
> *of the wicked. The anger of the LORD shall not return, until he*
> *have executed, and till he have performed the thoughts of his*

heart: in the latter days ye shall consider it perfectly. I have not
sent these prophets, yet they ran: I have not spoken to them,
yet they prophesied. But if they had stood in my counsel, and
had caused my people to hear my words, then they should have
turned them from their evil way, and from the evil of
their doings. (Jer. 23:18–22)

Several days after this experience, I was shown Acts 2:1–4, which says:

And when the day of Pentecost was fully come, they [the disciples]
were all with one accord in one place. And suddenly there came a
sound from heaven as of a rushing mighty wind, and it filled all
the house where they were sitting. And there appeared unto them
cloven tongues like as of fire, and it sat upon each of them. And
they were all filled with the Holy Ghost, and began to speak with
other tongues, as the Spirit gave them utterance.

Wow! What happened to the disciples is almost precisely what happened to me and my cousin, except I did not see any fire. God heard my prayer, and He responded. But now what? What was I supposed to do?

I felt I needed to tell others about what had happened. Surely everyone would like to know that God is real. Upon my return home, I shared my story with everyone in my high school. To my dismay, people laughed at me. My high school teachers, many of whom were secular humanists,[3] mocked me and said, "Just because a door blows open doesn't mean that God is involved, Rick."

Well, of course they wouldn't understand. They were not believers. Then I went and told my Christian friends. But they, too, told me this was wrong. They said that God did not do that sort of thing anymore, and that demons had deceived me. They said speaking in another language meant I had demons in me.

At the time, that idea was not very comforting. However, to calm my nerves and seek the truth, I turned to the "Book of Truth" and found this Scripture:

> *If a son shall ask bread of any of you that is a father, will he give him a stone? or if he ask a fish, will he for a fish give him a serpent? Or if he shall ask an egg, will he offer him a scorpion? If ye then, being evil, know how to give good gifts unto your children: how much more shall your heavenly Father give the Holy Spirit to them that ask him? (Luke 11:11–13).*

In this Scripture, Jesus taught that if a person calls on God, there is no way God will let evil intervene. Although my friends' traditional theology told me different, God's Word promised protection from evil.

This verse gave me hope that what I'd experienced in Florida was real and had nothing to do with being possessed. People's response to my story (both Christians and non-Christians) was a matter of their frame of reference. Their reactions made me realize that everyone has their own personal theology.

Theo, in Greek, means "God," and *ology* means "knowledge." Everyone has their own "knowledge of God" (theology). But unless God's Word is the foundation of their theology, it's just their individual opinions.

Even an atheist has a theology. People replace God with what they consider human reasoning and science, based, of course, upon their seemingly unlimited, all-knowing intellectual trinity of "me, myself, and I." The bottom line is that no matter how much you know, how much you study, how intellectual you appear to be, there is always more to learn. God is omniscient (all-knowing), and the Bible says, "The secret things belong unto the LORD our God: but those things which are revealed belong unto us and to our children for ever, that we may do all the words of this law" (Deut. 29:29).

WHERE DO YOU WANT ME TO GO?

I enrolled at Oral Roberts University (ORU) within a year of this experience. By 1977, I had graduated with an undergraduate business degree and a fully endorsed commercial pilot's license. I had built up my flying time by flying Oral Roberts' associate evangelists to various speaking engagements and flying missions teams to Haiti and Jamaica. Although I planned to stay in Tulsa and fly missions with a missionary company based there, God had other plans for me. After being refused a work visa, I received a letter from the US government telling me I had thirty days to exit the country. There were too many unemployed pilots during that time, and the government decided they did not need any Canadians to take those jobs.

Reluctantly, I drove home to Canada and joined my father and brother in the business of distributing Blue Bird school buses in the Canadian province of Ontario. It was the last job in the world I wanted to do and the last place on earth I wanted to live.

We lived in a little town (population 3,000) on what seemed to be the edge of the planet, where the average age was "deceased." It was quite a culture shock from living for four years in a state-of-the-art university populated by enthusiastic students who were taught to dream big. At the time, I thought this was what John must have felt like when he was banished to the Isle of Patmos.[4] However, somehow I knew this was what God was directing me to do. But how could this possibly be the answer to my vow only five years earlier?

My first job was to sweep and clean a couple of hundred school buses to prepare them for customer delivery. From piloting aircraft, sweeping out buses was quite a letdown. However, my vow was to do whatever God told me. As I swept out buses, a famous sermon called "The Fourth Man" came to mind. It was a sermon about how God uses inanimate objects to release people's faith. From Abraham's ram to Isaac's wells, Jacob's scepter to Moses's rod. From Gideon's fleece to Samuel's horn of oil, David's slingshot to Hezekiah's sundial, God used ordinary "points of contact" to do extraordinary miracles in people's lives. But unless they acted in obedience, the miracles never came. In the flash of a moment, I realized this was just a test. I discovered in Scripture that serving God means serving man, especially those you work for and with (Col. 3:22–24):

> Servants, obey in all things your masters according to the flesh;
> not with eyeservice, as menpleasers; but in singleness of heart,
> fearing God; and whatsoever ye do, do it heartily, as to the Lord,
> and not unto men; knowing that of the Lord ye shall receive the
> reward of the inheritance: for ye serve the Lord Christ.

I surmised from this discovery that if I obeyed God in the simplest of things, He might be pleased with my obedience and deliver me from this job and the location of its misery. It would only be a matter of time, I thought. But I had no idea that God's timing is not my timing.

A RENEWED VISION

Nine years later, Charles Harris, my alma mater's regional representative, called me. The university was looking for board members and wondered if I would be interested in serving. Within a week, I was on a plane heading to Tulsa to attend a meeting.

The university was initiating a medical missions program and was in desperate need of money. A conviction came all over me. In my nine years of working, I had grown weary of "well doing" (Gal. 6:9). I wasn't tithing a tenth of my income and was not interested in serving God all that much. I directed all my energy into making money. Now, I was associating once again with people totally sold out to serving God, just as I used to be. I was doing well in business, was living a clean life, but not one of pure dedication. I looked at my savings account and asked God what I should contribute. The amount given to me was ten percent of my net worth. I reluctantly obeyed and sent the missions project my financial "seed of faith." From that moment on, something happened to me, something very similar to Cornelius's experience in Acts 10:

> He [Cornelius] saw in a vision evidently about the ninth hour of the day an angel of God coming in to him, and saying unto him, Cornelius. And when he looked on him, he was afraid, and said, What is it, Lord? And he said unto him, Thy prayers and thine alms are come up for a memorial before God (Acts 10:3–4).

Cornelius was instructed to go and see Peter, who eventually explained the story of the Gospel, and Cornelius became the first Gentile in Scripture to be grafted into the vine of the Jewish faith and become a follower of Jesus. This significant moment marked the beginning of Gentiles coming to the Jewish rabbi Jesus to receive salvation, "for salvation is of the Jews" (John 4:22).

However, in my case, the visitation that lasted seven days was not about salvation. It was about America's role in Bible prophecy. This vision, or dream, involved a war in the Middle East that would drastically affect America. It was about the falling away of America and her covenant with God. It was about ancient Babylonian spirits that were invading this country. It concerned Russia and what they were going to do to both Israel and America in the days to come. And it was about a revival that would sweep the nation before her judgment.

I had no idea all these things were in the Bible. My experience was similar to King Nebuchadnezzar's prophetic dream of 603 BC, and "made me afraid, and the thoughts upon my bed and the visions of my head troubled me (Dan. 4:5)."

The prophet Daniel had dreams as well. After one of his dreams, he explained, "And I Daniel alone saw the vision: for the men that were with me saw not the vision; but a great quaking fell upon them, so that they fled to hide themselves. Therefore I was left alone, and saw this great vision, and there remained no strength in me: for my comeliness was turned in me into corruption, and I retained no strength (Dan. 10:7–8)." When another Old Testament prophet, Ezekiel, received his vision concerning things to come, he stated, "And when I saw it, I fell upon my face, and I heard a voice of one that spake (Ezek. 1:28)." Perhaps this all seems somewhat sensationalized to you, but I can assure you, these men were speaking the truth.

Several weeks after receiving the revelation you are about to read, I flew to Tulsa, Oklahoma, to seek spiritual guidance from Oral Roberts. The experience I had, accompanied by the revelation God gave me, left me awestruck. My head troubled me, fear overwhelmed me, and I had no understanding of what I was shown. After placing his right hand on my head, Oral Roberts emphatically stated, "You have definitely heard from God, son. This is the Holy Spirit, and you are very close to your calling right now. If this were demonic, the Lord would have shown me."

For the next twenty-one years, I served on the university's Board of Regents, primarily on the seven-member executive board. In this capacity, I traveled on multiple medical missions and evangelistic crusades throughout the world. The good news is, I am no longer afraid, and I have no doubt whatsoever that what you are about to learn in this book is a God-given prophetic interpretation of Scripture, straight from His heart. I encourage you to listen for His Spirit as you read this book.

THE MOST HIDDEN SECRETS ARE THOSE OF THE FUTURE
Who but God knows what is coming in the future?

> *Howbeit when he, the Spirit of truth, is come, he will guide*
> *you into all truth: for he shall not speak of himself; but*
> *whatsoever he shall hear, that shall he speak: and he will shew*
> *you things to come (John 16:13).*

I have shared with you some of my testimony of how my quest for God began. But there is much more that I will share as we journey into the future of Bible prophecy. For those of you who have studied traditional prophecy, I must warn you. Secrets from Scripture are going to be revealed that have never been taught in any other generation. They will contradict what you have been taught. Why is that? Because no other generation has ever experienced what we are getting ready to experience.

The prophet Amos said, "Surely the Lord GOD will do nothing, but he revealeth his secret unto his servants the prophets" (Amos 3:7). God has revealed this prophecy to me. I understand that what you read here about America's major role in Bible prophecy will be challenged by the same traditional theology that tells you God no longer does miracles or performs in us other gifts of the Spirit. My only response to my dear cessation theology brethren is the words spoken by Jesus two thousand years ago when he said, "let the dead bury their dead" (Matt. 8:22).

In 630 BC, God instructed Jeremiah to "to root out, and to pull down, and to destroy" what men of his generation were teaching concerning the future of Judah (Jer. 1:10). God called Jeremiah from the womb. He was touched by an angel and was spoken to audibly by God. We will quote other prophets who had similar experiences: one-of-a-kind, individualized, and specifically designed for their character and personality.

If I had not had an experience similar to that of Jeremiah, Ezekiel, Daniel, and Isaiah, I would never have the courage to write this book, go on television, nor deliver this message. But this prophetic insight cannot be based on my personal experiences. It must be founded on the Word of God, which confirms the revelation you are about to read. How a person receives their revelation, even if it sounds sensational, should never replace or supersede God's written Word.

God is real. He is speaking, and He is in total control of world events. If you just whisper the name of Jesus, He has promised that he will answer. He is omnipresent (everywhere), He is omniscient (all-knowing), and He is closer to you than your breath. You don't need someone to tell you what God is saying. You only need a Bible in your hand, a sincere hungering for Him, and ears willing to listen for His voice. So welcome aboard—you are about to have your eyes radically opened!

CHAPTER ONE

THE STILL, SMALL VOICE

IN OUR EVER-CHANGING North American society, many people have wondered, "What in the world is going on?" But have you ever considered asking, "What in the *Word* is going on? The answer can be found in the writings of the prophets.

> *Raise your students up to hear My voice, to go where My light is dim, My voice is heard small, where My healing power is not known, even to the uttermost bounds of the earth. Their work will exceed yours and in this I am much pleased.*[1]

These words, mandated by God to one of America's most controversial twenty-first-century evangelists, the late Oral Roberts, have echoed throughout the ages in some form or another to every generation of peoples around the globe.

TO HEAR GOD'S VOICE?

From the forty authors who penned the Scriptures over a 1,500-year period to the 2.5 billion Christians today who claim to have a personal relationship with Jesus Christ, the fact or delusion that God speaks to people is a topic of debate that has never stopped since the creation of man. Being a graduate of Oral Roberts University and having been a member of its Executive Board of Regents for over twenty years has given me a reflective view of this mandate God gave to the university's founder.

To hear God's voice? To call out to Him, and for Him, the Creator of the Universe, to respond to us on an individual basis is absolutely awesome. But the biggest question that I have queried in life thus far is not whether God is speaking. The biggest question is, who is listening? Who is hearing, and who is repeating the words that come from the mouth of God today?

> *The secret things belong unto the LORD our God: but those things*
> *which are revealed belong unto us and to our children for ever,*
> *that we may do all the words of this law. (Deut. 29:29).*

The Old Testament prophets were some of the most provocative people who ever lived. Many of the biblical prophets were the most misunderstood and eccentric spiritual activists of their generation. What was their purpose, and why is it so essential for us to study them and the prophecies they gave as far back as 2,800 years ago? The answers to these questions rest in the fact that these individuals heard God's voice and spoke it, as they frequently foretold future events. Some of the prophecies they proclaimed have already come to pass. Others, however, are being fulfilled in our generation—right under our noses.

Before we look to the prophetic future, we need to take a journey into history and review the foundational structure of the callings, purpose, and fascinating lifestyles of these heroes of the faith.

The first person to be given the title of "prophet" in the Hebrew Scriptures was Abraham, or Abram.[2] In Genesis 20:3–7, God spoke to

Abimelech, king of Gerar, in a dream. He warns him about a woman (Sarai) whom he has taken as his wife, but who is already married to "a prophet" named Abram.

The Hebrew word used for "prophet" in this passage is *nābî*. The word "prophet" is repeated more than 320 times in the Old Testament and 160 times in the Greek (*prophētēs*) New Testament. The Hebrew word *nābî*, or "prophet," is defined as: "an inspired teacher or proclaimer of the will of God; a person who predicts (or forth tells) the future."[3] Warren Wiersbe wrote, "They were primarily *forth-tellers* who declared God's Word to the people. Sometimes they gave a message of judgment, but it was usually followed by a message of hope and forgiveness."[4]

INAUGURATION OF THE PROPHETIC MINISTRY

For four hundred years, Abraham's descendants (Gen. 15:13; Acts 7:6) found themselves under the pharaoh's authoritarian rule, and then, for nearly 125 years, the servanthood of slavery to the Egyptians. Living in "a land that is not theirs" fulfilled the word the Lord had spoken to Abram (Gen. 15:13–16). During this time, God raised up one of Israel's most famous prophets, Moses (Ex. 3).

After Israel's miraculous exodus from Egypt through Moses' leadership, the prophet's official inauguration was showcased at Mt. Horeb. It was here that, for the first and only time in Scripture, God spoke audibly (Deut.18:16) to two million Children of Israel. However, due to the people's fearful response, asking God not to speak directly to them again, "lest we die," God inaugurated the office of prophet for the remainder of humanity as we know it. The Lord promised to raise up prophets like Moses from that time forward and to put His "words in his mouth; and he shall speak unto them all that I shall command him" (Deut. 18:18).

Thus the words spoken by God to the prophets were identified as "the Hebrew word, *galah*, "to uncover,"[5] or the Greek word *apokalupsis* "reveal or to unveil,"[6] . . . from which we get the English word "revelation." Since then, the Lord has equipped his prophets with a *divine disclosure* or *spoken word* as it relates to nations, future events, or personal direction.

"For the Lord GOD does nothing without revealing His secret to His servants the prophets" (Amos 3:7 ESV). It is fascinating that Scripture also laid down strict guidelines for how these prophets were to inquire of the Lord and hear His voice.

Matthew 22:14 states, "For many are called, but few are chosen (ESV)." Though many are called in the prophet's world, they are often reluctantly "drafted" into the prophetic ministry. Abraham Heschel, a prominent Jewish theologian, stated that prophets "must have been shattered by some cataclysmic experience in order to shatter others."[7] Frequently, these common men were not seeking to hear from God; instead, God manifested Himself to them in ways so dramatic they were compelled to deliver His "sure word of prophecy" to His people (2 Pet. 1:19). They were ordinary people like you and me who had a supernatural experience with an extraordinary God—the Great I Am.

The Hebrew word *massa* means "load" or "burden."[8] Most significantly, it was used in the Old Testament to describe the message the Lord laid upon His servants, the prophets. God directed the "messages" or "burdens" the prophets received toward both nations (Isa. 13:1; 14:1; Dan. 7:17; Jer. 1:5) and individuals (2 Sam. 7:4–5; 12:5; 1 Kings 13:21). Many prophets became overwhelmed because of the weight (or seriousness) of the word given to them. Prophets were often called to deliver a message that the people did not want to hear. However, the success of a prophet's ministry was not based on what the people wanted to hear, but instead on what the Lord wanted to say. In other words, prophets perform for an audience of One.

WHO WERE THESE MEN OF GOD?

Before we go too far, we need to know a bit about these prophets, who carried such an enormous burden. Let me introduce you to four of them:

ISAIAH (739 BC–680 BC)[9]

Isaiah was a prophet in the eight century BC, during the reigns of the Judean kings Uzziah, Jotham, Ahaz, and Hezekiah. Inspired by God, he wrote the Book of Isaiah. He was the son of Amoz (Isa. 1:1), and many believe he was King Amaziah's brother. Isaiah grew up in Jerusalem and was well educated. He became a political and religious counselor of the nation. He had contact with the monarchs and seemed to have been the Judean court's historiographer for several reigns (2 Chr. 26:22; 32:32).

A seraph brought a message to Isaiah regarding his call. A seraph is a six-winged angel; they are mentioned several times in Scripture. Isaiah felt unworthy to speak God's Word because he was a man of "unclean lips." (Isa. 6:5–9). However, the angel took a coal from off God's altar and physically touched it to Isaiah's mouth.

Never before or after has anyone been called exactly like Isaiah was called.

"Isaiah worked to reform social and political wrongs. Even the highest members of society did not escape his censure. He berated soothsayers and denounced wealthy, influential people who ignored the responsibilities of their position. He exhorted the masses to be obedient rather than indifferent to God's covenant. He rebuked kings for their willfulness and lack of concern."[10]

God's message to Isaiah reflected a heartfelt theme of holiness and God's majesty. He wrote against idolatry as well as the people's insincere approach to God. He often prophesied about impending judgment on the idolatrous Judeans:

Then I said, "How long, O Lord?" And he said: "Until cities
lie waste without inhabitant, and houses without people, and
the land is a desolate waste, and the LORD removes people far
away, and the forsaken places are many in the midst of the land.
And though a tenth remain in it, it will be burned again, like a
terebinth or an oak, whose stump remains when it is felled." The
holy seed is its stump (Isa. 6:11–13 ESV).

Isaiah was warning the people, as he knew their doom—their judgment—was sealed.

Isaiah "forth-told" the coming of the Messiah, the "peaceful prince," and the ruler of God's kingdom (11:1–11). He described the Messiah as a suffering, obedient servant (53:3–12). He prophesied the destruction of multiple nations within his generation that fell to God's judgment.

Isaiah's death came at the hands of cruel and hateful family members. According to the Jewish Midrash,[11] he was swallowed by a cedar tree and sawed through at the command of his grandson, King Manasseh.[12] But before his death took place, Isaiah prophesied about a great nation that would rise up in the last days. It would be the wealthiest, most powerful nation known to mankind and a nation that would fall out of covenant with God and be deposed in one day by weapons of warfare unknown at the times of his prophecy.

JEREMIAH (627 BC–586 BC)

Often called "the weeping prophet," Jeremiah was born in the village of Anathoth, about three miles northeast of Jerusalem. His father's name was Hilkiah, and he belonged to the tribe of Benjamin. His call came in the thirteenth year of King Josiah (640–609 BC).[13] In Jer. 1:4–5, God told Jeremiah:

Before I formed thee in the belly I knew thee; and before thou
camest forth out of the womb I sanctified thee, and I ordained
thee a prophet unto the nations . . . Then the LORD put forth
his hand, and touched my mouth. And the LORD said unto me,
Behold, I have put my words in thy mouth. See, I have this day
set thee over the nations and over the kingdoms, to root out, and
to pull down, and to destroy, and to throw down, to build, and
to plant (Jer. 1:5, 9–10).

The Lord, or an angel of the Lord, appeared to Jeremiah and called him to the task of speaking God's Word. Jeremiah was used to dramatically proclaim Israel's judgment by the nation of Babylon. He was instructed by God to "make bonds and yokes and put them upon thy neck" (Jer. 27:2). This sign was an object lesson for Israel and neighboring countries to warn that they were coming under the yoke of the Babylonians. Can you imagine being in the leadership of Israel and seeing this prophet walking around with a yoke on his neck?

The other prophets of that day denounced Jeremiah and proclaimed that Israel would defeat this enemy Babylon. Hananiah, after declaring such a prophecy, was rebuked by Jeremiah and died eight weeks later (Jer. 28:16). The Lord told Jeremiah,

Hearken not unto the words of the prophets that prophesy
unto you: they make you vain: they speak a vision of their own
heart, and not out of the mouth of the Lord . . . I have not sent
these prophets, yet they ran: I have not spoken to them, yet they
prophesied. But if they had stood in my counsel, and had caused
my people to hear my words, then they should have turned
them from their evil way, and from the evil of their doings
(Jer. 23:16, 21–22).

Only after the fall of Jerusalem did the people realize this man with the yoke around his neck carried God's "sure word" of prophecy to their nation. However, one hundred years after Isaiah, Jeremiah also prophesied about the seventh great providential nation that God will raise up in the latter days before the Messiah comes.

DANIEL (604 BC–535 BC)

Daniel was a celebrated Jewish scholar and master interpreter of dreams. As a youth, he was exiled to Babylon by the Babylonians after the Holy Temple's destruction in Jerusalem. He is famous for successfully interpreting the proverbial "writing on the wall," which led to the deposing of historical Babylon and his miraculous survival in the lions' den.

The book of Daniel is a narrative woven with mystery and prophecy, containing cryptic descriptions of future events, the mystical interpretation of dreams, profound visions about the coming Messiah, and the revival of the dead at the end of days. Many of his experiences with God and with angels left Daniel distraught and confused. God told him to "shut up the words, and seal the book, even to the time of the end . . . none of the wicked shall understand; but the wise shall understand" (Dan. 12:4, 10). Perhaps Daniel's most significant contribution was his interpretation of King Nebuchadnezzar's infamous dream, which laid out the past, present, and future of eight providential nations that God would raise up throughout history. Like Isaiah and Jeremiah, we also find hints from Daniel of the latter-day country of Babylon the Great (a nation that will precede the last and final empire on the earth). His writings are the primary source used by many Jewish and Christian scholars for calculating the approximate date of the future redemption.

Daniel displayed genuine self-sacrifice and unyielding faith in the face of immense adversity. He held on to his beliefs and religious practices despite the isolation of exile and the spiritual darkness surrounding him. Daniel served as a shining example of genuine devotion to God.[14]

EZEKIEL (650 BC–CA. 565–570 BC)

Known as one of the four greater prophets, Ezekiel was the son of a priest named Buzi. He was taken captive in the first Babylonian captivity of Jehoiachin, eleven years before Jerusalem's destruction. As a contemporary of Daniel, he was a member of a community of Jewish exiles who settled on the banks of the Chebar, a river or stream of Babylonia. He began prophesying in 595 BC and continued until 570 BC, a period of more than twenty-two years. In addition to Daniel's futuristic providential nations that would rise and fall, Ezekiel adds nations that will attack Israel in the latter days, including the most powerful country in that generation. This war has not yet happened, but we will discuss the specific details in future chapters.

Ezekiel was called through a vision of God while he was standing by the rivers of Chebar in Babylon. Ezekiel 2 records that the Spirit of God spoke to him audibly and then entered into Ezekiel and set him upon his feet.

While prophets often died before they saw the fulfillment of the prophetic words they delivered, many of Ezekiel's prophecies came to pass during his lifetime. The prophecies regarding the geographical region of the earth known today as Russia, however, remain unfulfilled. We will study these prophecies in the following chapters. We may be the generation to see those words fulfilled before our very eyes.

The time and manner of Ezekiel's death are unknown. His reputed tomb is located in the neighborhood of Baghdad, at a place called Keffil.[15] He may have been murdered in Babylon.

THE METHOD OF GOD SPEAKING

Throughout Scripture, we find four specific ways in which God communicated with His prophets:

- Visions
- Dreams
- Direct revelation (i.e., audible voice) (Num. 12:4, 6–8)
- The written (*logos*) Word of God

Visions and dreams are part of both the New and Old Testaments as well as the ancient world:

> *Belief in the reality and significance of dreams and visions was widespread in ancient times. The people of the Greco-Roman world believed that dreams and visions were ways of receiving divine messages, prophecy, and healing.*[16]

WHAT IS A VISION?

A prophetic vision from God occurs when a person is wide awake. Human endeavor cannot initiate visions; neither can they be induced by drugs or potions. Visions from God are created solely by the work of the Holy Spirit. He and He alone is the giver and interpreter of all godly visions. Communications by vision are referenced nearly ninety times in the Old Testament[17] and twenty times in the New Testament.

WHAT IS A DREAM?

Distinct from visions, dreams occur when one is asleep. The Bible teaches that God made man of body, soul, and spirit, and that God, who is the Father of spirits "will neither slumber nor sleep" (Ps. 121:4 ESV). He can speak to us through dreams even while our bodies sleep and our souls are at rest—nothing is impossible with God. When He desires to speak to an individual, there is no place to hide, as many of the prophets reluctantly experienced.[18]

As a young man, Joseph had dreams. God gave him a clear picture of his future, and his remembrance of the dreams God gave kept him going during his times of testing (Gen. 37–50).

WHAT IS DIRECT REVELATION?

Direct revelation is hearing the audible voice of God. Abraham experienced a direct revelation when God told him to leave his homeland (Ur) and go to a land God would show him. In front of the burning bush and on top of Mt. Sinai, Moses clearly heard God's voice. Of course, Jesus heard directly from His Father, and "the gospel Paul preached and taught was neither a human invention nor a human tradition, but was given to him directly by God **through a revelation of Jesus Christ. Revelation** is from *apokalupsis* and means an unveiling of something previously secret."[19]

Christians cannot afford to bury their head in the sand. We must carefully and prayerfully read and study the God's Word and be open to fresh revelation from within its pages.

WHAT IS THE WRITTEN WORD?

This divine communication is probably the most obvious. I don't know about you, but I often find that when I read the Bible, something—a new understanding or a new direction for me—leaps out. Proverbs 22:17–19 (ESV) reminds us:

> *Incline your ear, and hear the words of the wise, and apply your heart to my knowledge, for it will be pleasant if you keep them within you, if all of them are ready on your lips. That your trust may be in the LORD, I have made them known to you today, even to you.*

God's Word reveals so much—pleasure, knowledge, inspiration, trust, promise, and faith. And we have His written Word so accessible today.

WHAT ABOUT SIGNS AND WONDERS?

Besides the four methods defined above, the Old Testament often utilized symbols. These acts were "signs and wonders" given to God's prophets to get the message across to the people. A dramatic display would emphasize God's power, the source of the word that was coming forth.

In Isaiah 20:2, the prophet was instructed to "loose the sackcloth from off thy loins." He was to walk naked and barefoot for three years, wearing only a loincloth. This odd instruction was a prophetic sign of the fall of Egypt to the nation of Syria.

Almost one hundred years later, God told Jeremiah to take a fine linen cloth and bury it. He was to then dig it up after several days and wear it as a sign to Israel that her sins had made her filthy in the eyes of the Lord. As I wrote above, under the kingship of Jehoiakim, Jeremiah was told to "make thee bonds and yokes, and put them upon thy neck" (Jer. 27:2) to forth-tell the coming Babylonian captivity. This form of "enactment prophecy" delivered the word of warning to three ruling kings of Judah spanning a period of twenty-two years. Babylon ransacked the nation in 586 BC and "slew the sons of King Zedekiah before his eyes, and put out the eyes of Zedekiah, and bound him with fetters of brass, and carried him to Babylon (2 Kings 25:7)."

God used these and other signs through the prophets as personal illustrations or spectacles, drawing people's attention to the delivered word. When they saw the sign, they wondered. The sign caused them to stop and think about what they were seeing and hearing. And those signs did not stop with just a few prophets. Many people received signs throughout the Bible, and a specific sign was never repeated. Signs were uniquely designed as a personal, one-of-a-kind enactment, specifically delivered within each generation. As we discussed previously, from generation to generation, God has given signs to draw attention to His message.

In the New Testament, Paul used handkerchiefs and aprons (Acts 19:12) to transfer the healing anointing. Even the passing of Peter's shadow (Acts 5:15) brought deliverance to the people. These signs were significant contact points that God used for people and his servants to release their faith unto God. Strange, unusual, and beyond man's rationale, God's ways are higher than our ways, and His thoughts are higher than our thoughts. Working through the prophet's obedience and personal humility, God made sure that no flesh would glory in His sight as they delivered His miraculous, "sure word" (2 Pet. 1:19–21) of prophecy to the people.

JESUS IN PROPHECY

Jesus said in Matthew 5:17, "Think not that I am come to destroy the law, or the prophets: I am not come to destroy, but to fulfill." Not only did Jesus come to fulfill the word of ancient prophecy, He *was* the Word of ancient prophecy: throughout His life, many scholars believe that more than three hundred prophecies came to pass.[20]

It was written that He would come to us as a human (Gen. 3:15), be born of a virgin (Isa. 7:14), and a descendant of Abraham, Isaac, and Jacob, from the tribe of Judah (Gen. 22:18). He would appear after the time of Babylonian captivity and Jerusalem's rebuilding (Dan. 9:25). He would be born in a town called Bethlehem (Mic. 5:2) and be called out of Egypt, where his father Joseph had taken him (Hos. 11:1). He would be a light unto the Gentiles in Galilee (Isa. 9:1–2). A forerunner (John the Baptist) would precede His ministry (Isa. 40:3–4). He would teach in parables (Ps. 78:2), and miracles, signs, and wonders would confirm His Word (Isa. 35:4–6). He would be humble and meek (Isa. 42:2–3) and ride into Jerusalem on a donkey (Zech. 9:9). He would be called the Son of God (Isa. 9:6–7) by those who followed Him, yet be rejected by those who mocked Him (Isa. 53:1–4; Dan. 9:24–26) and despised by those who opposed him (Ps. 2:1–12).

Over the three days of His trial, crucifixion, and resurrection, Jesus Christ of Nazareth fulfilled over thirty ancient prophecies.[21] The odds of one man fulfilling this many prophecies are less than one in one trillion.[22]

Isaiah 53, written 750 years before the birth of Christ, perfectly describes Jesus and what He came to do. Jesus established a whole new communication system, or relationship, between God and people. We no longer need a prophet in order to hear God's voice.

Jesus said, "Behold, I stand at the door and knock. If any man hears my voice and opens the door [to his heart], I will come in to him and will eat [communicate] with him, and he with me" (Rev. 3:20 ESV). God still has prophets, but the good news is that no man can stand between you and God. Jesus is now our Prophet and High Priest (Heb. 3:1). And, as 1 Peter 2:5–9 reminds us, we are both a holy and royal priesthood. We have Jesus as our High Priest, and we are priests as well. We don't need any mediator. You can call out to Him directly, and He will answer you. Bible teacher Wayne Grudem wrote, "There can no longer be an elite priesthood with claims of special access to God, or special privileges in worship or in fellowship with God."[23] Psychologists may refer to that communication as a conscience, but the prophets called it His "still, small voice" (1 Kings 19:12).

The fulfillment of ancient biblical prophecy continues today. God promised us that in the last days young men will see visions and old men will dream dreams (Joel 2:28; Acts 2:17). God still speaks to us; He is getting ready to fulfill prophecies for the last days, which will come in rapid succession. Nations of the world are lining up, waiting for their appointed time to fulfill His Word.

However, according to Scripture, we in North America are about to be rudely awakened, as we play a significant role in biblical prophecy. We live in a secular society that refuses to acknowledge God's existence. Yet He is at the same time fulfilling ancient prophecies precisely as He spoke them. In a divided nation where "the heathen rage, and the people imagine a vain thing" (Ps. 2:1), God is still speaking through prophecy to those who "have ears to hear" (Mark 4:23). He is about to raise up a shout against those who oppose His Word, showing the world that "there is none [no god] like me, declaring the end from the beginning and from ancient times things not yet done . . . I have spoken, and I will bring it to pass; I have purposed it, and I will also do it" (Isa. 46:9–11).

In 850 BC, the prophet Elijah desperately sought to hear God's voice. He had called fire down on Mount Horeb, proving to the Baal worshippers that the God of Israel was the Most High God. After cutting off the heads of 450 priests of Baal, he received word from Queen Jezebel, "So let the gods do *to me*, and more also, if I make not thy life as the life of one of them by tomorrow about this time" (1 Kings 19:2). Elijah was now running for his life. He was desperate. He was hurting and thought that he was alone. He needed to hear from God. It was on a lonely mountainside hiding in a cave that Elijah discovered what a remnant in every generation has found:

> *And, behold, the Lord passed by, and a great and strong wind*
> *rent the mountains, and brake in pieces the rocks before the*
> *Lord; but the Lord was not in the wind: and after the wind*
> *an earthquake; but the Lord was not in the earthquake: And*
> *after the earthquake a fire; but the Lord was not in the fire:*
> *and after the fire **a still small voice**. And it was so, when Elijah*
> *heard it, that he wrapped his face in his mantle, and went out,*
> *and stood in the entering in of the cave. And, behold, there*
> *came a voice unto him, and said, What doest thou here, Elijah?*
> *(1 Kings 19:11–13).*

So I ask that you open your mind and consider, "What are we doing here?" Can we learn from the past, meditate on the present, and listen for that still, small voice of what God's Word has foretold is coming in the future?

God promised Daniel that in the latter days, "the wise shall understand" (Dan. 12:10). He told Habakkuk, "for the vision is yet for an appointed time . . . wait for it" (Hab. 2:3). And when that God-given vision or prophetic word comes to fruition, God emphatically promised Jeremiah, "For I know the thoughts that I think toward you, saith the LORD, thoughts of peace, and not of evil, to give you an expected end" (Jer. 29:11). Listen carefully. The Ancient of Days is about to speak directly to your heart as we begin our journey to unveil the hidden mystery of America's role in Bible prophecy.

CHAPTER TWO

PROVIDENTIAL NATIONS

SIX HAVE FALLEN, TWO MUST RISE

FOR YEARS, TRADITIONAL prophecy teachers have questioned whether America is in the Bible. The word "providential" describes a nation or person raised up by divine utterance or mandate. The prophet Daniel wrote, "Blessed be the name of God forever and ever . . . He changeth the times and seasons; he removeth kings, and setteth up kings" (Dan. 2:20–21).

In the first chapter of this book, we learned that prophets like Daniel were called to "go forth and tell" whatever the Lord spoke to them. In other words, they were "forth-tellers" of things to come. As we study their prophecies, we need to keep in mind that any nation they spoke of before it appeared is a providential nation raised up by God's divine utterance.

The prophet Isaiah wrote in Isaiah 46:9–11 (ESV):

I am God, and there is none like me, declaring the end from the beginning and from ancient times things not yet done,

saying, My counsel shall stand, and I will accomplish all my
purpose,' calling a bird of prey from the east, the man of my
*counsel from a far country. **I have spoken, and I will bring it to***
pass; I have purposed, and I will do it.

The prophet Amos wrote, "For the LORD **God does nothing without revealing his secret** to his servants the prophets" (Amos 3:7 ESV).

The Lord reveals His secrets to the prophets, and what He reveals, He will bring to pass. If He gives the prophet insight into the coming Messiah, they "forth-tell" it, and God brings it to pass. If He reveals His secrets about providential nations, we can be assured He purposed it and will bring those nations to pass. God never breaks His promises (Ps. 89:33–35; Heb. 6:18–20).

Psalm 33:9 reminds us that God's utterances created a universe out of nothing. God created the universe by speaking. He spoke into what was empty and void and created something new. Here, the psalmist reflects on the full power of God's voice as He speaks, and out of His utterance, the world and humankind were created (Gen. 1 and 2).

God can call things that do not exist as though they do. He can also provide the prophets with words of forth-telling about things that never existed, but will (Rom. 4:17). "Just as the Jews might have held to 'Abraham said it, I believe it, and that settles it,' Paul [in the verse from Romans] is now saying that God promised it, Abraham believed it, and that settles it."[1]

Likewise, the Lord spoke about nations before they came into existence. We remember the story of Abram (later Abraham). God promised to do something for him—He promised to make him a great nation long before the Jewish people were united into a nation. When the Children of Israel were freed from Egyptian bondage, God held true to His promise. He blessed them and made them a nation.

We can read Daniel 2 and find a secret revealed to Daniel in a night vision. This vision is an example of divine revelation—God revealing His great knowledge and purpose.

DANIEL'S FIRST VISION (Daniel 2)

In 600 BC, God gave the prophet Daniel the interpretation of King Nebuchadnezzar of Babylon's dream.

God initiated the dream, which consisted of the image of a man whose body parts were differentiated by specific types of metal. Each body part represented one of four providential nations that would reign upon the earth over the following one thousand years: Below is a model of the image the king saw in the dream, accompanied by the nations each body part represented.

1) Golden Head: Babylon
2) Silver Chest: Persia
3) Bronze Thighs: Greece
4) Iron Legs: The Roman Empire

Babylon
605-539 BC

Persia
539-334 BC

Greece
334-168 BC

Rome
168 BC-476 AD

DANIEL'S FIRST VISION (DAN 2, 603 BC)

The feet and toes represented kings or nations that would rise from a revised Roman Empire in the last days. As you read the description of the feet and toes, you will find they are made of clay and iron, a mixture of soft and weightier substances. This mixture could represent the types of governments that will be brought together in the last days. They will possibly be a mixture of democratic, autocratic, theocratic, and fascist regimes joining the collective and forming the final global governments.

This collection of leaders would form a "new world order." Additional revelation from Daniel 9:27 measures this governance for a span of seven years, ending with Christ's return (Dan. 2:44), pictured as a crushing stone, and the ultimate rule of Jesus Christ as King of Kings and Lord of Lords.

DANIEL'S SECOND VISION (Daniel 7)

Close to forty years after Nebuchadnezzar's dream, Daniel received another vision confirming the interpretation of the nations described in Nebuchadnezzar's dream. This time, however, those providential nations were represented by four distinct animals. Below, you will see both dreams compared and the years the providential nations fulfilled their roles in bible prophecy.

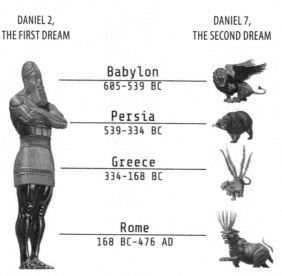

DANIEL 2,
THE FIRST DREAM

DANIEL 7,
THE SECOND DREAM

Babylon
605-539 BC

Persia
539-334 BC

Greece
334-168 BC

Rome
168 BC-476 AD

1) Lion with wings: Babylon, whose national symbol was a winged lion.

2) Bear with three ribs: Persia, who would conquer Lydia, Babylon, and Ethiopia.

3) Leopard with four heads: Greece, and after the death of Alexander the Great, the four generals who divided his empire into the four territories they ruled.[2]

4) The Beast with ten horns: This ancient kingdom of Rome became divided into east and west, signified by the two legs, but would eventually come together again as a ten-nation confederacy (the ten toes). It is speculated by most prophecy students that the geographical area of this last kingdom will be in the same region as the old Roman Empire. The ten horns on the beast together with the ten toes on the image represent the coalition of a "New World Order" governed by ten kings or regions.

Both of Daniel's visions address the same topic; they use different illustrations as their description. The ten toes or ten horns represent the last kingdom of man's rule on earth. In Scripture, ten frequently represents authority and government. For example, the ten plagues God gave Egypt that systematically dethroned ten major Egyptian gods. God gave us the Ten Commandants, the foundations of all Judeo-Christian laws. The ten horns and the ten toes will be man's last government to defy God's kingdom on earth. This final attempt will be dethroned by God, just as the ten Egyptians gods were dethroned.

According to most interpretations of prophecy, the last kingdom Daniel describes will come into power during the seven-year tribulation period. It is important to note that pagan practices of ancient Babylon,[3] which already exists today in our society, will continue throughout the seven-year tribulation. Her one world government will serve their leader, known as the Antichrist, from a ten-nation conglomerate. These spirits are destined to rule the earth and those who have rejected Jesus Christ as their Savior. We will refer to this empire as the **New World Order**.

It took one thousand years, ending with the fall of Rome in AD 476, for these four providential nations to "rise and fall." However, there are still more nations to come.

JOHN'S FIRST VISION (Revelation 13)

Jesus said, "When the Spirit of truth is come, He will guide you into all truth, and he will show you things to come" (John 16:13). The Holy Spirit that showed Daniel things to come is the same Spirit that revealed many "forth-tellings" to the Apostle John. He is the same Holy Spirit that speaks to each and every one of us today, just as Jesus promised: "My sheep hear my voice" (John 10:27).

During the Roman reign, circa AD 85, God gave the Apostle John further insight into the last ten nations and the New World Order (which has yet to appear). In Revelation 13, John is given a vision of a beast made up of the same animals described in Daniel's second vision (Dan. 7).

JOHN'S FIRST VISION (REV 13)

In John's revelation, the lion (the fierce power of Babylon), the leopard (the speed of Alexander's conquests makes this fit Greece perfectly), the bear (representing the ferocity and strength of Medo-Persia), and the beast (Rome incorporates all the viciousness, swiftness, and strength of the other empires), have all come to pass. These empires have fulfilled their role in history, but now we see them intermingled into the last ten-horned empire that will rise (Rev. 13:1). These ten constituents, coming from all nationalities, will someday form the New World Order.

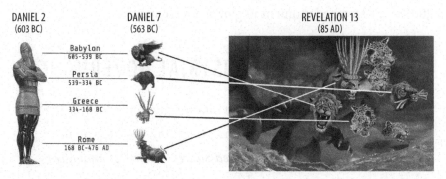

DANIEL 2 (603 BC)
DANIEL 7 (563 BC)
REVELATION 13 (85 AD)

Babylon 605-539 BC
Persia 539-334 BC
Greece 334-168 BC
Rome 168 BC-476 AD

Habakkuk 2:2–3 (ESV) says, "Write the vision; make it plain on tablets, so he may run who reads it. For still the vision awaits its appointed time; it hastens to the end—it will not lie." Are we currently living in the "appointed time" of the rise and reign of the ten-horned New World Order?

It would appear that the leading financial, industrial, and economically driven nations are desiring some form of global governance. "Governance" means all the processes that coordinate and control an organization›s resources and actions. Its scope includes ethics, resource-management processes, accountability and management controls.[4]

THE G20: GLOBAL FINANCIAL GOVERNANCE

In 1999, in the wake of the Asian financial crisis, the **G20** was formed to unite finance ministers and central bankers from twenty of the world's largest **established** and emerging economies. A decade later, at the height of the global economic crisis, the G20 was elevated to include heads of state and government. But it faces challenges from US protectionism and the growth of emerging powers. US President Donald J. Trump clashed with many of the group's members over trade, climate, and immigratoin policy.

However, after its financial rescue of the global economy in 2008, Stewart Patrick stated the overall purpose of the G20 is for global governance. "For this reason, Patrick describes the elevation of the G20 in 2008 as a watershed moment in global governance."[5]

THE G7 GLOBAL INDUSTRIAL GOVERNANCE

*The Group of Seven (G7) is an informal bloc of industrialized democracies—Canada, France, Germany, Italy, Japan, the United Kingdom, and the United States—that meet annually to discuss issues such as global economic governance, international security, and **energy** policy.*

Russia belonged to the forum from 1998 through 2014, when the bloc was known as the Group of Eight (G8) but was suspended following its annexation of Crimea. The G7's future has been challenged by continued tensions with Russia, disagreements over trade and climate policies, and the larger Group of Twenty's (G20) rise as an alternative forum. Meanwhile, [former] U.S. President Donald J. Trump has deepened divisions within the bloc, raising questions over cooperation on various policies.[6]

THE UNITED NATIONS: 2030 AGENDA

The United Nations is an international organization founded in 1945. It is currently comprised of 193 member nations. The mission and work of the United Nations are guided by the purposes and principles contained in its founding charter.

Due to the powers vested in its charter and its unique international character, the United Nations can take action on issues confronting humanity in the 21st century such as peace and security, climate change, sustainable development, human rights, disarmament, terrorism, humanitarian and health emergencies, gender equality, governance, food production, and more.

In September 2017, an article appeared in the *Independent News* titled "Nine Members of the UN Human Rights Council Accused of Violating Human Rights." The author wrote that "nine of the 29 countries listed are actually members of the Human Rights Council, a Geneva-based group made up of 47 UN member countries. These are Burundi, Egypt, Rwanda, Cuba, Venezuela, China, India, Saudi Arabia, and the United Arab Emirates."[7]

"According to the U.N.'s top human rights body, Israel is the worst human rights violator in the world today. That's the result of the latest session of the U.N. Human Rights Council which wrapped up in Geneva on Friday by adopting five times more resolutions condemning Israel than any other country on earth."[8]

WORLD HEALTH ORGANIZATION

The WHO is a UN agency founded in 1948, only several years after the UN itself was formed. The agency was created to coordinate international health policy, particularly on infectious disease.

The organization is comprised of and run by 194 member nations. Each member chooses a delegation of health experts and leaders to represent the country in the World Health Assembly, the organization's decision- and policy-making body.[9]

Although 15 percent, or approximately $400 million in 2019, of the

WHO funding comes from the US, in April 2020, that funding came to a complete halt. The reason was emphatically stated by President Donald Trump:

> "Had the WHO done its job to get medical experts into China to objectively assess the situation on the ground and to call out China's lack of transparency, the outbreak could have been contained at its source with very little death," he told reporters. "This would have saved thousands of lives and avoided worldwide economic damage. Instead, the WHO willingly took China's assurances to face value . . . and defended the actions of the Chinese government."[10]

It is abundantly clear that the United States, depending upon each administration's bent to embrace or oppose certain aspects of the United Nations global initiatives either supports or opposes Israel. However, the United Nations' stand toward Israel is at odds with America's historical determination to stand strong with Israel.[11] That was abundantly clear in 2017 when America moved its embassy to Jerusalem, declaring it as the eternal capital of Israel. However, because of the four-year cycle within America's electoral process, their supportive stand with Israel could differ between administrations. So what exactly is the United Nations agenda?

In 2015, every United Nations member state unanimously agreed to a fifteen-year plan to implement their "2030 Agenda for Sustainable Development."[12] Could this desire for global governance be the initial stages that will eventually form the beast of ten horns, or ten kings, that John described?

As recently as Nov 24, 2020 Prime Minister Justin Trudeau addressed the United Nations concerning the COVID-19 pandemic. He stated, "This pandemic has provided an opportunity for a reset. This is our chance to accelerate our pre-pandemic efforts to re-imagine economic systems that actually address global challenges."[13]

Canadian journalist Rex Murphy put it in a more transparent format: "Nevertheless, the raging pandemic, having wrecked the world's economies, is being taken as a cue by various eminent globalists to pursue a totally unrelated agenda. Rather than being described as an opportunity, this should be seen as opportunism, pure and simple."[14]

Murphy went on to say, "A combination of United Nations satraps, tech billionaires and, naturally, the apocalyptic environmental contingent have decided that this time of anxiety and disruption is the perfect moment to push their agenda."[15]

The United Nation's website boldly proclaims that "progress is being made in many places, but, overall, action to meet the goals is not yet advancing at the speed or scale required. 2020 needs to usher in a decade of ambitious action to deliver the goals by 2030."[16]

The "Decade of Action" calls for accelerating sustainable solutions to all the world's biggest challenges—ranging from poverty and gender to climate change, inequality and closing the finance gap." A transformative recovery from COVID-19 should be pursued, one that addresses the crisis, reduces risks from future potential crises and relaunched the implementation efforts to deliver the 2030 Agenda and SDGs during the Decade of Action."[17]

COVID-19 THE GREAT RESET

The founder of the World Economic Forum 1971, Klaus Schwab, termed the phrase "the Great Reset" in his recent book, *COVID-19: The Great Reset*. It is because of Schwab's writings that the United Nations and Trudeau's recent speech have accelerated their initiatives for the Decade of Action. Although the world economic forum has had a major effect on the UN and its global achievements, another forum runs parallel if not foundationally upon Schwab's writings.

THE CLUB OF ROME: ENTER THE TEN KINGS

As early as 1965, Italian industrialist Aureilio Peccei (1908–1984) and the director-general for scientific affairs at the Organization for Economic Co-operation and Development (OECD), Alexander King (1909–2007), began researching the sustainability of the planet, eventually forming the Club of Rome (COR) in 1968. With the help of core-minded thinkers from MIT, computer scientists studied the exponential global growth scenarios of "**population, agricultural production, non-renewable resource depletion, industrial output and pollution.**"[18] These studies laid the foundation for the UN's 2030 future agenda for planet sustainability. However, also originating from the Club of Rome was the concept that the creation of a New World Order would be "**represented in terms of interacting regions with provisions made to investigate any individual country or subregion.**"[19] In this governance, the globe would be divided into ten specific regions covering the seven continents of the world. It would integrate nations, languages, multitudes, and peoples.

Interestingly, one of the Club's original members was the late Prime Minister of Canada Pierre Elliot Trudeau. "COR cofounder Alexander King commented that soon after its establishment in 1968 Trudeau 'stimulated our thinking on the Club's philosophy and methods.'" Trudeau's interest led to the Canadian government sponsoring a COR meeting at Montebello in 1971. . . it was the critical meeting that led to The Limits to Growth report becoming a reality."[20]

"The Club of Rome is advancing the agenda of Thomas Malthus, who argued that population was held within resource limits by two types of checks: 1) positive ones, which raised the death rate, and 2) preventative ones, which lowered the birth rate. The positive checks included hunger, disease and war; the preventative checks, abortion, birth control, prostitution, homosexuality, postponement of marriage, and celibacy."[21]

Their vision, as stated in their 1991 publication, *The First Global Revolution: A Report to the Club of Rome*, reads, "In searching for a new enemy to unite us, we came up with the idea that pollution, the threat of global warming, water shortages, famine and the like would fit the bill. All these dangers are caused by human intervention, and it is only through changed attitudes and behavior that they can be overcome. The real enemy then, is humanity itself."[22]

"Today, the Club continues to be at the forefront of challenging and controversial global issues."[23]

THE LEADER OF THE NEW ORDER

According to Scripture, a one world government, or New World Order, will only come together at God's appointed time. And it will only come together by the sinister orchestration of a world leader (Rev. 17:16). Pastor Warren Wiersbe, describing this beast, wrote, "God does not see him as a man, made in the divine image, but as a wild animal, under the control of Satan. He is a man (Rev. 13:18); but he is energized from hell, for he comes out of the pit (Rev. 11:7; 17:8). Just as Jesus Christ is God in the flesh, so "the beast" will be Satan in a human body (see John 13:2, 27).[24]

The beast, as described by John and Daniel, is formidable and frightening. Can you imagine him as head of this New World Order?

The leader would be the dragon, Satan himself. (Rev. 20:2). He will do as he pleases during the seven-year Tribulation period. We will soon learn that it will only be after the seventh providential nation is deposed that the eighth and final nation can rise and the Antichrist will appear on the stage of Bible prophecy. But what kind of man will lead such an uprising?

In his Bible commentary, Oral Roberts describes this leader called the Antichrist as:

> *a man of superhuman economic and political brilliance, with ability to settle world problems and to adjust the collapsed economic conditions in the nations of the world. This man will be a 'complete' man from this world's point of view. Politically and economically, he will epitomize the essence of the world's humanistic philosophies. His appearance will be timed to meet the most terrible emergency the world has ever known.*[25]

Nearly six hundred years separates Nebuchadnezzar's dream, Daniel's vision, and John's vision. Yet, they all describe the same providential nations that will rise and fall at their appointed times. However, the rise of the last or eighth kingdom will not be easy. It will have great opposition before it appears on the stage of biblical prophecy, and that opposition is found in John's fourth vison of these latter-day providential nations.

THE SEVENTH PROVIDENTIAL NATION: A WOMAN APPEARS

> *Then one of the seven angels who had the seven bowls came and said to me, "Come, I will show you the judgment of the great prostitute who is seated on many waters, with whom the kings of the earth have committed sexual immorality, and with the wine of whose sexual immorality the dwellers on earth have become drunk." And he carried me away in the Spirit into a wilderness, and I saw a woman sitting on a scarlet beast that was full of blasphemous names, and it had seven heads and ten horns. The*

woman was arrayed in purple and scarlet, and adorned with gold and jewels and pearls, holding in her hand a golden cup full of abominations and the impurities of her sexual immorality. And on her forehead was written a name of mystery: "Babylon the great, mother of prostitutes and of earth's abominations." And I saw the woman, drunk with the blood of the saints, the blood of the martyrs of Jesus. When I saw her, I marveled greatly. But the angel said to me, "Why do you marvel? I will tell you the mystery of the woman, and of the beast with seven heads and ten horns that carries her" (Rev. 17:1–7 ESV).

John's fourth and final vision introduces another providential nation that appears while the New World order is attempting to rise from the sea of humanity. She is called "Mystery, Babylon the Great" (Rev. 17:5). This nation is not mentioned in any of the other dreams or visions.

When we closely examine the detailed time sequence John gave us in Revelation 17, it provides a completely new interpretation from those of traditional Bible teaching. For the last five centuries, traditional teaching has speculated that this woman is a commercial city that rules with the Antichrist. But Martin Luther, in his work titled *The Babylonian*

Captivity of the Church, in referring to Gen. 10:8–9, he wrote, "I now know for certain that the papacy is the kingdom of Babylon, and the power of Nimrod,[26] the mighty hunter."[27] Although Luther's premise that Babylon is an apostate religion that carries on throughout the tribulation, it does not alleviate the descriptions that she is also a commercial entity dominating world commerce before the AntiChrist rises to depose her. The Babylonian religious spirits are not hindered by the physical destruction of Commercial Babylon. They simply continue operating in other regions of the world after their reprobate influence pulls judgment down on Commercial Babylon.

Standing on the premise that traditional interpretation is incorrect, we will discover in upcoming chapters that the portrayal of this woman as a religion pales in comparison to the multiple descriptions of her being the richest, most influential population center in the world.

BABYLON THAT GREAT CITY

Through his understanding of Babylon, Luther set in motion the concept that Babylon is not only a religion but a city: "And the woman which thou sawest is that great city, which reigneth over the kings of the earth" (Rev. 17:18). Furthermore, the city according to Luther sits on seven hills. Rome is the "city of seven hills." Traditional theology has taught this for 500 years.

However, the word used here for "city" is *polis*, where we get the words politician, politics, and metropolitan. The meaning of *polis* is "population center." *Harpers Bible Dictionary* defines cities as "large areas of high population density . . . In the Old Testament, cities were walled."[28] Today, we do not have cities protected by walls, but we have large population centers protected by Air Defense Identification Zones. If you don't believe me, try penetrating the US ADIZ by aircraft and see how long it takes for an F35 fighter jet to pull up beside you. In summary, Babylon is not a city as we know it, but a "population center" protected by electronic walls. It is **a nation**.

Furthermore, the woman Babylon sits on seven mountains (Rev.17:9). Traditional theology interprets the seven mountains (*oros* in Greek) as hills, justifying that Rome, the city of seven hills[29], is this great city. Unfortunately, this city (*"polis"* in Greek) meaning population center, does not sit on hills. To emphasize that point, both Luke 3:5 and Luke 23:30 talk about hills (*buonos*) and mountains (*oros*), clearly differentiating the two words The mountains (*oros*) that the woman sits upon rise from waters of "peoples, and multitudes, and nations, and tongues" (Rev. 17:15). Mountains in Scripture "are a high land mass projecting above the surrounding area."[30]

We have made this comparison to clarify that Rome, the city on seven hills, does not sit on seven mountains. The mountains, or land masses of which there are seven in total, correspond with the seven continents (land masses) which we currently define within current geography. At the time of John's writing, people did not even know of the seven continents.

Revelation 17:12 gives us a snapshot time sequence of what will precede the beast, or New World Order, before it comes into power. During this vision, the beast and his ten-nation conglomerate have "not yet" (*oupo* in Greek) received power or authority to rule. This Greek word *oupo* verifies that before the beast is released, God will raise up a powerful providential nation. But contrary to the pictorial narration of an animal to describe it, God refers to this nation as a woman (Rev. 17:3).

This woman (or nation) sits upon the waters and also upon the beast. The Greek word used for "sit upon" in Revelation 17 is the word *kathemia*, which is also used to speak of a dignitary who sits in public as a judge or a queen.[31] This is the same word used to describe Jesus when He sits upon His throne as King of Kings and Lord of Lords (Heb. 1:13; Matt. 22:44).

This providential nation of Babylon the Great "sits upon"—or rules or presides—over the beast before the beast is released upon the world. Revelation 17:16 tells us the beast and the ten horns will hate Babylon the Great (the woman).

POLICEMEN OF THE WORLD

I was recently on vacation in Florida, walking down the beach with another Canadian friend. We were talking about world events. He said, "Who do these Americans think they are that they should police the world?" His statement flustered me, and I quickly responded with, "Who would you like to police the world? Russia? Iran? Perhaps China?" He looked somewhat perplexed as I said, "No matter what generation man has lived in, there has always been a predominant nation or nations that led the smaller nations."

I furthered my statement with a question: "What would happen if Canada was invaded by a hostile nation? What if a country like Russia or China decided that they needed our wheat fields in the central plain, our oil sands of the west, or our factories near the Great Lakes? What if they said, 'We are not going to buy, we are not going to trade, we are not going to negotiate, we are just going to take them, and if you resist, we will crush you with our military, with our weapons of mass destruction, and with our superior air power.'? Canada is a wonderful, friendly country, but with a population of only 35 million, we do not have the military might of other larger nations." My friend looked at me with a puzzled expression, so I quickly answered the question.

"Canada would make one phone call to 1600 Pennsylvania Avenue in Washington D.C. We would explain what was happening, and within ten minutes, US F35 and F22 fighter jets would fill our skies. Within hours, US military equipment and US soldiers would cross our borders, willing to fight our enemies and sacrifice their lives for our freedom. And once the aggressor nations knew that America was on our side, they would fully retreat from their evil intentions. The US jets would return home, the military and personnel would graciously remove themselves from our country and eventually extend a warm hand of friendship and say, 'Now let's do some business.'"

I continued, "There has never been a nation historically that has given so much to so many and been appreciated by so few as the United States of America. The only thing I have to say to our friends south of the border is '**God Bless the United States of America**' . . . and He certainly has."

My friend looked at me and said, "You know, Rick, I have never thought of it that way before, but you're right."

Since the waters that this "lady of kingdoms" (Isa. 47:5) sits upon represent peoples, multitudes, nations, and tongues, we have a global description of God allowing the woman to police the world, presumably for the freedom of many.

SEVEN HEADS ARE SEVEN KINGS

The Apostle John's second vision gives us a full panoramic view of all eight providential nations God would raise up throughout history.

Revelation 17:9–11 says, "The seven heads are seven mountains, on which the woman sitteth. And there are seven kings: five are fallen, and one is, and the other is not yet come; and when he cometh, he must continue a short space. And the beast that was, and is not, even he is the eighth, and is of the seven."

This may seem confusing upon first reading. However, we can put together a coherent and systematic time sequence of the eight providential nations that are being revealed to John.

THE EIGHT PROVIDENTIAL NATIONS

REV. 17:10 – "FIVE ARE FALLEN"
1. Egypt 1900–1450 BC
2. Assyria 722–630 BC
3. Babylon 605–539 BC
4. Medo-Persia 539–334 BC
5. Greece 334–168 BC

"ONE IS"
6. Rome 168 BC–476 AD

"OTHER IS NOT YET COME; WHEN HE COMETH, HE MUST CONTINUE A SHORT SPACE"
7. The Woman 1776–? AD
8. The Beast 10 Kings

ISRAEL, THE PROVIDENTIAL NATION

In looking at providential nations in Scripture, we can easily see six of the eight kings or empires described in Revelation 17:10. Each world empire is connected directly to Israel's history. The first being Egypt, which fulfilled Abraham's prophecy of 400 years of Jewish slavery (Gen. 15:13). The second is Assyria, which judged Israel for her idolatry and made her a vassal state, fulfilling Isaiah's prophecies (Isa. 10:5–12). And so on. But why is it that every nation throughout history to which Scripture refers has a direct correlation with Israel? It is because when it comes to Bible prophecy, in God's eyes, Israel is the geographical center of the earth.

God weighs the value of other nations by how they treat Israel. In Genesis 12:3, God stated, "I will bless those who bless you and curse those who curse you." He even stated concerning Israel, "And in thy seed shall all the nations of the earth be blessed; because thou hast obeyed my voice." But how exactly has Israel blessed the world?

Israel was the providential land that God promised to Abraham. Every Old Testament prophet came out of Israel. Israel was the providential land from which Jesus and the disciples came. Jerusalem, the eternal capital of Israel, is where Jesus was crucified for the sins of the world. But Israel and Jerusalem are also the nation and city to which He will return and become King of Kings and Lord of Lords. "For salvation is of the Jews (John 4:22)."

We are now waiting for the seventh and eighth kingdoms to appear. Remember what we wrote earlier in this chapter, "Whatever God purposes, He will bring to pass."? Waiting is never easy, but God's Word can assure us that these kingdoms will appear.

The prophet Isaiah reminds us:

> *The LORD of hosts has sworn: "As I have planned, so shall it be, and as I have purposed, so shall it stand" (Isa. 14:24).*

What an incredible verse this is! We can rest in the fact that whatever God determines, it will come to pass. He is a determined God. When He begins things, He finishes them. We can wait with peace and assurance because God is in control of the rise and the fall of nations.

Jesus said to the seven churches in Revelation, "He that hath an ear, let him hear what the Spirit saith unto the churches" (Rev. 3:13). This expression is a personal challenge for each of us. Interestingly, Jesus said these words eight times in the gospels and eight times in the Book of Revelation.[32] He's saying, "Folks, it's not enough that you have ears. They are not there to merely hold up your glasses. You need to hear My voice. You need to hear the voice of the Holy Spirit."

One of God's greatest commands through Moses began with, "Hear, O Israel (Deut. 6:4). This verse is a prayer that many Jewish people pray every morning and evening to remind themselves to listen for the voice of God. We, too, need to listen actively for God's voice.

We at Prophecy USA are praying that you have an ear to hear what we believe the Holy Spirit is saying to our generation. We believe a clear understanding of who we are and where we fit on God's prophetic time clock will sound the alarm within you. We desire that this awakening in your spirit will allow the Holy Spirit to personally unveil the hidden mystery of America's role in Bible prophecy. This unveiling will be sobering and perhaps even frightening, but rest assured, God is in control, and His word is a lamp unto our feet (Ps. 119:105).

CHAPTER THREE

TIMING IS EVERYTHING

MANY PEOPLE ARE wondering if we are in the "last days." Have you ever wondered if America is mentioned in the Bible? After all, if we are in the last days—as many prophecy experts believe—why wouldn't the most wealthy and powerful nation in the world be mentioned?

AN OVERVIEW OF THE BOOK OF REVELATION

The first sign that America is in the Bible is the mandate that she must be a providential nation.

The Book of Revelation contains twenty-two chapters. However, just as the Bible is not in chronological order, neither are the visions John recorded in Revelation 17 and 18. Chapters 17 and 18 take a detour from the narrative's chronological flow, digressing to describe the world system before Satan is given full control of the planet through Antichrist and the false prophet. The chronological narrative then continues in chapter 19.

From Revelation 6 through 16, we are given specific events within that period known as the Great Tribulation, when Antichrist will rule. This tribulation is a seven-year period, according to Daniel (Dan. 9), described by Jesus (Matt. 24:21), that would be a "great tribulation, such as was not since the beginning of the world to this time, no, nor ever shall be." Using the imagery of seven seals, seven trumpets, and seven vials (bowls), the Bible describes the plagues and natural disasters during these seven years as angels pour out His wrath upon the earth. According to Revelation 16, this tribulation ends with the pouring out of the seventh vial and a voice from heaven saying, "It is done" (Rev. 16:17).

At this point, the final battle of Armageddon will take place among the nations. The war ends with an earthquake that divides the holy city of Jerusalem into three parts. It is also when Christ returns, planting his feet once again on planet earth in Jerusalem. Revelation 16:17–21 says:

> And the seventh angel poured out his vial into the air; and
> there came a great voice out of the temple of heaven, from the
> throne, saying, It is done. And there were voices, and thunders,
> and lightnings; and there was a great earthquake, such as was
> not since men were upon the earth, so mighty an earthquake,
> and so great. And the great city was divided into three parts,
> and the cities of the nations fell: and great Babylon came in
> remembrance before God, to give unto her the cup of the wine of
> the fierceness of his wrath. And every island fled away, and the
> mountains were not found. And there fell upon men a great hail
> out of heaven, every stone about the weight of a talent: and men
> blasphemed God because of the plague of the hail; for the plague
> thereof was exceeding great.

A BREAK FROM TRADITIONAL MINDSET

Traditional theology has always interpreted prophecy by saying that Babylon the Great will be part of the Antichrist's world system, explaining that Babylon's destruction will take place at the end of the Tribulation. However, God's time sequence of events—what we find in His Word—does not say this. This scriptural evidence will be the foundation on which we will build our premise in discovering America's role in Bible prophecy. To verify our position, we will drill down into the Word of God and show you our findings and clarify our interpretations.

THE FIRST TIME-SEQUENCE HINT

In Revelation 16:19, the angel makes a reference to Babylon: "and great Babylon came in remembrance before God, to give unto her the cup of the wine of the fierceness of his wrath." The Greek word for remembrance in this verse is *mimneskomai,* meaning, "to recall information from memory" or to "recollect" or "remind oneself." In other words this "remembrance" is referring to a "past tense" event.[1] Additionally, the phrase "give unto her" is the Greek word *didomi,* translated "to make her drink."[2]

The English Standard Version Bible translation gives us a further insight, interpreting the passage in this way: "God remembered Babylon the great, **to make her drain the cup of the wine of the fury of His wrath.**" The wine in this verse is *oinos,* and is translated "punishment that God inflicts on the wicked."[3] From this narrative we now realize that the seventh vial of judgment being poured out is **not** the beginning of Babylon's judgment but is the **final** and 'last drop' of God's fury. This last drop is judging all the world who have followed the Babylonian spirits.

But if the seventh vial contains God's last drop of fury, where is the first drop?

To further explain this time sequence, God sent John an angel.

THE SECOND TIME-SEQUENCE HINT

Revelation 17:1 says, "And there came one of the seven angels which had the seven vials, and talked with me, saying unto me, Come hither; I will shew unto thee the judgment of the great whore that sitteth upon many waters."

Notice in this verse the angel taking John away is **not** the seventh angel that had the seventh vial, but instead, it is *one of* the seven angels who had already poured out its vial. John is being taken away from the original time sequence, in which the seventh vial of destruction has just been poured out, to view a previous event in the time sequence, the destruction of Babylon the Great.

From this point on (Rev. 17:1–11), this angel describes Babylon as a mystery. The word for mystery—*mysterion*—means "mysteries, religious secrets, confided only to the initiated and not to be communicated by them to ordinary mortals."[4] Furthermore, Babylon is described as being a rich, proud, powerful woman riding on the back of the seven-headed beast with ten horns (Rev. 17:1–11).

THIRD TIME-SEQUENCE HINT: THE FIRST CONFIRMATION

Revelation 17:12 says:

> And the ten horns which thou sawest are ten kings, **which have received no kingdom as yet**; but receive power as kings **one hour** with the beast.

In this passage, we see that the angel confirms the first two time-sequence hints by showing us the relationship between the ten horns and the beast.

Next, Revelation 17:13–15 tells us:

> *These have one mind, and shall give their power and strength*
> *unto the beast. These shall make war with the Lamb, and the*
> *Lamb shall overcome them: for he is Lord of lords, and King of*
> *kings: and they that are with him are called, and chosen, and*
> *faithful. And he saith unto me, The waters which thou sawest,*
> *where the whore sitteth, are peoples, and multitudes, and*
> *nations, and tongues.*

Neither the Antichrist (the beast) nor his kingdom have come into power, but they are waging war with the Lamb (and His bride), and the Lamb is overcoming them, because when you touch God's people, you are touching God. The woman (Babylon the Great) is sitting (ruling over, policing) "multitudes, nations, and peoples" throughout the earth, and the beast, who has not yet received authority to rule, is attempting to overcome, but the woman is thwarting his agenda.

As we saw in the first verse of Revelation 17, everything described here takes place *before* the tribulation begins. The beast and the ten horns hate the woman who is holding him down. Why? Because he has not yet deposed the seventh providential nation that is opposing his efforts for a New World Order. However, this pre-tribulation time sequence dramatically changes at God's appointed time.

THE TRIBULATION BEGINS AT GOD'S APPOINTED TIME

> *And the ten horns which thou sawest upon the beast . . . shall*
> ***hate*** *the whore [Babylon] and shall make her desolate . . . and*
> *burn her with fire. For God hath put in their hearts to fulfil **His***

will, and to agree, and give their kingdom unto the beast, until
the words of God are fulfilled (Rev. 17:16–17).

As we stated in Chapter Two, these time-sequence verses further confirm Babylon's existence before the beast or the New World Order arrive. The coming New World Order cannot fulfill God's Word until He gives authority to **depose** the seventh providential nation and begin the seven-year tribulation period.

This becomes clear in Revelation 17:12, when it states that the beast and the ten horns have "not yet" received their appointed time of authority. Then in Revelation 17:16, the "hour" is appointed for them to depose "the great whore," Babylon the Great.

Revelation 17:15 tells us that the waters from "where the whore sitteth, are peoples, and multitudes, and nations, and tongues." The people come from what we will describe as the "sea of humanity," and the seven heads represent the land masses on which they dwell. The ten horns represent ten kings who will join the beast, and together they will form the eighth and last kingdom to rule over the earth before Christ returns. But could these ten kings, or the concept thereof, be the ten regions of earth originally conceived in 1968 by the Club of Rome? If so, it would mean that Babylon the Great is not part of those ten regions, because by then she will be deposed.

To review, as mentioned in the previous chapter, the woman rides on top of the beast. She polices or rules over the beast before he comes into power. Interestingly, the woman is not a king. She is completely different from the other kingdoms who ruled the earth under a kingly dictatorship, represented by the animals in Daniel and John's visions.

"Babylon is mentioned in two hundred sixty verses in Scripture and is second in importance only to Jerusalem."[5] However, ninety of those mentions are directed not toward ancient Babylon, but toward this latter-day providential nation who sits upon the beast.

Historically, over a period of one thousand years, ancient Babylon and the surrounding area were the crossroads of civilization. In fact, Babylon may have been one of the most important city-states in the ancient Middle East. To get a better understanding of not only John's references, but also of providential nations, let's examine ancient Babylon, historical Babylon, and Babylon the Great.

ANCIENT BABYLON (APPROXIMATELY 2000 BC)

After the Flood, the descendants of Ham, Noah's son,[6] moved to the area around the Euphrates River in present-day Iraq. It was here that Nimrod, Ham's grandson, formed the nation called Babylon and, with his wife, Semiramis, founded the pagan, idolatrous Babylonian religions, which still impact our societies today. There is no doubt that under Nimrod and Semiramis's leadership, Babylon became the center of idolatry and the creator of every heathen and pagan system in the "then and there," and they exist hidden within our modern culture in the "here and now."

It was also in ancient Babylonia that the Lord confounded the speech of the Babylonians as they built the Tower of Babel (Gen. 11) toward the heavens in an attempt to establish themselves as gods. "In the Bible this city increasingly came to symbolize the godless society, with its pretensions (Gen. 11), persecutions (Dan. 3), pleasures, sins and superstitions (Isa. 47:8–13), its riches and eventual doom (Rev. 17, 18)."[7]

HISTORICAL BABYLON (605 BC–539 BC)

In the sixth century BC, ancient Babylon was rebuilt by King Nebuchadnezzar. [After he attacked the Jewish kingdom of Judah for the third time] "Nebuchadnezzar took the holy articles from the temple of God in Jerusalem and carried them back to Babylon, where he laid them up in the temple of his god. It was a way of declaring that, in Nebuchadnezzar's judgment, the gods of Babylon were superior to and more powerful than the Jewish God, Jehovah."[8] His nation (historical Babylon) provided a mirror image of the power and wealth that the seventh nation, "Mystery, Babylon the Great" (or "the woman"), would possess.

In 1803, archaeologists found a stone tablet among the ruins of Babylon. It contained ancient writing about Nebuchadnezzar and the false gods he once worshiped. An excerpt reads, "I am Nebuchadnezzar, king of Babylon, the exalted prince, the favorite of the god Marduk, the beloved of the god Nabu." The tablet is known as the East India House Inscription.[9] Nebuchadnezzar had taken what Nimrod started to a new level of idolatry and false gods.

It was in historical Babylon that the famous story of Shadrach, Meshach, and Abednego took place (Dan. 3). Three young Hebrew boys were thrown into Nebuchadnezzar's burning, fiery furnace for refusing to bow to his pagan golden image. Miraculously, a "fourth Man" appeared within the flames and robbed the flames of their violence. And "upon whose bodies the fire had no power, nor was an hair of their head singed, neither were their coats changed, nor the smell of fire had passed on them."[10]

Belief in God has been challenged within every generation, but within each generation there has been a remnant of believers who stand tall and refuse to bow to pagan gods. Historical Babylon fell in 539 BC, but according to Scripture, her religious practices will test the faith of believers once again in the "latter days" (Dan. 10:14).

In 539 BC, the Persians, led by Cyrus the Great, captured Babylon and then marched further west to continue their conquests. After Babylon's defeat, her temples were destroyed. However, this didn't stop the spread of the Babylonian religion. It found a new home in Pergamos in Asia Minor and was later headquartered in Rome.

MYSTERY, BABYLON THE GREAT (PRESENT DAY)

Babylon the Great is described as a woman who sits on the beast before he comes to power. Within the Bible, there are more than fifty distinct descriptions of her. She is called a "great city" in Revelation 17:18, and we find the kings of the world allowed her to influence them. The name written on the forehead of the woman is, "**Mystery, Babylon the Great**" (17:5). Babylon is described in both chapters 17 and 18 as being evil and wicked, yet there is a remnant of believers within her who will "come out" from the sins of her pagan religions (Rev. 18:4).

Scripture says that Babylon the Great will appear before a ten-nation New World Order comes into global power. Remember that in 2015 the United Nations implemented their seventeen-goal plan to reach their "Sustainable Development Agenda" by 2030. The G20, the G7, and the WHO are striving for global governance, even as we speak.

We already know that the Bible tells us the coming New World Order is the eighth and final kingdom to rule on earth. But before we have an eighth nation, doesn't it make sense we will know who the seventh nation is?

If that seventh nation existed today, she would surely be a providential nation, divinely structured to meet every description of the woman who is called Mystery, Babylon the Great.

TWO BIBLE STUDY TOOLS

To better understand prophetic Scripture, we will use two of my favorite Bible study tools, which in layman terms, I define as:

- Attempting to understand what was in the mind of the author at the time of his writing—the "**then and there**."
- Attempting to interpret what was said **then and there** and what it means to us today—the "**here and now**."

You may recall that God's Spirit told Daniel to shut the books of his writing because it was sealed until the time of the end. By this understanding, we can see that the seventh nation was termed a mystery as in "Mystery, Babylon the Great" because at the time of John's prophecy in AD 85, the future was a mystery. At that time, people did not even know the world was round. Most could not read. Christopher Columbus and the nation of Spain did not exist. It's doubtful any prophet knew it would take 2,000 years before God would raise a nation to fulfill one thing, and this is what God said in Isaiah 46:10:

> *Declaring the end from the beginning, and from ancient times*
> *the things that are not yet done, saying, My counsel shall stand,*
> *and I will do all my pleasure.*

God had given his words of prophecy and, providentially, He would someday make His Word come to pass. This verse in Isaiah is the first hint qualifying that America is in the Bible.

AMERICA IS A PROVIDENTIAL NATION

Many presidents made it clear that America was founded on Judeo-Christian principles and that they leaned heavily on the Scriptures to form the new nation of the United States of America:

George Washington, commander-in-chief of the American Revolution and one of the signers of the US Constitution, said in New York City on October 3, 1789, as he proclaimed a day of thanksgiving, that "it is the duty of all nations to acknowledge the providence of Almighty God, to obey His will, to be grateful for His benefits, and humbly implore His protection and favor."[11]

In 1837, at the July 4th ceremony in Newburyport, Massachusetts, statesman and diplomat **John Quincy Adams** said, "Is it not that the Declaration of Independence first organized the social compact on the foundation of the Redeemer's mission upon the earth? That it laid the cornerstone of human government upon the first precepts of Christianity?"[12]

Theodore Roosevelt, twenty-sixth president, proclaimed, "The teachings of the Bible are so interwoven and entwined with our whole civic and social life that it would be impossible for us to figure to ourselves what life would be if these standards were removed. We would lose almost all the standards by which we now judge both public and private morals; all the standards which are, with more or less resolution, strive to raise ourselves,"[13]

It is abundantly clear that the United States of America was established providentially on the Judeo-Christian faith. Quoting George Washington, this time from his first inaugural address:

No people can be bound to acknowledge and adore the invisible
hand which conducts the affairs of men more than the people
of the United States. Every step by which they have advanced
to the character of an independent nation seems to have been
distinguished by some token of providential agency.[14]

THE COVENANT

"A 'covenant' is an agreement enacted between two parties in which one or both make promises under oath to perform or refrain from certain actions stipulated in advance."[15] A typical covenant in the ancient

Middle East usually implied that each party would receive certain benefits. A covenant with God always invokes the benefits of His provision, guidance, and protection. For example, those who blessed Abraham would be blessed by God, and those who cursed Abraham would be cursed by God (Gen. 12:3).

Whether the Founding Fathers of America knew it or not, they were *providentially* entering into a covenant with God when they founded the United States upon biblical principles. At the same time, they invoked God's benefits of divine provision, guidance, and protection because of their faith and obedience.

We can read Deuteronomy 28:1–6 and discover the blessings or benefits that would be invoked upon Israel if she followed God's covenant—"if you faithfully obey the voice of the LORD your God, being careful to do all his commandments that I command you today, the LORD your God will set you high above all the nations of the earth (28:1 ESV)."

The Bible tells us that if Israel obeyed God's covenant, it would invoke His blessing, and they would be:

- "High above all nations of the earth." Israel would have preeminence about the world's nations (see Deut. 28:1–14).
- "Blessed shalt be in the city." She would have the blessing of location.
- "Blessed shalt you be in the field." She would have the blessing of provision.
- "Blessed shall be the fruit of the body, and the fruit of thy ground, and the fruit of thy cattle, the increase, of thy kine, and the flocks of thy sheep." She would have the blessing for family and their possessions. A blessing of growth and prosperity.
- "Blessed shall be they basket and thy store." She would have the blessing that not only their herds would increase, but

they would prosper materially. The Lord would provide food and possessions—not a wealth, but a blessed provision of what they needed.

- "Blessed shalt thou be when thou comest in and blessed shall thou be when thou goest out." She would have the blessing of protection as they journeyed in and out.

"These blessings would lift Israel far above all the other nations (Deut. 26:19) and make Israel "a light to the Gentiles" (Isa. 49:6). This would give the Jews opportunities to tell the other nations about the true and living God (Deut. 28:10)."[16]

As a providential nation, the United States has a similar opportunity. The Founding Fathers of the United States of America integrated the same divine principles into her foundation as those laid out by Moses for the nation of Israel in Deuteronomy 28. Have you ever considered that the foundations of America's laws, schools, and government were written covenants, making declarations of faith to God? These declarations invoked divine benefits.

The divine principles written into America's economic policies, as well as in her declaration "that all men are created equal, that they are endowed by their Creator with certain unalienable rights, that among these are life, liberty and the pursuit of happiness," have allowed America to fulfil her providential role in Scripture? She truly has become a "lady of kingdoms." (Isa. 47:5)

CAPITALISM WAS GOD'S IDEA

Perhaps you think America's prosperity is based on capitalism. If so, you are correct. But did you know that capitalism is based on biblical principles?

In 2 Thessalonians 3:10, Paul states "For even when we were with you, this we commanded you, that if any would not work, neither should he eat." God's plan is to provide for our needs through our work.

3 John 1:2 says, "I wish above all things that thou mayest prosper and be in health." God is concerned about us. He wants us to *prosper* (meaning "to have a good journey") to enable us to serve.

Luke 6:38 states, "Give, and it shall be given unto you; good measure, pressed down, and shaken together, and running over." Notice that this passage doesn't say to protest and it shall be given unto you. It doesn't say to strike and it shall be given unto you. It doesn't say to lie, cheat, deceive, or steal and it shall be given unto you. It says give! Give of your time, talents, investments, money . . . give something first and serve others to help meet their needs!

2 Corinthians 9:10 tells us, "Now he that ministereth seed to the sower both minister bread for your food, and multiply your seed sown, and increase the fruits of your righteousness." We need to realize that the apostle Paul's words focused on us using our gifts, talents, and ideas. What the Holy Spirit gives us, no matter which gift or talent it may be, we are to use it for someone else's benefit (Rom 12:6). We don't have spiritual gifts or natural talents for our own exclusive benefit. God tells us to use those talents and gifts to benefit others and, in the process, we will find that God will begin to bless us, and that He "shall supply all your need according to his riches in glory by Christ Jesus (Phil. 4:19)." You see, the nearest of God's helping hands is usually found at the end of your own wrist.

I heard the story of a man who, in his later years of retirement, bought himself a brand-new sports car. A Christian neighbor came over and looked at the car and said sarcastically, "I wonder how many families you could have fed with what you paid for that car."

The man pondered the thought and said, "Well, I know the engineers who designed the car got paid. And the over 250 people on the assembly line who put it together got paid. I know the dealer got paid because I personally handed him the check. But every person who got paid worked hard to give me exactly what I wanted, and they deserved every penny they got . . . because I love my new car!"

Capitalism and a work ethic were God's ideas. Greed, laziness, and entitlement were not.

"The United States has been the world's largest economy since 1871. The nominal GDP for the United States is $21.44 trillion. The US GDP (PPP) is also $21.44 trillion. Additionally, the United States is ranked second in the world for the approximate value of natural resources. In 2016, the US had an estimated natural resource value of $45 trillion."[17]

While communist and socialist countries build walls to keep people in, the US builds walls to keep unwanted people out. Why? Because of her wealth and the freedom to make it.

> And the woman was arrayed in purple and scarlet colour, and decked with **gold** and **precious stones and pearls**, having a **golden cup** in her hand full of abominations and filthiness of her fornication (Rev. 17:4).

The early leaders of the United States knew God's hand was on their nation. They therefore set out to base the government, the economic system, and the culture around basic Judeo-Christian principles. While the culture wars continue to try and disengage the United States from those principles, God continues to bless the nation.

THE LADY OF KINGDOMS

Interestingly, the Statue of Liberty sits upon the waters of Ellis Island with seven spikes on her head. The designer of the Statue of Liberty (which was originally named Liberty Enlightening the World), Frederick Bartholdi, designed the seven spikes to represent the seven seas and seven continents of the world[18] to which the woman illuminated her voice of liberty, calling out to the "nations, tongues, and peoples" of the world.

Out of the 835 seaports in the world, the US has 360 stretched across 12,000 miles of Coastline, giving jobs to over 13 million citizens.[19]

And every shipmaster, and all the company of ships, and sailors,
and as many as trade by sea (Rev. 18:17).

Wherein were made rich all that had ships in the sea by reason
of her costliness [wealth]! (Rev. 18:19).

From her ports in New York City, Lady Liberty stands watching the merchants of the earth trade their wares. Of course, what isn't traded upon the waters is traded at the world's largest financial center, the New York Stock Exchange, located only several miles from Ellis Island. It is here that the lady of kingdoms stands daily, fulfilling ancient prophecy as she faces southeast, silently watching the little city of Babylon—New York City.

Through multiple commodity ETF funds, the markets trade . . .

The merchandise of gold, a silver, and precious stones, and
of pearls, and fine linen, and purple, and silk, and scarlet,
and all thyine wood, and all manner vessels of ivory, and all
manner vessels of most precious wood, and of brass, and iron,
and marble, and cinnamon, and odours and ointments, and
frankincense, and wine, and oil, and fine flour, and wheat, and
beasts, and sheep, and horses, and chariots (Rev. 18:12–13).

Unfortunately, these products are not the only commodities Babylon the Great has traded. Included in these is her ninth description—she has traded in "slaves and the souls of men" (Rev. 18:13).

"An estimated 750,000 soldiers died in the [Civil] war."[20] Both black and white gave their lives in battle to free America from slavery. By 1863, Abraham Lincoln was a weary leader whose wife's seamstress, Keckley, claimed in her book, *Behind the Scenes in the Lincoln White House*, that he "was empowered as he studied and pondered the Bible, played a critical role in his life, especially during the catastrophic Civil War." Keckley added her own sense of wonder: "What a sublime picture was this! A ruler of a mighty nation going to the pages of the Bible with simple Christian earnestness for comfort and courage and finding both in the darkest hours of a nation's calamity. Ponder it, O ye scoffers of God's Holy Word, and then hang your heads for very shame!"[21]

At the end of this darkness, the Thirteenth Amendment was signed, and the Emancipation Proclamation banned slavery in the US Constitution.

Despite this fact, human sex trafficking in the US has hit record numbers. Slavery, while it may look different today, is unfortunately still alive and well in America:

> *Each year, an estimated 14,500 to 17,500 foreign nationals are trafficked into the United States. The number of US citizens trafficked within the country each year is even higher, with an estimated 200,000 American children at risk for trafficking into the sex industry.*[22]

However, through her capitalistic endeavors, the US also meets the tenth description of Babylon the Great, as she makes merchants of the earth rich through the abundance of her delicacies:

> *And every shipmaster, and all the company in ships, and sailors, and as many as trade by sea . . . Wherein were made rich all that had ships in the sea by reason of her costliness! (Rev. 18:17, 19).*

Is it any wonder that in 1944, "delegates from forty-four Allied countries met in Bretton Wood, New Hampshire . . . and decided that the world's currencies would be linked to the US dollar, which at that time was built upon the gold standard?"[23]

The arrangement, which came to be known as the Bretton Woods Agreement,[24] paved the way for America to fulfill her eleventh description in Holy Scripture, placing her global financial dominance on the "seven mountains, on which the woman sitteth" (Rev. 17:9):

> *And the woman which thou sawest is that great city [population center], which reigneth over the kings of the earth. . . . and the kings of the earth, who . . . lived deliciously with her shall bewail her . . . and the merchants . . . who were made rich by her, shall stand afar off (Rev. 17:18; 18:9, 15).*

John, Jeremiah, and Isaiah were visited by angels who gave us more than fifty descriptions of this lady of kingdoms, Babylon the Great, as far back as 2,750 years ago. Here are the first eleven:

1) (Jer. 51:7) She is providentially raised up by God as a "golden cup in the hand of the Lord."
2) (Rev. 17:10, 12) She is the seventh of eight providential nations.
3) (Isa. 47:7; Rev. 17:5; Dan. 12:10) She is a mystery; *mysterion*—a secret revealed to a small group of people.
4) (Rev. 17:10, 12) She appears before the Antichrist and the ten nations emerge.
5) (Isa. 47:5, 7; Rev. 17:3; 18:3) She is recognized by the world with the symbol of a woman.
6) (Rev. 17:3, 4; 18:16) She is the wealthiest of all nations.

7) (Rev. 18:17, 19) She trades with merchants at her deep-water ports.
8) (Rev. 18:12) She trades all twenty-seven products listed in Scripture.
9) (Rev. 18:13) She has traded in "slavery and souls of men."
10) (Rev. 18:19) She makes merchants of the earth rich through the abundance of her delicacies.
11) (Rev.17:9, 18; Rev. 18:9, 15) She has a world currency that dominates the "seven mountains of the earth."

Proverbs 25:2 tells us, "It is the glory of God to conceal a thing: but the honour of kings is to search out a matter."

Revelation 1:5–6 says, "Unto him that loved us, and washed us from our sins in his own blood, And hath made us kings and priests unto God and his Father."

As kings and priests, let us hold fast to our spiritual mandate and search out the matter. Remember, God will speak directly to you. You no longer need a prophet to hear His voice. Press on "for He will show you things to come" (John 16:13), and be assured God's vision to you "is yet for an appointed time . . . it shall speak, and not lie" (Hab. 2:3).

CHAPTER FOUR

WHAT POPULATION CENTER IS LIKE THIS GREAT CITY?

HAVE YOU EVER wondered why America is the richest nation in the world and has the world's most powerful military? Do these two things have any correlation with America's role in Bible prophecy?

Although the Bible specifically states that God "removes kings and sets up kings" (Dan. 2:21 ESV), Scripture also offers deeper insights. The Bible states in Ephesians 6:12 that mankind "wrestles not against flesh and blood" but against spiritual entities called "principalities, powers and rulers of the darkness of this world, against spiritual wickedness in high places."

This battle against spiritual entities is often called spiritual warfare. "*Spiritual warfare* is war with sin and sinful personalities. While all human beings are victims of spiritual warfare, its primary combatants are God, His angels and His followers, who are opposed by Satan and his demons. It is warfare between the kingdom of God and the kingdom of the Devil."[1]

We first learn of spiritual warfare and its origins in Ezekiel 28 and Isaiah 14. These two prophets described a war that broke out in heaven as Lucifer, the anointed cherub of worship, led a rebellion against God and His ordinances. Lucifer, whose name means "light bearer," did not want to worship God, but instead wanted to be like God. Through his rebellion, Lucifer and one-third of the angelic host were cast out of heaven and sent to earth.

Lucifer's name was also changed to Satan, meaning "adversary," "accuser," or "slanderer."[2] In Genesis 1—as if to humiliate Lucifer and let him know that without God he was nothing—God scooped His hand into the earth, formed man into His own image, and then breathed into man the breath of life. God anointed the dirt to worship him because an angel would not. From that point on, man became "a living soul," and the new worship leader on earth.

But Satan, the adversary of man, soon convinced Adam and Eve to rebel against God's ordinances, and so the battle began. Mankind would forever be conflicted about whether to walk in God's ways and laws or to rebel and fight against them. It was not until God sent His only begotten son, Jesus Christ—who overcame Satan's temptations (Matt. 4:1–11), died on the cross, and rose from the dead—that mankind was given a way back to God through merely asking Jesus for forgiveness.

Fifty days after His resurrection, on the Day of Pentecost,[3] the Spirit of Jesus was released upon His believers, who were now equipped to overcome the lies of Satan. The Spirit of Jesus entered the believers and began breathing out of them. As His Spirit breathed through "lips of clay," they spoke in over fifteen languages about the wonders of God (Acts 2:1–4). Since that day, the Greater One—the Lord Himself— has empowered believers in many ways.

WAR IN TODAY'S SOCIETY

"We are at war. As to the origin of this war, all we know is what the Bible tells us. It began in the cosmic realm, evidently before the creation of man, in an angelic rebellion against the Lordship of God (Job 4:18; Matt. 25:41; 1 Cor. 6:3; 2 Pet. 2:4; Jude 1:6; Rev. 12)."[4]

Today we are fighting a war. John 10:10 gives us a contrast: There's a thief who wants to kill and destroy us, but on the other side is Jesus, who wants to give us an abundant life. Our war is a spiritual struggle between the ultimate good (Jesus) and the ultimate evil (Satan, or the devil). We may not see this war, but it's here, actively going on in our minds and within our culture.

We have progressives and conservatives, Republicans and Democrats, pro-life and pro-choice, traditional marriage and gay marriage. We have men and women, and now—according LGBT groupthink—we have multiple genders within the new progressive ideology.[5]

The Bible does not talk about genders, but it does say, "So God created man in his **own image**, in the image of God created he him; male and female created he them. And God blessed them, and God said unto them, Be fruitful, and multiply" (Gen. 1:27, 28). The purpose of His creation was to multiply. However, the New World Order's purpose is not to multiply but to be "sustainable."[6] It is not God's will for believers to judge others' lifestyles (Matt. 7:1), but that's not always the attitude of nonbelievers. We will showcase this perspective in future chapters.

We also have capitalism, in which everyone gives and receives (Luke 6:38), meaning that you work to receive a salary. At the opposite end of the spectrum, we have socialism, in which financial entitlement is a human right.

What we need to remember in the midst of this battle is that spirits operate through people. Satan is a deceiver and a slanderer. Just as he convinced Eve by saying, "Did God really say that?" he can convince you and me to waiver in our faith and deviate from the path God intended for us and our nation.

So how do we handle this war? We fight it. As the Apostle Paul said, "Do not be conformed to this world, but be transformed by the renewal of your mind, that by testing you may discern what is the will of God, what is good and acceptable and perfect" (Rom. 12:2 ESV). To overcome spiritual warfare and the cultural wars, we need to determine to not be conformed to the world's thinking. We can't allow our minds to drift into the mold Satan wants us to live in. Instead, we need to be transformed (changed from the inside). God alone can transform us and our nation in this way.

Deuteronomy 28:1–15 is an interesting passage of Scripture. In it, Moses is speaking to the Children of Israel. These are his parting words before he dies and the generation moves into the Promised Land. He's speaking to individuals, and he's speaking to the new nation. Moses is giving them a choice—they can be blessed or they can be cursed. He's speaking from his heart, because if they want to fully achieve all that God has for them in the Promised Land, they must do certain things—they must be a people (individuals) and a nation that:

- faithfully obeys the voice of the Lord by doing all His commandments (v. 1)
- sees their enemies defeated and fleeing (v. 7)
- lives a holy life, keeping His commandments and walking in His ways (v. 9)
- is set apart from other nations; who sees that they are called by the Lord (v. 10)

In these passages, God is giving this fledgling nation a formula for ultimate success in the Promised Land, and He's instructing them about governing themselves. God is pro-government **if** (and "if" looms large in Moses's speech) that government holds strong to His principles, His way, and His laws.

GOVERNMENT IS GOD'S IDEA

In their book *Effective Stewardship*, Jonathan and Amanda Witt quote Ronald J. Sider on the subject of government. Sider elaborates on the idea that government is a good and necessary element of God's created order. "Since persons are communal beings created in the image of the Trinity, we naturally create a variety of different institutions," he writes. Government is one of those institutions. "It is not the only or even the most important institution of society, but it is a crucial element of a good society." In short, government, "is a gift from God, not an invention of Satan."[7]

Some might think that America's rise to power is just a coincidence, but our research team at Prophecy USA are convinced that America's present role in Bible prophecy is no coincidence. Clearly her role is mandated by God, and it is one of the ways we can read the prophetic time clock as it relates to Bible prophecy.

Daniel 2:21 states that God "changes times and seasons, He deposes kings and he raises up kings."

Romans 13:1–5 (ESV) reads:

> *Let every person be subject to the governing authorities. For there is no authority except from God, and those that exist have been instituted by God. Therefore whoever resists the authorities resists what God has appointed, and those who resist will incur judgment. For rulers are not a terror to good conduct, but to bad. Would you have no fear of the one who is in authority? Then do what is good, and you will receive his approval, for he is God's servant for your good. But if you do wrong, be afraid, for*

he does not bear the sword in vain. For he is the servant of God,
an avenger who carries out God's wrath on the wrongdoer.

Paul is reminding us that we should, as citizens, be subject to the governing authorities. And we do this because they are appointed by God and serve a purpose in His overall plan. What's interesting is that Paul wrote this while the Roman Empire was in control of most of the known world. The Roman government was known for its ferocity, and it was no democracy. The people had no vote and Christians were severely persecuted. Yet, Paul still sees this government as the people's legitimate authority. He knows God—not the Roman leaders—was in control. However, there are consequences based on the types of people who set governance and policy within government:

When the righteous are in authority, the people rejoice: But
when the wicked beareth rule, the people mourn (Prov. 29:2).

One of the biggest mistakes within modern Christianity is the false concept that the Church, or believers, should not be "worldly," which includes not being involved in politics. If that dogma is correct, then Joseph should have never counseled Pharaoh, Moses should have never challenged Egypt, Samson and David should have never fought the Philistines, Nathan should never have confronted David with accusations of adultery, Elijah should not have taken on Queen Jezebel, Isaiah shouldn't have warned dozens of nations that they were about to fall under God's hand of judgment, and Daniel shouldn't have counseled Nebuchadnezzar and his nemesis Cyrus. Every major Old Testament prophet was involved in either counseling or warning kings and queens.

Meanwhile, in the New Testament, John confronted Herod, Jesus stood before Pontius Pilot, and Paul battled the gates of hell to stand before Caesar only to eventually be "beheaded in Rome during the reign of Nero AD 64–67."[8]

THE MIGHT OF THE USA

Although some of the nations that have risen and fallen throughout history are seen as either good or evil, most of these nations have been a combination of both. No nation in history has established a government that fully reflects the ordinances of God's spiritual kingdom.

However, when a nation does embrace the ordinances of God, that nation invokes His benefits to help it fight evil. The Founding Fathers of the United States of America were second only to Israel in deliberately and enthusiastically embracing God's ways within their nation's Constitution.

America's prosperity has been second to none in the history of mankind. In his book *The Economy from a Biblical Perspective*, Stephen McDowell agrees. He wrote that, "freedom and the ability to benefit from one's labor caused the United States to be the most inventive, progressive, and prosperous nation in history."[9] That prosperity has in turn enabled her to "police" or "rule over" nations whose fascist governments have oppressed their people.

If not for the involvement of the United States in World War II, the nations of Europe would have fallen to one of the most terrible dictators in history, Adolf Hitler. Fascist dictators like Stalin, Mao, and Hitler brutally murdered well over 100 million people[10] throughout history in their attempts to replace God's ordinances with secular humanist governments.

STANDING IN THE GAP

Scripture tells us that the seventh kingdom, which will rule before the beast is released on earth with his New World Order, will "sit upon the beast" to hold him down until his appointed time comes into play. The tremendous prosperity the United States currently enjoys has equipped her with the military power to do exactly that. She stands in the gap between good and evil, supporting other nations around the world who want liberty and freedom from fascist regimes.

America has played an incredible role in her short 240-plus years of existence. The prophetic time sequence in which we now live, the prosperity America has enjoyed, and her influence around the world all play a part in fulfilling the description of the seventh kingdom mentioned in Revelation 17:10–11.

According to Scripture, the wealth one receives from being in covenant with God is not just for personal enjoyment. This wealth is to be used to establish *His* covenant (Deut. 8:18). It's a covenant that He has never broken. This "power to get wealth" also allows that nation to receive and deploy God's benefits (His guidance and His protection), further His eternal purpose, and fulfill the task of Romans 13 in being a godly government.

Deuteronomy 28:7, 13 (ESV) tells us:

> *The LORD will cause your enemies who rise against you to be defeated before you. They shall come out against you one way and flee before you seven ways. . . . And the LORD will make you the head and not the tail, and you shall only go up and not down, if you obey the commandments of the LORD your God, which I command you.*

But what benefits has God given America to maintain her status as being the "head and not the tail"? How does He cause her enemies that rise against her one way to flee before her seven ways? And how exactly does this allow the mystery woman in Revelation 17:12 to rule over the beast and the seven continents before they are released into power?

- "In 2019 the United States spent around 718.69 billion **US dollars** on its **military**."[11]
- This expenditure is roughly the size of the next seven largest military budgets in the world.[12]
- With "nearly 800 military bases in more than 70 countries and territories abroad, from giant "little Americas" to small radar facilities."[13]
- America invests "more on national defense than China, India, Russia, Saudi Arabia, France, Germany, United Kingdom, Japan, South Korea, and Brazil, combined."[14]
- America's Air Force boasts of approximately "13,000 military aircraft. Comparatively, China and Russia, the world's next-largest aerial powers, have a total of only 2,000 to 3,000 military aircraft each."[15]
- Although the People's Republic of China (PRC) has the largest navy in the world, surpassing the **US Navy**,[16] the **United States** has eleven aircraft carriers, the largest military vessels in the world, while China and Russia each have only one."[17] These carriers give the US superior air power globally with her 13,264 military aircraft compared to Russia and China's combined total of 7373."[18] This gives the US "more than twice the deck space of every other foreign carrier combined."[19]
- The United States, as of November 2018, had 830 registered space units in orbit. That number almost exceeds the combined total of the rest of the top ten. China follows with 280, and Russia is third with 147.[20]

In summary, the USA, like no other nation in world history, dominates the air, the land, and the waters—peoples, and multitudes, nations, and tongues (Rev. 17:8).

Of course after such monumental scientific achievements, in June 2019, "to ensure long-term sustainability of outer space activities, the UN Committee on the Peaceful Uses of Outer Space (COPUOS) is drawing up best practice guidelines,"[21] specifically "for the Long-term Sustainability of Outer Space Activities."[22] Once again, we see a "world government entity" trying to force their will on an independent nation.

Is it any wonder that the enemies of America—a nation whose riches, wealth, and military might are second to none in the world; whose founding purpose was to achieve a government structure that would invoke God's blessings upon her; who honors God on her currency; who once mandated prayer in public schools, the posting of the Ten Commandments, and Bible reading in her education system, and was once called a "Christian nation" by the men who founded her—hate her?

According to Revelation 17:12 and 16, the beast and the ten kings who have not yet received power hate the seventh kingdom, described as a woman ruling over them. Is it because this woman uses her wealth not only for her own benefit, but to be a beacon of light and protection for smaller nations—nations who also want their God-given, unalienable rights to "life, liberty, and the pursuit of happiness?"

Meanwhile, hostile regimes would like nothing better than to invade weaker neighboring countries and rob them of their land, their possessions, and their freedom to prosper. All we can say at Prophecy USA is: "God bless the United States of America for not letting this happen!"

Is it any wonder that the angel said to John, "the woman which thou sawest is that great city, which reigneth over the kings of the earth" (Rev. 17:18)?

Perhaps the greatest advantage of America's wisdom has been the tremendous technical advances and inventions she has provided to the world. Since the early 1900s, the US has brought the following to the world:

1903: The airplane[23]

1912: The first assembly line[24]

1926: Liquid-fueled rockets

1940: Digital computers

1945: The atomic bomb

1946: Bank-issued charge cards

1958: Integrated circuitry

1960: Internet[25]

1965: Compact discs

1966: The Lunar Module

1969: The first man on the moon

1971: Personal computers

1973: Cell phones

1978: Microwave ovens

1981: The Space Shuttle

1988: Stealth bombers

1989: Handheld GPS[26]

1991: Wi-Fi

2004–2006: Facebook, Twitter, YouTube

2007: The smart phone

2010: The iPad[27]

2015: The SpaceX reusable rocket[28]

According to statistics from the 2020 Union of Concerned Scientists' (UCS) satellite database, the US has a combined total of 1,425 military and commercial satellites, traveling as high as 22,000 miles above the earth.[29] Global satellite technology delivers real-time audio and video, live streaming to and from anywhere in the world. With the help of digital telescope technology, the US military can identify and monitor objects as small as a milk carton from thousands of feet above the earth.

No other nation in the history of the world has achieved this level of riches nor incredible scientific advancements within a mere 240-plus years since its beginning. So, at this point, we at Prophecy USA ask you to rationally consider this question: Do the descriptions so far of Babylon the Great look like a small city in Italy, located 70 miles inland? A city with no ports, no global commerce, and no military? Does traditional teaching from five hundred years ago, from men who never knew the existence of electricity, GPS satellites, the Internet, or America, even come close to fulfilling the prophecies "then and there" and the realities "here and now?"

THE TURNING POINT

All of this wisdom, scientific achievement, and military power is wonderful. But the Bible tells us that for every nation, there comes a turning point . . . even for Babylon the Great. Isaiah 47:10 (ESV) reveals to us that her prosperity comes with a price: "Your wisdom and your knowledge led you astray, and you said in your heart, "I am, and there is no one besides me."

Here we see a turning point for this seventh providential nation known as Mystery, Babylon the Great. **When prosperity, wisdom, knowledge, and pride enter the picture and become of utmost importance, things change, and not for the better.** In Isaiah's mind, the nation made several mistakes. She was so prideful and arrogant that she never thought anything could steal her prosperity from her. She felt a certain immunity, probably because of her size and military might. But in the end, nothing could save her from the upcoming disaster. "A society built on luxury, wantonness, pride and callousness to human life and personality is necessarily doomed, even from the human point of view."[30]

Writing about the turning point and Isaiah's prophecy, Irish biblical scholar J. Alec Motyer wrote:

Here is the astonishing optimism of all who say there is no
God and no life to come. They opt for a world without moral
consequences. Such is a misleading wisdom (in the practical
guidance of life) and knowledge (the conceptual background or
philosophy of life). These in turn arise out of a view of oneself:
self-sufficiency (I am) and unaccountability—no-one besides
me; in this context, no authority outside myself to which I must
render an account.[31]

BLESSINGS AND CONSEQUENCES

The first fifteen verses of the Mosaic covenant in Deuteronomy 28 list the blessings of those who keep covenant with God. They are followed by the consequences of breaking that covenant.

For every verse that promises blessing if you obey His voice, there are three verses that warn of what will happen if you break the covenant with God. Whether you obey His word or disobey His word, there are guaranteed consequences. Rabbinical sages wrote that the power of blessing and cursing is in your hands. You have free will to carry on with either. You can choose blessing or you can choose evil.[32]

Lucifer was once anointed to choose and carry out God's purposes in heaven, but he lifted himself up in pride and decided he did not need God; in fact, he thought he was a god unto himself. He chose to disobey God's words. According to the apostle Paul, at that point the "mystery of iniquity"—sin—was birthed (2 Thess. 2:7) within this archangel, and he lost favor with God.

According to the Bible, Mystery, Babylon the Great falls into the same iniquity that caused Lucifer's fall. In fact, the same spirits that fell with Lucifer begin to manifest their presence through the inhabitants of Babylon.

As you may recall, the Bible warns us that "we wrestle not against flesh and blood, but against principalities, against powers, against the rulers of the darkness of this world, against spiritual wickedness in high places" (Eph. 6:12). Paul is describing our fight against Lucifer and his fallen spirits.

The New Testament word "fallen" is the Greek word *piptos*, which means to fall from one level to another level.[33] Revelation 18:2 specifically states that Babylon will fall from one level, that of spiritual relationship with God and His favor, to another level, where she is invaded and controlled by evil spirits. Of course, not everyone in Babylon falls into this trap. It appears there will be a major battle over the soul of the nation, which John explains in Revelation 18:4–5:

> *And I heard another voice from heaven, saying, Come out of her, my people, that ye be not partakers of her sins, and that ye receive not of her plagues. For her sins have reached unto heaven, and God hath remembered her iniquities.*

From her riches to her power and her pride, Babylon the Great will become set up for a spiritual fall. In this chapter we can add five more descriptions of her greatness:

12) (Rev. 17:9, 18) She has the greatest military force in the world.
13) (Rev. 17:3) She uses her military to "police" or "rule over" the seven mountains of the earth.
14) (Isa. 47:10) She has wisdom and knowledge above other nations.
15) (Isa. 47:8) She is proud, haughty, and "says in her heart, I am, and no one else besides me."

16) (Isa. 47:10; Rev. 18:7) She says, "I sit a queen and shall see no sorrow."

CULTURE WARS?

At the beginning of this chapter, we wrote about the spiritual warfare that is occurring around us and, in many cases, to us. This warfare is real. The difficulty in many western churches is that people don't know there's a war going on. They don't see the consequences of curses. They don't read or study their Bibles. They believe they live in a prosperous and safe world and are minimally aware of the two kingdoms that are struggling for power. In some cases, the spiritual world is less real, less tangible, than the materialistic world in which they live. They, like Babylon, succumb to pride and arrogance. They put their trust in self or in idols they've created.

Mainstream news networks have used the term "culture wars" in defining our nation's political and social differences. The Bible, however, does not talk about culture wars. The Bible talks instead about two specific kingdoms that are battling each other on earth: God's kingdom of light and another kingdom, referred to as the kingdom of darkness. Do you think the battle between these two kingdoms could be at the root of what our news agencies refer to as "the culture wars"?

CHAPTER FIVE

FALLEN, FALLEN, BABYLON HAS FALLEN

HAVE YOU EVER wondered why there is such diversity of opinion in American politics today, or why those expressing certain opinions are often met with such hostility? This chapter unveils the root of the hostility, the hatred, and the volatile emotions of a nation driven into darkness.

In our previous chapters, we highlighted sixteen descriptions of the seventh kingdom called "Babylon the Great," which will rise and fall before the eighth kingdom comes onto the world scene. The only nation that meets these descriptions today is the United States of America.

We also learned that the Constitution, developed by America's Founding Fathers, mirrored a godly covenant, which brought God's blessings upon this country. She has become the richest, most powerful, most educated, and most technically advanced nation in the history of mankind. Her education system, judicial system, and government structure were all founded upon Judeo-Christian principles.

The Bible states that after the seventh kingdom (Babylon the Great) has enjoyed unequaled technological and material blessings, she will fall away from the biblical tenets that made her great. It will not happen overnight, but something will happen gradually within Babylon that will drastically change her covenant relationship with God. We at Prophesy USA believe that America is currently in this stage of transition. A battle is raging between those who hold fast to the biblical foundations of the Constitution and those who desperately want to change it—from "In God We Trust" to "In Government We Trust."

In 2 Timothy 3:16, the Bible tells us, "All scripture is given by inspiration of God, and is profitable for doctrine, for reproof, for correction, for instruction in righteousness." Likewise, Romans 15:4 (ESV) states: "For whatever was written in former days was written for our instruction." Both these verses, written by the Apostle Paul, give us a hint into what can cause a nation or a person to fall. When a nation fails to recognize the basic tenants of God's building blocks, it is subject to a fall. As we discussed in our last chapter, there is a turning point, and the United States is there, balancing between a country led by biblical principles and one led by self-indulgence, self-governance, and an overwhelming trust in government rather than in God.

Chuck Colson, in his landmark book, *Kingdoms in Conflict,* shared this historical turning point concerning the United States:

> As recently as 1954 the Supreme Court explicitly rejected the
> contention that government should be neutral toward religion.
> Justice William O. Douglas stated that "we are a religious people
> whose institutions presuppose a Supreme Being." But only nine
> years later, barbed wire was flung up on the "wall of separation"
> between the two as the court reversed itself in its landmark
> school-prayer decision. Though the expulsion of formal prayer
> from the schoolroom did not impede people's ability to talk to
> God whenever they wished, the decision reflected the shifting

public consensus about the role of religiously based values in
public life. It set off major tremors along long-dormant fault
lines in America's political landscape.[1]

In the same book, Colson quotes author Russell Kirk, who said, "Without Christian culture and Christian hope, the modern world would come to resemble a half-derelict, fun-fair, gone nasty and poverty-racked, one enormous Atlantic City."[2]

We discussed earlier the fall of Lucifer from heaven before man was created (Ezek. 28; Isa. 14). Lucifer began looking at his own gifts instead of at the Father of Lights, who is the Giver of all good gifts. At that point, the "mystery of iniquity"—or sin—was birthed in his soul, and God cast him and one third of the dark angels to earth. Lucifer's name was changed to Satan, meaning "adversary." Current evangelical theology deems Satan an adversary today, an enemy who opposes anything and anyone who would follow after the ordinances of the Father.

One of this adversary's goals is to dismantle the biblical values the United States' Founding Fathers thought were critical, not only to the nation's independence from England, but as foundational principles that would propel the country to be different from others. A country blessed of God that did things based on His principles. We are not naïve to think that the US is a perfect nation, filled with perfect people who are the walking examples of Jesus on earth. However, the founding principles of the Ten Commandments undergird the standard by which each citizen in the US is judged. It is those principles by which the backbone upon which all moral and civil laws were originally based. The freewill of man has much to do with whether the nation or individuals care to follow that protocol.

Jesus taught his disciples in John 10:10 (ESV), "The thief [devil] comes only to steal and kill and destroy. I came that they may have life and have it abundantly."

When people or a nation have biblical values as their underpinnings, there's an opportunity to have "life and have it abundantly." When those underpinnings are chipped away by a diabolical enemy, that opportunity disappears, and it is often replaced by a complacent spirit, a focus on self, and complete trust in the government rather than God.

PRIDE GOETH BEFORE A FALL

In historical Babylon of 605 BC, King Nebuchadnezzar fell into the same trap as Lucifer did when, after being empowered by God to build the great city of Babylon, he said in Daniel:

> *Is not this great Babylon, that I have built for the house of the*
> *kingdom by the might of my power, and for the honour of my*
> *majesty? While the word was in the king's mouth, there fell a*
> *voice from heaven, saying, O king Nebuchadnezzar, to thee it is*
> *spoken; The kingdom is departed from thee. And they shall drive*
> *thee from men, and thy dwelling shall be with the beasts of the*
> *field: they shall make thee to eat grass as oxen, and seven times*
> *shall pass over thee, until thou know that the most High ruleth*
> *in the kingdom of men, and giveth it to whomsoever he will*
> *(Dan. 4:30–32).*

Daniel 4:33 says that at that same hour, Nebuchadnezzar fell mentally ill with a rare clinical illness that psychiatrists call boanthropy, in which one believes himself to be a bovine animal. "They" drove him from his dwelling, and "they" made him eat grass like a beast for a period of seven years. According to Scripture, even Nebuchadnezzar's hairs grew as eagle's feathers and his nails like bird's claws (Dan. 4:33).

Although this took place in ancient Babylon in 600 BC, Dan 4:31-33 states that this same pride will swell within the hearts and minds of many in Babylon the Great. Instead of recognizing the blessings of God, many inhabitants of this seventh nation will follow the example of King Nebuchadnezzar. They will fall away from the biblical principles of their founders and begin to take God out of the equation of their lives. They will believe the lie that their wealth and prosperity were created by their own wisdom and intelligence.

Concerning Babylon the Great of the latter days, Scripture says:

> Get thee into **darkness** . . . for thou shalt no more be called, The
> lady of kingdoms. . . . For thou hast trusted in thy **wickedness**:
> thou hast said, None seeth me. Thy **wisdom** and thy **knowledge**,
> it hath **perverted** thee; and thou hast said in thine heart, **I am**,
> and none else beside me. Therefore shall **evil** come upon thee;
> thou shalt not know **from whence** it riseth: and **mischief** shall
> fall upon thee; thou shalt not be able to **put it off**: and **desolation**
> shall come upon thee suddenly, which thou shalt not know
> (Isaiah 47:5, 10–11).

By using a word study, we can see what was in the mind of Isaiah "then and there" in 850 BC; and it is shocking for what it interprets to us in the "here and now."

Darkness (*hosek*): Darkness is subsequently a master image for chaos, separation, and death, and a synonym of sin and evil.[3]

Wisdom (*hokma*): Intellectual wisdom; experience; shrewdness. The word can also refer to technical skills or special abilities in fashioning something.[4] The word is also connected to military skill (Isa. 10:13).

Knowledge (*Da-at*): knowledge. a knowledge, perception, skill. Discernment, understanding, wisdom.[5]

Perverted thee (*shuwb/shoob*): of spiritual relations; to turn back (from God), apostatize. to turn away (of God).[6]

"**I Am**": In Exodus 3:14, Moses said, "whom shall I say sent me and the Lord said, 'I Am has sent you.'" Secular humanists think they are gods because they are reliant on themselves and "science." Lucifer fell from heaven because the mystery of iniquity in his heart said, "I shall be like God."

Evil (*rah*): misery, distress, injury[7]

Whence (*hothen*): from what place or origin[8]

Mischief (*hovah*): NASB Dictionary: ruin, disaster[9]

Put if off (*kaphar*): To cover, purge, make an atonement, make reconciliation, cover over with pitch[10]

Desolation (*shoah*): ravage, devastation, ruin, waste[11]

Suddenly (*pithom*): Surprisingly, suddenly, or suddenness[12]

Utilizing modern terminology, the verses from Isaiah read:

Your skill in technical matters and shrewdness and knowledge of me has turned you away from me. For you think you are a god. Therefore disaster and misery shall come upon you from a place you don't know of. Ruin and disaster shall come and you cannot make amends nor be pardoned for the desolation shall surprise you and come suddenly.

Although the wording of these verses focuses on destruction of material goods, the book of Revelation gives us the spiritual foundation of who is working behind the scenes, waiting to kill, steal, and destroy (John 10:10).

Babylon the great is fallen, is fallen, and is become the habitation of devils, and the hold of every foul spirit, and a cage of every unclean and hateful bird (Rev. 18:2).

It appears from these scriptures that the same "principalities, powers and rulers of darkness" that overtook ancient Babylon and made

Nebuchadnezzar lose all rational thought would find their way into Babylon the Great in the latter days. This new mindset would put man ahead of God. It would glorify the creature above the Creator and give no acknowledgement whatsoever to God for His role in making America a providential nation.

Although atheism has been here since the beginning of mankind, this religion of "me, myself, and I" is identified with a new name; most people would recognize it as "secular humanism."

"Secular Humanism begins with denial or doubt concerning the existence of anything supernatural—including God—but then goes well beyond that secular stance by positively affirming and valuing the potential of human beings to be kind, enact justice, solve problems, and make the world a better, safer, greener, and more humane place."[13]

Secular humanism throws away the laws of the God. It ignores biblical principles and embraces relativism, human thinking, and "self" as the center of the universe. It seeks to separate us from God, godly thinking, and is a philosophy rooted in the enemy's diabolical plans for this world.

This falling away and the resulting separation from God is caused by the same principalities, powers, and rulers of darkness that were released when "they" drove Nebuchadnezzar out of his mind and "they" made him eat grass. These same spirits have tried to control mankind throughout history, denying God and rebelling against the simplest of His commandments.

Scripture states that once Babylon the Great is removed, "they" will be given a seven-year period on earth with the beast (the eighth kingdom) to rule as "they" choose. It will be the darkest time of mankind's existence. Before that happens, however, "they" will first appear in Babylon the Great—and their appearance will be obvious to those who understand the "signs of the times."

In 1 Chronicles 12:32, the Bible introduces us to "the children of Issachar." They were men "that had understanding of the times, to know what Israel ought to do." Bible commentator Matthew Henry wrote of these men, "Those of that tribe were greatly intent on public affairs, had good intelligence from abroad and made a good use of it. They knew *what Israel ought to do:* from their observation and experience they learned both their own and others' duty and interest (emphasis mine)."[14]

It's a good thing for us to know the "signs of the times." We need to study our Bible and know biblical truth. We need to be able to discern whether decisions are made using biblical values or if secular humanism is forcing policies and an ungodly culture upon us.

NOTHING NEW UNDER THE SUN

Ecclesiastes 1:9 (ESV) says, "there is nothing new under the sun."

Spanish philosopher George Santayana coined the phrase, "Those who cannot remember the past are condemned to repeat it."[15]

We learned of how ancient Babylon fell because King Nebuchadnezzar, in his arrogant pride, refused to acknowledge that God was the reason for the wealth and blessings of his nation. His pride blocked the knowledge he needed to keep his nation prosperous and safe. His only frame of reference came from self-interest. He didn't remember when past kingdoms were destroyed by outside or inside forces.

I heard a story once of a young atheist who was debating with his university professor about the existence of God. In frustration, the professor asked the student, "Out of all the history in the world, do you think you know ten percent?"

"Maybe," said the young student.

"Okay," the professor replied, "out of all the science in the world, do you know ten percent?"

"Maybe," said the young man.

"Okay, out of all the science, physics, biology, mathematics, and history in the world, do you know ten percent?"

"No," said the young man, "that would be impossible."

"Fine," said the professor. "Let's say that you did know ten percent of all knowledge. Is it possible—just possible—that in the ninety percent of knowledge you don't know, a higher power exists?"

The audience clapped while the young man became angry. "That is ridiculous!" he said.

"Okay, let's make it simple," the professor said. "Have you ever met my parents?"

"No, I have not, but how does that have anything to do with this?"

"Well," said the professor, "just because you have never met my parents does not mean they don't exist! The truth of the matter is this: My parents don't exist in your world, but they are alive and well in mine."

Hosea 4:6 says, "My people are destroyed for lack of knowledge: because thou hast rejected knowledge, I will also reject thee." Likewise, Isaiah 5:13 proclaims, "Therefore my people are gone into captivity, because they have no knowledge." The prophets are emphasizing the knowledge of God—His character, His will, and His power.

In Ephesians 1:17, Paul prayed, "That the God of our Lord Jesus Christ, the Father of glory, may give unto you the spirit of wisdom and revelation in the knowledge of him." He also wrote in Romans 8:7, "Because the carnal mind is enmity against God: for it is not subject to the law of God, neither indeed can be." When a person or a nation takes the knowledge of God out of their own library of wisdom, disaster is inevitable—especially if that nation was founded upon a covenant with God.

Luke 12:48 (ESV) states, "to whom much was given, of him much will be required." Proverbs 16:18 also cautions, "Pride goeth before destruction and an haughty spirit before a fall." 1 Corinthians 8:1 warns us to be careful because "knowledge puffeth up."

Narcissism and pride are peculiar diseases. They "puff up" a person (or a whole nation) to think he or she knows everything. They are the strangest of diseases because they make everyone in the room feel sick to their stomach—everyone, that is, except the person who is full of it.

Psalm 53:1 tells us, "The fool hath said in his heart, 'There is no God.'"

There are three groups of people reading this book:

- Those who have no belief whatsoever in a higher power—the **Athiest.**
- Those who honestly don't know whether God exists or not—the **Agnostic.**
- Those of you who, at some time in your life, have called out to God and heard His still, small voice (1 Kings 19:12). He knows you and you know Him. He speaks to your heart through your conscience. You hear His wisdom in Bible reading, sermons, in teachings, and you have no doubt whatsoever that He exists—you are a **Believer.**

Many times, other people don't understand the God-given knowledge given to you as a believer. It is like the little boy who was flying a kite. He let it go high into the clouds. An elderly gentleman walked by and said, "What are you doing, son?"

"I am flying my kite," the boy answered.

The man looked up and said, "Well, I don't see any kite."

"Oh, but it's there, sir—I can assure you."

"How are you so sure it's there, son?"

"Because I can feel the tug, sir. I can feel the tug."

Like the little boy's kite, your knowledge as a believer is there. You have the love of the Father, the power of Jesus Christ, and the wisdom of the Holy Spirit residing in you. What you need to do is receive them and use them. Are you listening for the tug? That still, small voice? The discerner between good and evil?

Remember Job? There's a man who lost everything—his family, his wealth, and many of his friends. He was in such bad shape at one point, he sat on a dung heap and used a shard of pottery to scratch the sores on his body. Psalm 107, written long after Job, is a psalm of deliverance. In it, the psalmist celebrates God's deliverances. The psalm itself was probably sung by a person who experienced times of danger and stress, much as Job did. But Job, like the psalmist, found strength in the knowledge of God. He understood in his heart that the "tests" he experienced would deepen his relationship with his Creator. He trusted in the knowledge God gave him. He knew He had a purpose for him, and he rested deeply in that truth.

THE REAL BATTLE FOR AMERICA'S SOUL

There is a battle raging today over the soul of America. Most people believe the battle is an economic battle between socialism and capitalism, or a political battle between Democrats and Republicans. But according to Scripture, it is a battle between remaining in covenant with God and His ordinances and walking away from the concept of "one nation under God."

On one side of this battle are conservatives, who lean toward America's Founding Fathers and the Judeo-Christian principles on which America was founded. On the other side are progressives, who, like Nebuchadnezzar, don't believe that God has anything to do with their blessings. They don't want God, the Ten Commandments, or prayer in school or government. In fact, they even want to monitor your speech to prevent the name of God from being mentioned in public places.

DARK AGENDA

In his book *Dark Agenda*, David Horowitz, a self-proclaimed agnostic, explains the battle raging in America brought about by secular humanists:

They see themselves a liberators—pioneers of a new millennium
for the human race. They envision a future in which religion has
been vanquished and rationality prevails. They want a world in
which humanity is finally free from myths and superstitions. The
believe in a vision of "new men and women," liberated from the
chains of the past. Science will enter in a utopian age of reason,
enlightenment and social justice.[16]

When Horowitz wrote these words, he had no idea he was preaching a message straight from the Bible concerning things to come. This battle is no coincidence. The prophecies of Scripture predicted this would happen to Babylon the Great. The same spirits that convinced Nebuchadnezzar he was a god in ancient Babylon invade the culture of Babylon the Great today.

When Isaiah said, "Sit thou silent, and get thee into darkness" (Isa. 47:5), he was not talking about somebody turning off the lights. He was referencing a spiritual condition that would come upon Babylon's people, a condition that history has seen happen time and time again with nations that have been "deposed by God and raised up by God."

INTO DARKNESS

We will focus on two scriptures concerning Babylon the Great and her identification with the United States of America:

1) Isaiah 47:5: " Sit thou silent, and get thee into darkness, O daughter of the Chaldeans: for thou shalt no more be called, The lady of kingdoms."

2) Revelation 18:2: "Babylon the great is fallen, is fallen, and is become the habitation of devils, and the hold of every foul spirit, and a cage of every unclean and hateful bird."

We have already looked at how pride and a lack of biblical knowledge caused Babylon's King Nebuchadnezzar to fall from God's favor. Yet according to Scripture, Babylon the Great of the latter years will repeat Nebuchadnezzar's mistakes. Even the pagan religions that Babylon practiced will be repeated in the latter years, as America falls into darkness.

The word "darkness" in the preceding verse in Isaiah is the Hebrew word *choshek* (or *hosek*), meaning "the antithesis of understanding" or lack of understanding as well as "spiritual insensitivity."[17] Isaiah summed this up by saying, "Woe unto them that call evil good, and good evil; that put darkness for light, and light for darkness" (Isa. 5:20). This darkness affects society in two ways:

- Spiritual or religious darkness.
- Moral darkness.

Isaiah 47:12–13 lists several ancient Babylonian religions that will be found in Babylon the Great of the last days:

> *Stand now with thine enchantments, and with the multitude*
> *of thy sorceries wherein though hast labored from thy*
> *youth . . . Thou art wearied in the multitude of thy counsels*
> *[government]. Let now the astrologers, the stargazers,*
> *the monthly prognosticators [mediums, fortune tellers]*
> *stand up and save thee from these things that shall come*
> *upon thee.*

According to the *Easton's Bible Dictionary*, the "enchantments" in this passage had to do with "divination," which referenced "small images or cult objects used as domestic deities or oracles by ancient Semitic peoples."[18] In today's language, this would include anything to do with divination or occult paraphernalia, such as Ouija boards or tarot cards; calling up familiar spirits, mediums, and fortune tellers; witchcraft; and worship of the moon or planets.

"All kinds of enchantments were condemned by the Mosaic law (Lev. 19:26; Deut. 18:10–12),"[19] yet were common in ancient Babylon. Hollywood and the movie and television industry have made all of these practices widely acceptable—even encouraged—in our culture. Oddly enough, there are television series today simulating the myth of men and woman transforming their bodies into animals (boanthropy/ lycanthropy). Nebuchadnezzar suffered from this belief; it was considered his judgment for not acknowledging God or giving Him thanks for the financial blessings he had. Today, however, this mental illness, as well as the Babylonian religious practices are topics of entertainment within the North America movie industry.

SORCERY AND *"PHARMAKIA"*

Isaiah talks about "sorceries." In Hebrew, the word for sorceries (*kesheph*) means magic or witchcraft. When the Old Testament was translated into Greek, "*kesheph*" was translated into the Greek word "*pharmakia*." This is where we get the English word "pharmacy," which includes using drugs for altered states of consciousness.

Latter-day Babylon the Great is a drug-induced nation.

In an article posted on the *Science Daily* website, a University of Southern California study found that American drug overdose death rates are the highest among wealthy nations:

> *A new study found that the United States has the highest drug overdose death rates among a set of high-income countries. The study found that drug overdose death rates in the United States are three and one-half times higher on average when compared*

to seventeen other high-income counties. The study is the first to demonstrate that the drug overdose epidemic is contributing to the widening gap in life expectancy between the United States and other high-income countries.[20]

In the covenant God made with Israel through Moses, He specifically warned them:

There shall not be found among you anyone who burns his son or his daughter as an offering, anyone who practices divination or tells fortunes or interprets omens, or a sorcerer or a charmer or a medium or a necromancer or one who inquires of the dead, for whoever does these things is an abomination to the LORD (Deut. 18:10–12 ESV).

This darkness, or "lack of understanding," has a dramatic effect on Babylon's society, as showcased by her immoral lifestyle. Will the United States fall the same way?

Interesting to think about are those people who have a knowledge of God and Jesus yet still turn from Him. They suppress the truth, enabling them to continue with immoral lifestyles. "It is not that men and women have no knowledge of God at all and are condemned for what they 'innocently enough' do not know. It is rather that they do have knowledge of God but have rejected it because they do not like the direction in which such knowledge takes them.[21]

This seeming lack of knowledge is true for nations as well as for individuals. In the chambers of the United States House of Representatives are displayed several verses from the Bible. For example, the chapel of the House of Representatives contains an open Bible on an altar in front of a stained-glass window that depicts George Washington in prayer and the words, "Preserve me, O God, for in thee do I put my trust" (Ps.

16:1). The US is well aware of its biblical heritage, but like Babylon, they are abandoning it.

A REPROBATE SOCIETY

In Romans 1:18–21 (ESV), Paul describes the effects of this darkness in society:

> *For the wrath of God is revealed from heaven against all ungodliness and unrighteousness of men, who by their unrighteousness suppress the truth. For what can be known about God is plain to them, because God has shown it to them. For his invisible attributes, namely, his eternal power and divine nature, have been clearly perceived, ever since the creation of the world, in the things that have been made. So they are without excuse. For although they knew God, they did not honor him as God or give thanks to him, but they became futile in their thinking, and their foolish hearts were darkened.*

Here we see the word "darkened" again. The New Testament Greek word used this time is *skotizo*, which means being "to be darkened and unable to understand."[22] Paul continues: "And even as they did not like to retain God in their knowledge, God gave them over to a reprobate mind [that is, a society that has no moral compass as far as Scripture is concerned]" (Rom. 1:28). The Greek word for "reprobate" is *adokimos*, meaning "that which is depraved or without morals."[23] Once again, good becomes evil and evil becomes good. This describes a society that has total disregard for God's moral protocol (Isa. 5:20).

Romans 1 lists twenty-three characteristics to look for in a reprobate society, including: *They were filled with all manner of unrighteousness, evil, covetousness, malice. They are full of envy, murder, strife, deceit, maliciousness. They are gossips, slanderers, haters of God, insolent, haughty, boastful, inventors of evil, disobedient to parents, foolish, faithless, heart-less, ruthless. Though they know God's righteous decree that those who practice such things deserve to die, they not only do them (Rom. 1:29–32).*

In America today, we are seeing radical changes in morals, culture, and society. Is it possible that we are being invaded by the same Babylonian spirits that wreaked havoc in ancient Babylon before she was judged?

A FALLEN NATION

You might be thinking to yourself that other nations practice these pagan religions as well. You are correct; however, other nations did not build their constitution, judicial systems, and culture on Judeo-Christian principles and stand out as a providential nation like America. Other nations are not the richest nation in the world, nor are they recognized globally as a "lady of kingdoms." There is no nation that can come close to the military might of the United States as she confronts hostile, aggressive regimes throughout the world.

To be fair, we must address every description of Babylon in order to discover her identity. So, let's continue to unveil the mystery Scripture reveals.

Although she is described as a "lady of kingdoms," perhaps the most telling sign of her fall into moral depravity is found in Revelation 17:1–2:

> *Come hither; I will shew unto thee the judgment of the great whore [prostitute] that sitteth upon many waters [multitudes, tongues and peoples]: with whom the kings of the earth have committed fornication, and the inhabitants of the earth have been made drunk with the wine of her fornication.*

The nation that was called the "lady of kingdoms" is now called a whore (prostitute) and the distributor of fornication. Obviously, this describes her fallen state.

How could a nation that was founded on a covenant with God, that instituted the Bible into her education system, placed Judeo-Christian laws into her judicial system, and even displayed a statue of Moses in her Supreme Court building now be called a prostitute and a peddler of fornication throughout the world?

Since 1962, secular humanists have fought vehemently to take the Bible out of the education system, prayer out of the classroom, God out of government, and Judeo-Christian moral values out of our society entirely. We have taught grade school children that they come from monkeys and then wonder why they grow up to act like animals.

The word "prostitute" is *porne* in Greek. It is where we get the English word "pornography." In 2012, America was producing close to 89% of porn films globally.[24] Currently, America hosts 428 million porn Web pages, or sixty percent, of the worldwide total.

Meanwhile, 66 percent of the porn produced or hosted in the United States comes from California,[25] which makes sense, considering it's the center of both the technology industry and the porn industry. Hollywood is the world's top producer of pornographic films, producing one pornographic movie every forty minutes—twenty-four hours a day, seven days a week.[26]

Yet no matter how bad that may seem, Scripture tells us that there is still the voice of believers within Babylon, and they are to "raise up a shout" of warning. Babylon the Great has fallen, but God still has tremendous victory in store for those who call upon His name. If you are a believer in Christ, do not be alarmed: something good is about to happen to you, and it is one of Scripture's most hidden mysteries!

From the radical changes that have happened in America, it is evident she has fallen from her covenant position as a lady of kingdoms

(Deut. 28:1–15). She has come to a place where for the majority her people, obeying God's voice is far from their agenda (Deut. 28:15–45). We can now add the following descriptions as the progressive left (non-believers) fall into darkness:

17) (Isa. 47:1; Rev. 18:2) She "falls" spiritually in God's eyes.

18) (Isa. 47:5; Rev. 18:2) She is **driven** into darkness.

19) (Isa. 47:9, 10, 12) She embraces ancient Babylonian religions.

20) (Isa. 47:9) She has enchantments, pagan paraphernalia.

21) (Deut. 18:10–11; Isa. 47:12–13) She practices necromancy, has mediums.

22) (Isa. 47:13) She has stargazers (astrologers).

23) (Isa. 47:9; Rev. 18:2) She has witchcraft, including Satan worship.

24) (Rev. 17:1–2, 4, 5) She is a world leader in producing pornography.

25) (Rev. 18:3) She is a world leader in selling pornography.

26) (Isa. 47:9, 12; Rev. 18:23) She is a drug-induced nation filled with a "multitude of sorceries."

27) (Rom. 1:29–31) She meets the twenty-three characteristics of a reprobate society found in Romans 1.

28) (Deut. 28:12; Deut. 15:6) She becomes a debtor nation, not a lender.

29) (Rev. 18:2) She becomes the habitation of every form of immorality.

CHAPTER SIX

THE WORLD VERSUS THE WORD

WHAT HAPPENS WHEN those who are called to change the world with God's Word let the world start changing His Word. One famous North American preacher is credited with saying that "the Bible is no longer relevant in today's society." However, according to the Bible, that preacher's opinion is not relevant. The Bible calls this phenomenon "the apostasy."

THE APOSTASY

In the last few chapters, we outlined twenty-nine descriptions of Babylon the Great. So far, the United States of America meets every description. Her founding upon Judeo-Christian principles has made her a providential nation. The blessings she has received on account of her covenant with God are evident in her wealth, military, and global influence. She has become a "lady of kingdoms," exactly as Isaiah and John described. The fact that most providential nations depicted in Revelation 17 are symbolized by animals, with the seventh nation described as a woman, also leads us to believe America could be the seventh nation that stands in the gap and polices the world before the eighth and final kingdom arrives.

We also discussed three categories of people reading this book—atheists, agnostics, and believers. However, according to Scripture, there will be several types of believers evident in the last days. These believers will be weighed in the balance before Babylon's demise.

The Bible describes a spiritual transformation in Babylon: the angel declares to John, "Babylon the great is fallen, fallen" (Rev. 18:2). Unfortunately, what we see here is that instead of believers influencing Babylon to lessen its moral depravity, Babylon's moral depravity has affected believers, even to the point that they have fallen away from studying and following God's Word.

Paul warns us (2 Thess. 2:3) that there will be an *apostasia*, or spiritual "falling away," that will affect Jesus' followers immediately before a great tribulation comes upon the earth. That falling away, which is also interpreted as a "rebellion" (ESV), began in several churches during the time John wrote the book of Revelation. Jesus warned John about several belief systems that were seducing believers in several cities where each group (church) gathered.

Although those believers have passed away, the sins and the spirits with which they wrestled (the sins Jesus addressed in Revelation 2 and 3) still exist. The historical churches described in Revelation are an example of the theological tool known as typology. The believers "then and there" represent what believers in the last days will look like in the "here and now."

WHICH BELIEVER DO YOU REPRESENT?

In His admonition to the seven churches (groups of believers), Jesus said, "I know your works" (Rev. 3:8 ESV). He was speaking to practicing

Christians who were serving in the churches. And just as He warned them 2,000 years ago, He warns us today: "He that hath an ear, let him hear what the Spirit saith unto the churches" (Rev. 3:13). In essence, Jesus is not only speaking to first-century Christians, but directly to modern-day believers as well.

Revelation 18:4 tells us God's people are in Babylon the Great, and He warns them to "be not partakers of her sins." God is calling you and me to separate ourselves from those things that oppose God's moral protocol. Jeremiah wrote a warning: "Remove out of the midst of Babylon (Jer. 50:8)." The prophet goes on to write in the next chapter, "My people, go ye out of the midst of her [Babylon], and deliver ye every man his soul from the fierce anger of the LORD (Jer. 51:45)." I don't know about you, but I don't ever want to face the fierce anger of the LORD.

God wanted the first-century Christians—and He wants believers today—to untangle themselves from the sins of the world. That does not mean that you stop participating in government, politics, sports, the arts, or social events. Instead, we are to go into the world with the gifts and talents God has given us, mandated and sent, so that "the life also of Jesus might be made manifest in our body" (2 Cor 4:10). He calls us to live a life that is transformed (Rom. 12:2) and not to succumb to Babylon's sins by falling away from the true faith.

THE FIRST GROUP: EPHESUS BELIEVERS
(Revelation 2:1–7)

The first believers addressed by Jesus in the book of Revelation lived in Ephesus. In Revelation 2:4–5 (ESV), He says: "But I have this against you, that you have abandoned the love that you had at first. Remember therefore from where you have fallen; repent and do the works you did at first."

These believers fell from their "first love" for God. The New Testament Greek word for "love" in this passage is *agape*, used 118 times in Scripture to describe God's perfect love. Jesus said in the Gospels, "If you love me, you will keep my commandments" (John 14:15 ESV). He qualified that statement by saying, "So whatever you wish that others would do to you, do also to them, for this is the Law and the Prophets" (Matt. 7:12 ESV). The Ephesus believer needs to restore their love for God but their love for others even more.

John painted an interesting picture of this group of believers. Ephesus was the wealthiest and most splendid city in the area (modern-day Turkey). The word often translated "church" in our Bibles is the Greek word *ecclesia*. It means "called-out company." God expects His church to be separate, called-out by Him, not to the world but to Jesus Christ.

The word used for "works" in verse 2 of Revelation 2 is the Greek word *kopos*. It means "toil resulting in weariness, laborious, toil, trouble."[1] It describes an all-out effort that demands physical, mental, and emotional diligence. The Ephesians were not to be spectators.

But the Ephesians lost their love (*agape*), and in doing so, they lost their closeness to Jesus. Their lost love opened the door to apathy, indifference to others, and compromise with evil. Like many cancers, this loss of love may have started as a small spot, but it quickly grew to overtake the church. Their works overshadowed their love for Jesus, and they had orthodoxy without intimacy with their Savior.

Jesus calls them to remember and repent. They needed to remember the thrill of the early days. I'm reminded of the Prodigal Son, who suddenly "came to himself" after pondering his spiritual condition and remembered his Father and the home he had left behind (Luke 15:17).

Jesus also called the believers at Ephesus to repent and stop doing what blinded them to their first love. They needed to take personal responsibility for their failure and move forward to gaining back that love.

It's true for us today as well. We need to "come home" as individuals and as a nation. Let's not let the sins of Babylon blind us from our true love, Jesus Christ.

THE SECOND GROUP: SARDIS BELIEVERS
(Revelation 3:1–6)

Closely resembling the believers in Ephesus were those in Sardis:

In Revelation 3:1–3 (ESV), Jesus said:

> *I know your works. You have the reputation of being alive but you are dead. Wake up . . . for I have not found your works complete in the sight of my God . . . repent. If you will not wake up, I will come like a thief and you will not know at what hour I will come against you.*

In the first century, the city of Sardis was impregnable. It was also a prosperous city. The people were prideful because of their location and wealth. Jesus doesn't have much good to say to them. Unfortunately, the Sardis believers thought they were alive with a good reputation. Still, nominal Christians filled the church building, but there was no life in the believer. Jesus said they were dead. Paul's prayer that "the life of Christ might be made manifest in your mortal flesh" (2 Cor 4:11) was not happening to them personally. As a result, Jesus warned them to be watchful and to wake up.

What was their problem? They allowed traditional religious routines to replace a lifestyle of personal worship. They deceived themselves into thinking they were doing well as a group, but their intimate relationship with Christ was dead, as they rested in their wealth and laziness.

The apostle James, Jesus' brother, provides a solution for these believers:

But be doers of the word, and not hearers only, deceiving
yourselves. For if anyone is a hearer of the word and not a doer,
he is like a man who looks intently at his natural face in a mirror.
For he looks at himself and goes away and at once forgets what
he was like. But the one who looks into the perfect law, the law
of liberty, and perseveres, being no hearer who forgets but a doer
who acts, he will be blessed in his doing (James 1:22–25 ESV).

We can't be mere "hearers" of God's Word. We can listen but then never apply what we've heard. "Doers" put into practice what God is teaching them. Doers are awake. False teaching does not deceive them. John 8:31 reminds us, "Then said Jesus to those Jews which believed on him, if ye continue in my word, **then** are ye my disciples indeed." Doers don't stray from God's Word. The church in Sardis strayed, and Jesus gave them a divine wakeup call.

THE THIRD GROUP: SMYRNA BELIEVERS
(Revelation. 2:8–11)

In contrast to the believers in Sardis, doers of the Word were found in the next church Jesus addressed, which was found in Smyrna. However, there was a price they paid for serving God. Jesus said to the believers at Smyrna in Revelation 2:9–10:

I know thy works, and tribulation, and poverty, [but thou art
rich] and I know the blasphemy of them which say they are Jews
[believers], and are not, but are the synagogue of Satan. Fear
none of those things which thou shalt suffer: behold, the devil
shall cast some of you into prison, that ye may be tried; and
ye shall have tribulation ten days: be thou faithful unto death,
and I will give thee a crown of life.

The Smyrna believers were doers, but they were under tremendous persecution for not worshipping the emperor. They lived under pressure every day. If they didn't choose to worship the emperor, they were banned from making a living and were under constant pressure from the government. The Greek word for "tribulation" (or in some translations, "affliction") is *thlipsis*. It means to be under a crushing weight "due to the pressure of circumstances or the antagonism of persons."[2]

Jesus told the believers at Smyrna to be faithful. He reminded them that He transcends circumstances, and that through their deep connection with Him, they would overcome the pressure and difficulties. Jesus gave them hope and a crown of glory. Concerning this passage, Lewis Drummond, a close associate of Billy Graham, wrote:

> *Christ's admonition constitutes a wonderful promise, not only for the church of Smyrna in the first century, but for all of God's people of any age. Actually, it can be a blessed experience when God's people patiently endure pressure, persecution, and peril for the Lord Jesus Christ. As Peter said, "In this you greatly rejoice, though now for a little while you may have had to suffer grief in all kinds of trials. These have come so that your faith—of greater worth than gold, which perishes even though refined by fire—may be proved genuine and may result in praise, glory and honor when Jesus Christ is revealed" (1 Pet. 1:6–7 NIV).[3]*

APOSTASY (REBELLION) AND CULTURE WARS

These are the first three of the seven types of believers Jesus addressed in the first chapters of the book of Revelation.

Except for the persecuted believers of Smyrna, who held fast to their convictions and were encouraged to endure, even unto death, the believers, as a whole, were in a fallen state with regard to their spiritual practices. Instead of the believers influencing society with the Word of God, it appears that society influenced the believers, and there was a falling away, or *apostasia*, within the body of Christ.

Although the modern-day church does not exclusively live in "Babylon the Great," Scripture indicates that a large number of believers will be living in her before she is judged. We will discuss that judgment in a later chapter.

COME OUT OF HER, MY PEOPLE

Jeremiah 51:14 tells us: "Surely I will fill thee with men, as with caterpillars; and they shall lift up a shout against thee." The Babylonians lived for centuries worshipping idols and ancient mythology. Their erroneous beliefs would now be destroyed along with them.

Jesus gave Christians a warning about Babylon the Great in Revelation 18:4: "Come out of her, my people, that ye be not partakers of her sins."

"Come out of her, my people" is a call for God's people to disentangle themselves from the new norms of Babylonian culture that opposes their covenant with God's Word. "It may also be an evangelistic call to God's elect to come to faith in Christ and come out of Satan's kingdom (cf. Col. 1:13). In both cases, the message is to abandon the system."[4]

The United States has within her more Christians than any other nation in the world today.[5] Unfortunately, not all Christians are focused on the pure message of the Gospel. False teaching shifts morality, and pride, wealth, and malaise have crept into many churches and Christians' hearts. Therefore, the descriptions of the believers at Ephesus and Sardis can be found, to some extent, in Babylon the Great.

During the last two decades, political pundits have recognized intense political differences within the American population and have coined the phrase "culture wars" to describe the phenomenon. The

Bible does not mention the term "culture wars." It does, however, discuss two distinct spiritual kingdoms battling on earth, each kingdom opposing the other solely on the basis of its acceptance or rejection of God's Word. These opposing kingdoms are God's kingdom of light and knowledge, and Satan's kingdom of darkness and ignorance.

Most non-believers—who we call atheists or secular humanists—give no regard whatsoever to God's Word, deeming it insignificant within their worldview. However, believers are mandated by Scripture to base their entire worldview on the biblical moral protocol of Judeo-Christian doctrine. Yet this biblical worldview is held by only a remnant of believers in the last days. In the coming chapters, we will discover that sin corrupted five out of the seven groups of believers that Jesus addressed. His solution to every sin was to return to the Word—which should, of course, be the first love of all believers. For just as "the word was made flesh and dwelt among us" (John 1:14), that same Word should manifest in our personal lifestyles.

SYNAGOGUE OF SATAN

It is interesting to note that Scripture's description of the believers in Smyrna includes a reference to the "synagogue of Satan" that persecuted them: "I know thy works, and tribulation, and poverty . . . and I know the blasphemy of them [that] are of the synagogue of Satan" (Rev. 2:9).

In New Testament Greek, the word used for "synagogue" means "a house of assembly" or "a gathering place." "Assembly" can denote religious, political, or even social activist houses of assembly. Wherever people assemble and gather, a "groupthink," or common ideology, is considered a synagogue. This, of course, happens within all religious, social, or political parties whose members are like-minded and have common values.

Yet when an assembly is influenced by Satanic inspiration, it will always oppose biblical principles and defy biblical morals. The fruits of that ideology will sometimes manifest as violence, bigotry, hatred, and outright rebellion against biblical practices. It thus becomes a "synagogue of Satan" (Satan, meaning "adversary"). "These men [those who say they are believers but are not] *are a synagogue of Satan*. Their assembly for worship did not gather together God's people, but Satan's, who is 'the accuser of our brothers' (12:10)."[6]

It's important to keep this thought in mind while searching for the identity of Babylon the Great because, as Revelation 18:2 says, "Babylon the Great is fallen, is fallen and has become the habitation of devils, and the hold of every foul spirit, and a cage of every unclean and hateful bird (or demon)." Satan's ideology always opposes the authority of God's Word and especially those who follow it. That is why this ideology, likened unto the *apostasia*, will always oppose and hate Jews and Christians who are attempting to follow biblical principles.

The Bible reminds us that Satan continually opposes the authority of the Word, as well as "those who keep the commandments of God and hold to the testimony of Jesus" (Rev. 12:17 ESV). Jesus gives us a warning and a promise in John 10:10 (ESV), "The thief cometh not, but for to steal, and to kill, and to destroy I am come that they might have life, and that they might have it more abundantly."

Satan uses circumstances to steal our joy. We can't change some of our circumstances, but we can change our outlook. Remember, the Enemy comes to make our lives miserable (1 Pet. 5:8). We need to keep fighting for biblical principles and not let the gatherers at the synagogue of Satan rob us of the promise Jesus offers in John 10:10.

THE PERSECUTION OF CHRISTIANS

The World Atlas reports that Christians number 2.2 billion globally,[7] representing 32 percent of the world's population. In early November of

2012, German Chancellor Angela Merkel declared that Christianity was "the most persecuted religion in the world." Robert Shortt's research report for Civitas UK[8] confirms Merkel's claim.[9] Christianity is persecuted like no other religion in the world.[10]

Former American Vice President Mike Pence cited statistics from the Open Door Foundation noting that "83 percent of the world's population lives in nations where religious freedom is threatened or banned."[11] He singled out as "unparalleled" the brutal treatment of the 300,000 secret believers in North Korea who risk their lives to follow their Christian beliefs. Up to 70,000 Christians in North Korea have been sent to labor camps because of their faith.[12] The North Korean regime formally demands its officials to, in their words, "wipe out the seed of Christian reactionaries."[13]

According to the Open Doors Foundation, reporting in 2018, "Of the fifty countries on the Open Doors' World Watch List, thirty saw an increase in persecution during the reporting period. Our new research indicates that throughout the world, **approximately 215 million Christians experience high, very high, or extreme persecution for following Jesus.** Nearly one of every twelve Christians in the world lives in an area, or in a culture, in which Christianity is illegal, forbidden or punished."[14]

As I wrote a few pages ago, Jesus gives us the solution in His exhortation to the believers of Smyrna in Revelation 2:10 (ESV): "Be faithful unto death and I will give you the crown of life." The resources we have in Jesus Christ are completely adequate. They are the *only* resources we need to overcome the Adversary and his corrupt schemes.

Revelation 2:10 should speak loudly to the 1.5 million Middle Eastern Christians who have been forced to leave their homes or were martyred due to the ravages of ISIS.[15] A global jihad of hatred, very similar to what Adolph Hitler did, is being carried out against Jews and

Christians, but nothing today can be compared to what will happen in the tribulation period.

My wife and I recently traveled to Poland and toured several Nazi death camps. Our guide for the trip was Holocaust survivor Irving Roth. Irving shared with us how he and his family suffered in the Auschwitz death camp. He said he will never forget the day the Nazi guards were nowhere to be found. Suddenly, the door of his barracks was kicked open, and two American soldiers walked in—one white and one black—and said, "You are free!" Yet Irving shared something else with us that was just as alarming as what we saw at the death camps. He said that once Hitler and the National Socialist Party, also known as the Nazi party, gained power through the election process, the first thing they did was enforce a national boycott, divestment, and sanctions movement on all Jewish businesses. In fact, he said that this movement is exactly what some nations and activists are trying to enforce against Israel today (the BDS movement).

Something is happening around the world in the spiritual realm. Biblical prophecy predicted it, and we are watching its fulfillment through every form of international media. The "synagogue of Satan" is rising up; the demons who controlled Hitler are about to make another appearance in the history of planet earth. But we don't need to be afraid. Scripture tells us:

- Revelation 2:10 (ESV): "Be faithful unto death . . ."
- Psalm 116:15 (ESV): "Precious in the sight of the LORD is the death of his saints."
- First Corinthians 1:18 (ESV): "For the word of the cross is folly to those who are perishing, but to us who are being saved it is the power of God."

ACCUSATIONS AGAINST AMERICAN CHRISTIANS

Since America has the largest number of Christians of any nation in the world, certainly these verses must apply to us. As you may recall, Jeremiah 51:14 states, "For I will fill thee [O Babylon] with men, as with caterpillars . . . and they shall lift up a shout against her!" John added to that statement 750 years later: "Come out of her, my people, that ye be not partakers of her sins, and that ye receive not of her plagues" (Rev. 18:4).

Although many individuals, mainly children, have been sexually and mentally abused in both Satanic rituals and human trafficking, Christians have not yet experienced physical persecution in North America. We are, however, experiencing verbal accusations from vast numbers of people assembled in opposition to Judeo-Christian values. For example, if you:

Stand up for traditional marriage	You are labeled **homophobic**[16]
Stand against Muslim terrorism	You are labeled **Islamaphobic and racist**
Stand up for the life of the unborn	You are labeled as waging **war on women**
Stand up for capitalism	You are labeled a **greedy one-percenter**
Believe Jesus is the only way to heaven	You are labeled **non-inclusive** or **narrow-minded**

Jesus said in Revelation 12:10 that Satan is "the accuser of the brethren . . . which accused them before our God day and night." Holocaust survivor Irving Roth is well acquainted with this statement. He began our tour of Auschwitz by telling us that persecution always starts with words. Before the Jews were imprisoned in horrific concentration camps, there was a period of time during which the Nazi-controlled media used false accusations to stir up the general population against the Jews. There is nothing new about "fake news." The Nazis declared that the Jews were responsible for the poor economic climate of the day, the stock market crash of the 1930s, and the Great Depression. Hitler and his followers blamed everything bad on the Jews, and German people followed along—like sheep to the slaughter.

FIGHTING FOR THE SOUL OF AMERICA

In *Dark Agenda*, Horowitz explains that there is a battle over the soul of our nation. It is a battle between left-wing progressive groups who oppose biblical values and right-wing conservatives who hold to the Constitutional foundations of "one nation under God."

According to Horowitz, this battle began in the early 1960s, when the infamous atheist Madalyn Murray O'Hair, egged on by the American Civil Liberties Union (ACLU), succeeded in getting Bible reading and prayer out of the American school system by "overturing nearly two centuries of precedent and tradition, and change the life of a nation."[17]

Scripture warns us in Proverbs 22:6, "Train up a child in the way he should go: and when he is old, he will not depart from it." Senseless mass shootings, total disregard for others, drug addiction, and an immoral society that has no limits for sexual promiscuity: all these things have led to a confused generation, unhinged from any consciousness of the golden rule: "So whatever you wish that others would do to you, do also to them" (Matt. 7:12 ESV).

The word *babel*, from which we get the word Babylon, means confusion, or "to confuse."[18] Babylonian culture, as in the past (Gen. 11), will be overcome with the same confused generation.

The book of Isaiah states: "my ways are higher than your ways and my thoughts than your thoughts" (Isa. 55:9). In opposition to God's ways, Romans 1 tells us what a society will think like, once it forsakes God's ways.

> *Because that, when they knew God, they glorified him not as God, neither were thankful; but became vain in their imaginations, and their foolish heart was darkened . . . And even as they did not like to retain God in their knowledge, God gave them over to a reprobate mind, to do those things which are not convenient; being filled with all unrighteousness, fornication, wickedness, covetousness, maliciousness, full of envy, murder, debate, deceit, malignity, whisperers, backbiters, haters of God, despiteful, proud, boasters, inventors of evil things, disobedient to parents, without understanding, covenant breakers (Romans 1:21, 28–31).*

The American Democrat's platform since 2004 promised "faith and family, duty and service, individual freedom and a common purpose to build one nation." But a major revision to the that platform took place at the Democratic National Convention of 2012 when "former Ohio Governor Ted Strickland, mindful of the religious sentiment of his constituents, proposed to insert a reference to 'God-given potential' and also to restore the promise Obama had made (and not kept) to recognize Jerusalem as the capital of Israel. The amendment failed by voice vote three times, but the convention chair Antonio Villaraigosa ruled that it actually passed. "Democrats Boo God" became the headline of the day."[19] They booed when Villaraigosa called it for the "aye" voters. However, the fact remains that they removed all mention of God and Israel from the platform that day.

So what does this have to do with Bible prophecy? Everything, when it comes to America's role in Scripture.

TYPOLOGY: NEBUCHADNEZZAR'S PRIDE AND NARCISSISM

Previously, we explained the theological tool called typology. Typology happens when the history of the past repeats itself in the future. In other words, what happened "then and there" parallels what is happening "here and now."

On our tour of the Polish death camps, Holocaust survivor Irving Roth cited the example of Adolf Hitler and his use of boycott, divestment, and sanctions to eliminate the Jewish people. That same agenda is happening now, in real-time, in the modern BDS movement.

Biblical typology, however, goes back much further than a mere eighty years. In 600 BC, King Nebuchadnezzar ruled historical Babylon (a typological nation reflecting the same characteristics as the latter-day nation Babylon the Great found in the book of Revelation). Scripture states that God raised historical Babylon and made her great. Scripture also prophesies that He will raise latter-day Babylon and make her great. Both are providential nations, yet both nations will fall . . . and for the same reasons.

Shortly after Daniel interpreted King Nebuchadnezzar's dream and told him that God raised Babylon as a providential nation, Nebuchadnezzar forgot about God and decided to build an idol of his god. Consequently, if the people did not bow their knee to this god, they would be thrown into a fiery furnace. It was at this time that Shadrach, Meshach, and Abednego refused to bow. Nebuchadnezzar threw them into the fire, yet a fourth Man miraculously appeared in the flames and delivered the three Hebrew boys (Dan. 3). The Bible says that the fourth Man had an image as of the Son of God. Everyone was astonished at the miracle, and Nebuchadnezzar publicly professed his allegiance to the God of Israel.

Daniel 4:3 writes, "How great are his signs, how mighty his wonders!

His kingdom is an everlasting kingdom, and his dominion endures from generation to generation (ESV)."

Although Nebuchadnezzar acknowledged God at one point in his life, there was a turning point, after which he disregarded God. In Daniel 4, he looked over his great nation and said, "Is not this great Babylon, which I have built by my mighty power as a royal residence and for the glory of my majesty?" While the words were still in the king's mouth, there fell a voice from heaven that said, "O King Nebuchadnezzar, to you it is spoken: The kingdom has departed from you, and you shall be driven from among men, and your dwelling shall be with the beasts of the field. And you shall be made to eat grass like an ox, and seven periods of time shall pass over you until you know the Most High rules the kingdom of men and gives it to whom he will" (Dan. 4:30–31 ESV).

Pride and narcissism were at the root of Nebuchadnezzar's downfall in historical Babylon, and pride and narcissism will be at the root of the downfall of Babylon the Great. As stated in Isaiah 47:

> *Therefore hear now this, thou that art given to pleasures, that dwellest carelessly, that sayest in thine heart, I am, and none else beside me; I shall not sit as a widow, neither shall I know the loss of children: for thou hast trusted in they wickedness: thou hast said, None seeth me. Thy wisdom and thy knowledge, it hath perverted thee; and thou hast said in thine heart, I am, and none else beside me (Isa. 47:8, 10).*

As soon as Nebuchadnezzar declared that statement, the kingdom departed from him, and he was driven into insanity (Dan. 4:32). As mentioned earlier he was given over to a mental illness known as boanthropy. Significantly, the Bible says that as God handed him over to a darkened mind, "they" drove him into the wilderness, and "they" made him eat grass like a beast of the field. Who were "they"? The Bible says we wrestle not with flesh and blood but against principalities, powers, and rulers of darkness. Nebuchadnezzar has been dead for over 2,500 years, but the spirits that drove him into darkness are still alive and well on earth today.

PRIDE AND NARCISSISM IN BABYLON THE GREAT

Oddly enough, Bible prophesies that the narcissistic tendencies affecting Nebuchadnezzar will also be prevalent in the last days of Babylon the Great. Will they be caused by the same demonic spirits?

Revelation 18:2 says, "Babylon the Great is fallen, is fallen and has become the habitation of devils, and the hold of every foul spirit, and a cage of every unclean and hateful bird (or demon)." It seems people within Babylon the Great will be driven to darkness and become unhinged with their godless ideology. They will begin to act out their frustrations when God hands them over to a "reprobate mind"—that is, a mind that cannot discern between good and evil—according to Romans 1:28. Therefore evil will become good, and good will become evil. They will be driven to achieve their godless agenda at any cost, to others or to themselves.

Horowitz explains that the progressive left movement today is fueled by the teachings of the late Saul Alinsky. Ironically, Alinsky wrote in his 1971 book *Rules for Radicals*, "The first radical known to man who rebelled against the establishment and did it so effectively that he at least won his own Kingdom."[20] He was, of course, referring directly to Lucifer.

Alinsky's fourth rule states, "The most important weapon known to mankind are satire and ridicule."[21] Does this equate to the modern-day slurs of "war against women," "homophobic," "Islamophobic," and "xenophobic," which many apply to those who disagree with their progressive groupthink ideology?

Revelation 12:10 talks about the accuser, who accuses believers before God "night and day." Friends, we must clearly understand that Satan is the accuser of the brethren. He works continually to tempt us to sin, then turns around and accuses us before God and ourselves. He accuses us of things for which we are not guilty in an attempt to shame, humiliate, and bully us. While we need to remember that he's the accuser, we also need to remember that Satan is all about intimidation. Every believer wrestles with thoughts attitudes and opinions (spirits) that oppose the "word" (conscience) inside of us. However, God's Holy Spirit is about conviction and transformation. Satan is in the shame business. The Holy Spirit is in the conviction business, leading hearts and minds to repentance, forgiveness, and restoration. Satan can accuse us of many things, but in the end, the Holy Spirit will lead us to truth about ourselves and offer redemption through Christ.

There is therefore now no condemnation to them which are in Christ Jesus, who walk not after the flesh, but after the Spirit. For the law of the Spirit of life in Christ Jesus hath made me free from the law of sin and death (Rom 8:1, 2).

Recently I was having a conversation with a friend in Florida who is a die-hard Democrat. As a pondering question, I asked him, "If someone is wearing a red hat in support of a political party and another person comes out of nowhere and sucker punches them in the face, for no other reason than because they're wearing a red hat, is the person wearing the hat a fascist? Or is the person who punched them in the face the fascist?"

I could get no answer from my friend. Of course, some would say that wearing a red hat triggered the response. In other words, they are saying that if someone disagrees with you, you have the right to punch them in the face, riot in the streets, and burn and desecrate private property. The justification being that you were triggered, and those people deserved it. Hitler's brown shirts, from the Nazi Party, would probably agree with that logic.

Obviously, Jesus' teaching of, "Thou hypocrite, first cast out the beam out of thine own eye; and then shalt thou see clearly to cast out the mote out of thy brother's eye" (Mat 7:5) need not apply.

GOD'S AMAZING DISCERNMENT

In any warfare, you have intelligence and counterintelligence. These two aspects of warfare are also necessary for spiritual warfare, which is embedded in thoughts, attitudes, and opinions expressed. Two thousand years ago, when an unhinged crowd screamed, "Crucify him! Crucify him!" most people in the crowd knew that Jesus had done nothing wrong. However, God's wisdom and intelligence was amazingly discerning. First Corinthians 2 states: "But we speak the wisdom of God in a mystery, even the hidden wisdom, which none of the princes of this world knew: for had they known it, they would not have crucified the Lord of glory" (1 Cor. 2:7–8). There were no princes at the crucifixion; however, in the spirit realm, there were "principalities, powers and rulers of darkness" that worked through the assemblies gathered there.

Ironically, God knew and precisely prophesied what the free will of some men would do when they rejected His Son. But the demonic spirits manipulating those men were putting a noose around their own necks in the process. Without a crucifixion, there could be no resurrection. Without the shedding of innocent blood, there could be no redemption from sin. Without the price of death paid for those sins, there could be no eternal life for those who believed.

Those who oppose and reject the godly heritage and covenant of Babylon the Great are doomed to fulfill the very words of a God that they think does not exist.

"[I have] given [my people] into thine hand [oh Babylon]; thou didst shew them no mercy; upon the ancient hast thou heavily laid thy yoke" (Isa. 47:6).

With this chapter, we can now add several more descriptions of Babylon the Great, which all meet the criteria for America's role in biblical prophecy:

30) (Rev. 18:4; Jer. 51:14) She is a nation that has a large amount of God's people within her.
31) (Rev. 2:2–7) (Ephesus) She has Christians within her who have lost their "first love" for Christ.
32) (Rev. 3:1–6) (Sardis) She has Christians within her who have "dead works."
33) (Rev. 2:8-11) (Smyrna) She has Christians within her who are persecuted.

God has prophesied a specific outcome for Babylon the Great, but He also has an extraordinary plan for those who serve Him. Remember, He rewards those who diligently seek Him, and He never fails to fulfill His promises.

Something very good is about to happen to those who trust in God's Word and discipline themselves to choose to follow it in their everyday lifestyle. A day will soon come when God will fulfill multiple biblical prophecies in rapid succession. The miracle of Shadrach, Meshach, and Abednego will pale in comparison to what God has planned for his bride in Babylon the Great.

CHAPTER SEVEN

THE BELIEVERS OF PERGAMOS AND THYATIRA

IN THE PREVIOUS chapter, we discussed Jesus' warning that there will be an apostasy or spiritual "falling away" before He returns. This apostasy will affect believers immediately before a seven-year global tribulation begins. The flood of temptation in the last days will be blatantly clear. However, the sins of the believers in Pergamos and Thyatira are perhaps the most blatantly available in our world of high-tech social media.

The conclusion Jesus gave in each of his admonitions to the seven categories of believers—he who has an ear, let him hear what the Spirit says—makes it clear that He wasn't only speaking to those early believers. His warnings are not any less essential today. Those sins wrestled with 2,000 years ago are alive and well in Mystery, Babylon the Great. In our continued study of the seven churches of Revelation, this will become increasingly clear. But will we have an ear to hear?

We've examined the sins of the believers at Ephesus, Sardis, and Smyrna. Another church Jesus spoke to lived in Pergamos. They are the fourth group of believers we will study.

THE FOURTH GROUP: PERGAMOS BELIEVERS (Rev. 2:12–17)

From approximately 63 BC to AD 24, the city of Pergamos, located in the western portion of Asia Minor, was one of the most influential cultural and religious centers in the world. Located atop a hill, which offered an advantage in the event of an attack, Pergamos was known for her temples honoring Roman emperors and pagan gods, including Zeus. As a cultural center, the city was immersed in idolatry, especially the worship of Dionysus and Aphrodite (both connected with fertility and resulting immorality). It is no wonder that believers of Pergamos faced intense pressure to conform or even renounce their faith. Unfortunately, some did compromise, and fell into idolatry and sexual immorality.

Jesus spoke to the believers of this city in Revelation 2:

> *[These things I say unto Pergamos] I know where you dwell, where Satan's throne is. Yet you hold fast to my name . . . But I have a few things against you: you have some there who hold the teaching of Balaam, who taught Balak to put a stumbling block before the sons of Israel, so that they might eat food sacrificed to idols, and practice sexual immorality. So also you have some who hold the teaching of the Nicolaitans. Therefore repent. If not, I will come to you soon and war against them with the sword of my mouth . . . [but] to the one who conquers I will give him . . . a new name (Rev. 2:13–16 ESV).*

The book of Ecclesiastes says, "there is nothing new" under the sun. This exactly why Jesus can warn today's believers by referring to the same moral issues Pergamos and Thyatira battled 2,000 years ago. Yet Jesus goes back even further into history in His message to Pergamos. He connects their sin directly to those Children of Israel in the Old Testament who destroyed themselves by participating in sexual immorality. We will take a closer look at this in a moment. But first, let's read what Jesus said to the believers in Thyatira, who faced similar challenges with sexual immorality.

THE FIFTH GROUP: THYATIRA BELIEVERS
(Rev. 2:18–27)

Along a route that connected Pergamos and Sardis sat the city of Thyatira. Thyatira's economy revolved around trades and crafts. The city featured large trade guilds that met regularly to worship patron deities. People who refused to participate in these guilds were isolated both economically and socially.

The city hosted the cult of Apollo, and many felt the Roman emperor was an earthly manifestation of this god. Like Pergamos, the citizens of Thyatira had a problem with sexual immorality.

> *I know your works, your love and faith, and service and patient*
> *endurance [in this passage Jesus is talking to good people who*
> *love God and are working hard in the church for the Kingdom of*
> *God]. But I have this against you, that you tolerate that woman*
> *Jezebel, who calls herself a prophetess and is teaching and*
> *seducing my servants to practice sexual immorality [porneuo]*
> *and to eat food sacrificed to idols. I gave her time to repent, but*
> *she refuses to repent of her sexual immorality [porneia]. Behold,*

I will throw her onto a sickbed, and those who commit adultery with her I will throw into a great tribulation, unless they repent of her works, and I will strike her children dead. And all the churches will know that I am he who searches mind and heart: and I will give to each of you according to your works. But to the rest of you in Thyatira, who do not hold this teaching, who have not learned what some call the deep things of Satan, to you I say, I do not lay on you any other burden. Only hold fast what you have until I come (Rev. 2:19–25 ESV).

We see plainly from the letters to the believers at Pergamos and Thyatira that both were involved in idolatry and sexual immorality. But who are Balaam and the Nicolaitans in the letter to the Pergamos believers? And what was meant by the reference to Jezebel and the "deep things of Satan" in the letter to the believers in Thyatira?

WHO WAS BALAAM?

To the believers of Pergamos, Jesus mentioned Balaam and the Nicolaitans. So what in the world was He talking about? Who was Balaam? To answer this question, we must flip back to our Old Testament, to the portion of Israel's history dating more than a thousand years prior and recorded in Numbers 22–24.

Our story begins some time after Moses, through God's deliverance, led the Children of Israel from Egyptian slavery. They had nearly completed their wilderness journey, and Joshua was preparing to lead them into the Promised Land. On their way, however, they found themselves opposed by the Moabites, who sat between them and the Jordan River on their journey to Canaan.

Before we go any further in the story, we need to understand who these Moabites were. Moab was a tribe that descended from Lot's son

Moab. His name means "water of a father; i.e., seed, progeny; desire; progeny of a father; of the father. Waste; nothingness."[1] Why such a horrible name? Genesis 19:30–38 details the story of Lot's daughters and their fear that the entire world had perished. They felt it was their responsibility to repopulate the world, and so they got their daddy drunk and had sexual relations with him. The result of these immoral acts was two sons, Moab[2] and Ammon. Both Moab and Ammon's descendants eventually became enemies of the Children of Israel. And it is the Moabites that act as obstacles for Israel in Numbers 22–24.

As Israel prepared to enter the Promised Land, King Balak of Moab offered to the prophet Balaam a large payment to curse the invading Israelite army. Balaam was a pagan sorcerer and magician, and his family were specialists who blessed or cursed people for the right price. But God used Balaam for His purposes—He intervened against King Balak's request, and warned Balaam not to curse the Children of Israel. Balaam obeyed the Lord, much to King Balak's displeasure.

Israel eventually defeated the Moabites, but Balaam convinced the Israelites to refrain from killing the Moabite women and to take them as wives instead. Those wives eventually led Israel's men to embrace pagan gods, including the ancient Babylonian god known as Baal. Baalite worship ceremonies involved sexual activity with multiple partners. By leading the Children of Israel to other gods, Balaam proved himself to be a false prophet (Deut. 13:2, 3). His example is used in Revelation to warn believers today of what tactics to watch for, and especially of the god to which these false prophets like Balaam will lead them.

Numbers 25:1–3 warns:

> *And Israel abode in Shittim, and the people began to commit*
> *whoredom with the daughters of Moab. And they [the daughters*
> *of Moab] called the people unto the sacrifices of their gods: and*

the people did eat, and bowed down to their gods. And Israel
joined himself unto Baal.

Balaam knew he could not curse Israel, because God's presence protected them. So he schemed to have them curse themselves through immorality and idolatry—the promise of pleasure.

The Enemy is powerless to curse us, but he often puts things in front of us that direct us away from God. The only power he has over us is the power we give him through our free will—the choices we make.

The spirit manipulating Balaam knew God would judge Israel for their immorality and idolatry. The Lord's anger showed itself in a plague that began to strike down thousands among Israel and seemed as if it would continue until the whole nation was consumed.

"Though Balaam was a greedy prophet for hire, God nevertheless used him to make an accurate prediction of the coming Messiah: "A star shall come forth from Jacob, a scepter shall rise from Israel" (Num. 24:17)."[3]

Believers who practice Balaam's tactics today seem oblivious to the fact that any sexual involvement outside the bond of holy matrimony is a form of defiance against God's laws. It is putting one's own sensual appetite ahead of God's moral code of ethics and His best way for relationships to grow and prosper. The doctrine of Balaam is a doctrine of defiance.

So how do we overcome Balaam's doctrine?

- Resist the devil (1 Pet. 5:9; James 4:7).
- Stand firm against the schemes of the devil (Eph. 6:11).

We are called to resist the doctrine of defiance and be believers who focus on the mortal blow Jesus' life, death, and resurrection gave to Satan and the followers of Balaam.

WHO WERE THE NICOLAITANS?

Little is known about this group, but their connection to the doctrine of Balaam becomes evident in studying what we do know. Revelation 2:15 (ESV) explains that the doctrine of the Nicolaitans works hand-in-hand with the practices of Balaam: "So also you have some who hold the teaching of the Nicolaitans." The Nicolaitans promoted an acceptance of pagan practices and immoral behavior—a yielding of the separation (sanctification) to which the church was called. While the church at Ephesus was commended for rejecting the Nicolaitan's heretical teachings, the church at Pergamos was called to repentance for aligning with them.

The term "Nicolaitans" is derived from two Greek words: *nikos*, meaning "conquer" or "subdue", and *laos*, meaning "laity." *Laity* refers to laypeople of the church, distinct from the leadership. "Nicolaitan" is then a descriptive term for leadership who are motivated to conquer and subdue believers of Christ, enticing them to leave sound doctrine by appealing to their fleshly desires—another satanic tactic. This was the reason Jesus despised the doctrine and the deeds of the Nicolaitans. He knows that following their teachings will lead a person to utter destruction.

Nicolaitan teaching, or doctrine, works within the structure of the church from the top down, with leaders teaching heresies to those who will follow them. Nicolas of Antioch, introduced in Acts 6:5, is an example of this. Nicolas was a leader (deacon) within the church of Antioch. He converted from paganism to Judaism and eventually to Christianity. But according to early church records, it is apparent that Nicolas of Antioch remained immersed in occultism and sexual immorality.

Nicolas taught a doctrine of compromise, implying that total separation between Christianity and the practice of pagan rituals was not necessary. He had no problem integrating his belief systems into the church or aversion to enticing believers to participate in occultist practices. He taught a perverted form of grace by teaching and adhering to gnostic principles.

Nicolas perverted grace in the sense that he convinced believers they could knowingly live a lifestyle of continuous immorality and idolatry without suffering eternal consequences.[4] In other words, repentance was no more than just lip service with absolutely no commitment to discontinue the sins that they confessed.

John linked "the practices of the Nicolaitans with the practices of those who listened to Balaam (Revelation 2:14–15). Those who followed Balaam in Numbers used Midianite women to seduce the men of Israel and lead them to worship other gods. Examples of such acts have played out with Solomon, for instance, when his wives from pagan religions led him astray and after other gods" (1 Kings 11:1–5).[5]

Believers are warned in 1 Corinthians 6:9–10 (ESV) that "neither fornicators, nor idolaters, nor adulterers, nor men who practice homosexuality, nor thieves, nor greedy, nor drunkards, nor revilers, nor swindlers will inherit the kingdom of God."

God has called His people to be "set apart" from the world, beginning with Israel (Ex. 19:5–6) and then again with the church (1 Pet. 2:9–11). This separation is marred when we give in to outside pressures or internal temptations. Instead, Hebrews 12:1 says, "let us lay aside every weight, and the sin which doth so easily beset us, and let us run with patience the race that is set before us." The Greek word for "beset us" means "ensnares us" (NKJV rendering) or "clings too closely" (ESV rendering). So what are some present-day Nicolaitan doctrines that would obstruct us from entering into God's will?

Today we have liberal progressive church leaders who deny Scriptures concerning:

- the virgin birth of Jesus
- the death and resurrection of Jesus

- the deity of Jesus (they claim He was just a prophet, not the Son of God)
- the existence of hell
- the necessity of repentance from sin.

Perhaps the greatest departure from Scripture within our North American Judeo-Christian culture has been from the view that traditional marriage is marriage between one man and one woman. Nowhere in Scripture is marriage ever performed other than between a man and a woman. Yet today, many church leaders will marry anybody to anyone and call it holy matrimony. This has become a major bone of contention between North American culture and Judeo-Christian protocol.

It is no longer enough that adults live in sexual immorality and that their lifestyles are justified and even considered praiseworthy. We have now taken God's Word out of schools. Rather than passing out Bibles, we hand out condoms and teach courses on how to use them. Encouraging our children to break the moral codes set forth in Scripture, we even equip them for safe sex. Should someone get pregnant, they can just go down to the local Temple of Baal and sacrifice their baby for financial benefit and have no responsibility to raise him or her.

Jesus warned that in the last days, false teachers called Nicolaitans will once again utilize the deception of Balaam. Their doctrines or teachings will seduce Christians away from the Word of God. Jesus knew that following their teachings would lead a person to utter destruction.

In 2 Timothy 4:3 (ESV), we are told that a time is coming "when people will not endure sound teaching but [will instead have] itching ears." Many will turn away from the truth and wander off into myths. But did you know God encourages us to test and discern what we hear and are taught? The litmus test is always the Word of God.

TESTING THE SPIRITS

In 1 John 4:1 we read, "Beloved, believe not every spirit, but try the spirits whether they are of God." But how do we try (or test) the spirits, and what are some of the modern-day myths that the Nicolaitans are teaching today? What are they saying about Jesus and the Judeo-Christian values on which our society was established through the Founding Fathers' covenant with God?

1 John 4:1 tells us to "try [prove, discern, distinguish] the spirits whether they are of God." Today we have liberal progressive *church leaders* who deny the virgin birth of Jesus, His death and resurrection, the necessity of repentance from sexual immorality, and even the existence of hell. Some have stated that the Bible is no longer relevant for our culture. Yet according to prophecy, those who have "fallen away" are fulfilling the very prophecies they deny. Those who say the Bible is no longer relevant in our society don't realize that, according to the Bible, their opinions are no longer relevant to God. They are fulfilling exactly what Scripture said would happen in latter-day Babylon. They have followed the way of Balaam.

Many modern-day progressive interpretations of Scripture are no longer relevant to biblical practice. So-called "progressive" groupthink has, in fact, made our society regressive, causing many to commit the exact sins that Jesus prophesied would be commonplace before His return. And all this is marketed in the name of achievement, growth, and progressivism.

Of course, we know the truth—that these lies are not new and are propagated not simply by man, but by the spirits at work behind the scenes. The same spirits who have been at work for thousands of years. They are not new to their agenda, and as is so plainly evident in observing the "culture wars," their methods are incredibly effective. They worm their false teachings into hearts and minds by a variety of means, often portraying themselves as the godly choice. But by implementing God's directive to test those things which we hear and are taught, we can guard ourselves against their perverted "truths."

So let's test some of these doctrines with God's Word, and examine some popular modern-day "Nicolaitan" teachings.

WHAT IS THE TRUTH ABOUT JESUS?

Looking first at the Nicolaitan doctrine that claims Jesus was a prophet, not the Son of God, what can we find in the Scriptures regarding this idea?

Paul writes in Romans 10:9–10, "if thou shalt confess with thy mouth the Lord Jesus Christ, and shalt believe in thine heart that God hath raised him from the dead, thou shalt be saved. For with the heart man believeth . . . and with the mouth confession is made unto salvation." Indeed, salvation can only be achieved by confessing that truth.

According to 1 John 4:3, "every spirit that confesseth not that Jesus Christ is come in the flesh is not of God: and this is that *spirit* of antichrist, whereof ye have heard that it should come; and even now already is it in the world."

John 15:26 says, "but when the Comforter is come . . . he shall testify of Me."

In Matthew 12:34, Jesus says, "O generation of vipers, how can ye being evil, speak good things? For out of the abundance of the heart the mouth speaketh."

Remember, Jesus said if we confess Him as Lord and believe in our hearts that God has raised Him from the dead, we will be saved. But saved from what? If there is no hell, as some progressive church leaders teach, what have we been saved from? We will test this teaching against Scripture in a moment.

By searching God's Word, we learn that Jesus Himself claimed to be the Son of God and that this doctrine was also taught by Paul. We learn that He was crucified and rose from the dead for our salvation. If a spiritual leader does not preach the death and resurrection of Jesus Christ, they are teaching a Nicolaitan doctrine. It is not the spirit of Christ coming out of that vessel, but another spirit.

We have seen in multiple passages of Scripture, even from the mouth of Jesus that Nicolaitan doctrine sets itself against the truth and will not line up with what we read in God's Word. In this same way we have demonstrated here, we can use His Word as the litmus test for all Nicolaitan doctrine. The method works. But it also makes clear the critical importance for us believers to stay daily in the Word and study always what is written. Without a full and deep knowledge of the Scriptures, we will be susceptible to lies set against us.

GODLY FEAR VS. WORLDLY FEAR

We have listed and observed some of the teachings of liberal progressive church leaders. We have learned that Scripture clearly proves the idea that Jesus was not only a prophet but that He was resurrected from the dead to save us from sin. Let's now look at another of these Nicolaitan teachings, the idea that there is no hell. We will begin by distinguishing between the two types of fear described in the Bible: worldly fear and godly fear.

Paul admonished us in Philippians 2:12 to "work out your own salvation with fear and trembling." But why would the man who wrote two thirds of the New Testament tell us to work out our salvation with "fear and trembling"? We will examine Scripture to find out more.

Proverbs 1:7 tells us, "The fear of the LORD is the beginning of knowledge."

Likewise, Proverbs 9:10 says, "The fear of the LORD is the beginning of wisdom."

Did you know that according to Isaiah 11, fear is one of the seven spirits, or characteristics, of God's presence? But this is not the same fear we are accustomed to. *Fear* in this case means to have a "holy reverence."

According to biblical prophecy, the Messiah would supernaturally manifest those seven characteristics: "And the Spirit of the LORD shall rest upon him, the Spirit of wisdom and understanding, counsel and might, knowledge and the fear of the LORD" (Isa. 11:2). And we now know that He did. In fact, in Luke 4, Jesus referred to this passage of Isaiah, saying:

> *The Spirit of the Lord is upon me, because he hath anointed*
> *me to preach the gospel to the poor; he hath sent me to heal the*
> *brokenhearted, to preach deliverance to the captives,*
> *and recovering of sight to the blind, to set at liberty them that*
> *are bruised, to preach the acceptable year of the Lord*
> *(Luke 4:18–19).*

According to Isaiah 11:3 (ESV), "And his [Jesus] delight shall be in the fear of the LORD." There are two types of fear in the Bible: worldly fear and godly fear.

John writes in 1 John 4:18, "perfect love casteth out [worldly] fear . . . because [worldly] fear hath torment."

Believers are encouraged in 2 Timothy 1:7 that, "God hath not given us the spirit of fear but of power, and of love, and of a sound mind."

Jesus distinguished between the two kinds of fears in Matthew 10:28 (ESV), saying, "do not fear [worldly] those who kill the body but cannot kill the soul. Rather fear him [God/godly fear] who can destroy both soul and body in hell."

Jesus mentions hell four times in the New Testament:

- In Revelation 21:8 (ESV), He says, "But as for the cowardly, the faithless, the detestable, as for murderers, the sexually immoral, sorcerers, idolaters, and all liars, their portion will be in the lake that burns with fire and sulfur, which is the second death."

- In Revelation 2:11 (ESV), Jesus tells us: "He who has an ear, let him hear what the Spirit says to the churches. The one who conquers will not be hurt by the second death."
- In Matthew 13:41–43 (ESV) that "angels will gather out of his kingdom all causes of sin and all lawbreakers, and throw them into the fiery furnace. In that place there will be weeping and gnashing of teeth."
- In Revelation 20:10 (ESV) Jesus tells us that the lake of fire (furnace) will last "day and night, forever and ever"—in other words, eternity.

Since Jesus warned us of hell, how can modern-day teachers deny that hell exists? This is obviously another spirit at work (And I will give you a hint: it is *not* the Holy Spirit!).

If you want to be an overcomer, you must cast down the doctrines of the Nicolaitan spirit. You must decide whether to fear God and follow the Word or to fear man and follow the herd.

The good news of the gospel is that Jesus offers us victory over worldly fear if we walk first in godly love. When we walk in perfect love, we overcome the fear of man. Because "there is no fear in love, but perfect love casts out fear. For fear has to do with punishment, and whoever fears has not been perfected in love" (1 John 4:18 ESV).

FEAR OF MAN

The Nicolaitan spirit operates within Babylon the Great to push believers towards its secular humanist groupthink ideology by way of the sort of "outside pressures" mentioned previously. We read about this in the previous chapter, but it is worth discussing again here, especially in light of what we have learned about the believers of Pergamos and Thyatira.

There is an undeniable "fear of man" within our North American culture, particularly for those who do not follow the herd mentality of modern liberalism. The suffix word *phobia* is defined as "an exaggerated usually inexplicable and illogical fear of a particular object, class of objects, or situation."[6] In modern America, if you disagree or refuse to comply with a particular idea or belief held within the liberal agenda, you will be falsely accused of a multitude of phobias. Specific terminology and name-calling are used to intimidate dissenters and create this "fear of man."

We discussed in the previous chapter some of the terminology used to pressure and intimidate those who maintain a biblical worldview. We will look at a few examples again here.

As we've noted in an earlier chapter, you will be called:

- *Islamophobic*: if you disapprove of Islamic terrorism.
- *Homophobic*: if you disagree with current LGBTQ ideologies.
- *Xenophobic*: if you disagree with open-door immigration policies.

Of course, when we consider all the ways in which our modern Babylonian society and the Nicolaitan spirit try to bully believers away from following the Word of God, these names are just the tip of the iceberg.

We have now unveiled the mystery of Balaam and the Nicolaitan leaders—their influence on the historical church of Pergamos as well as on modern-day believers. We have seen some of the ways that their teachings affect a believer's sanctification. Now let's return to Jesus' message to the believers in Thyatira to explore the two terms referenced there.

WHO WAS JEZEBEL?

Jesus mentioned two more names in His address to the church of Thyatira in Revelation 2. We will first look at "that woman Jezebel."

> But I have a few things against you: you have some there who
> hold the teaching of Balaam . . . But I have this against you, that
> you tolerate that woman Jezebel, who calls herself a prophetess
> and is teaching and seducing my servants to practice sexual
> immorality [pornevu] and to eat food sacrificed to idols
> (Rev. 2:14, 20 ESV).

Who was Jezebel? And why did she call herself a prophetess?

In the ninth century BC, during the time of Elijah the prophet's ministry, Queen Jezebel ruled Israel with King Ahab. Jezebel was originally from Phoenicia. According to Scripture, she promoted Baal worship—which Jesus referred to as "the deep things of Satan"—throughout Israel and used the title of prophetess to deceive and persuade the people.

Elijah prophesied Jezebel's death (1 Kings 21), and we read later in 2 Kings 9:30–37 that she was thrown out of a window, and her body devoured by dogs, thus fulfilling the prophecy.

But what, you might ask, is Baal worship? What are these deep things of Satan?

THE HISTORY OF BAAL WORSHIP

During the nineteenth century BC, King Nimrod and Queen Semiramis founded (Gen. 10–11) and reigned in ancient Babylon along the Euphrates River (the location of present-day Iraq). This, of course, is where the Tower of Babel was built.

According to extra-biblical accounts, Queen Semiramis, "had a son

[Tammuz] with an alleged miraculous conception."[7] From the deification of this son came the fertility god known as Baal as, "the worship of Baal is related to the worship of Tammuz."

For many people living in ancient times who relied on the abundance of the land for survival, fertility was one of the core aspects of religious faith. Consequently, there was a focus on sexuality. Temple prostitution was a part of worship.

Baal's female counterpart was the goddess Ashtoreth (Asher). Worship of this fertility goddess continued throughout the generations, though she was identified in each culture by a different name:

- She became Ishtar both in Egypt and in historical Babylon (600 BC).
- She became Aphrodite to the Greeks in 334 BC.
- She became Venus to the Romans in AD 70.
- She was worshipped as Diana in the ancient city of Ephesus.

Ashtoreth was worshipped at poles—which historians believe were carved into the image of a woman—that had been driven into the ground. Both female and male Sodomite prostitutes were involved in the worship ceremonies. The rituals practiced around Ashtoreth poles involved multiple forms of sensual activity, encouraging worshipers to either watch or even participate in various sexual acts with the prostitutes or with each other. Every generation of Judeo-Christian believer has had to overcome this spirit.

- In 1600 BC, Joshua battled Baal worshippers when the Children of Israel entered the Promised Land (Josh. 1–5).
- In 1150 BC, God instructed Gideon to tear down of the altar of Baal and cut down the Ashtoreth poles in his fight with the pagan Midianites (Judg. 6:25).

- In 850 BC, Elijah called down fire from heaven at Mount Carmel and single-handedly killed 450 of Queen Jezebel's prophets of Baal (1 Kings 18:15–40).
- In 670 BC, King Josiah brought forty years of blessing upon Israel when he purged the sin of Baal worship from the land (2 Kings 23).

Thus, from the time of ancient Babylon in 2000 BC to the writing of the book of Revelation in AD 85, and even to today, God has continually warned His people against the sensual, erotic worship associated with the spirit He calls Baal.

THE WORSHIP OF ASHTORETH

Baal and Ashtoreth are still worshipped this very day. The "deep things of Satan" are now also slickly marketed throughout the multimedia world of the adult entertainment industry. The spirits of ancient Babylon have merely reinvented themselves within our secular humanist society—for "there is nothing new under the sun."

Most people today likely believe pole dancing was a North American invention. How little we have learned from nearly 5,800 years of Jewish history!

There are approximately 3,700 strip clubs in North America that proudly raise the pole of Ashtoreth. Today the poles are not carved into the image of a woman; instead, we have over 350,000 strippers hanging on those poles nationwide. One statistical magazine "expects industry revenue to increase at an annualized rate of 4.1% to $8.0 billion during the five-year period, including growth of 2.1% in 2019 alone."[8]

Did you know that the word *baal* in Hebrew means "master"? Millions of men today are slaves, addicted to this master, watching daily at their altars of Baal within their own households as "pornography sites attract more visitors each month than Amazon, Netflix, and Twitter combined . . . 30% of internet content is porn."[9]

"Countless personal accounts have shown that first exposure to pornography on a young, developing brain has the potential to lead to a lifelong toxic habit. Recently, research by security technology company Bitdefender found that kids under the age of ten now account for 22% of online porn consumption among the under-eighteen age."[10]

Hollywood is the number-one producer of the $3 billion global pornographic film industry, completing "thirty-seven pornographic videos" within the United States per day—24 hours a day, seven days a week.[11] Our lady of kingdoms truly has become a lady of prostitutes (*porne*), just as prophecy said she would. Believers in the church of Thyatira were deceived "then and there" by sexual immorality, just as many believers are deceived "here and now" by the same Babylonian spirits of erotic worship.

Jesus warned us in Revelation 2:22, "I will cast them that commit adultery with her [Jezebel] I will cast into great tribulation, except they repent of their deeds." Is it any wonder that the angel urges the believers within Babylon the Great in Revelation 18:4, "Come out of her, my people, that ye be not partakers of her sins, and that ye receive not of her plagues"?

DELIVERANCE FROM THE SINS OF BAAL

The key to deliverance from erotic Baal worship is sitting on the tip of your tongue. For there is no name given among men and women, in heaven or on earth, which is greater than the name of Jesus. Through His death and resurrection, He has provided a way to overcome any sin that "so easily besets you."

*If you will confess with your mouth the Lord Jesus Christ, He is
faithful and just to forgive you your sin and cleanse you of all
unrighteousness (Rom. 10:9–10 ESV).*

You see, there is not a sin, a spirit, a Nicolaitan leader, or any form of
sexual immorality that can overcome the cleansing power of His blood
if you call on His name and confess your sins. He has promised to reward those who diligently seek Him—and He never fails on His promises (Rev. 2:10).

Babylon the Great is a nation overflowing with moral confusion,
but that moral confusion does not have to flow into us. God has promised that He will show us the secret things that belong to Him (Deut.
29:29); His Holy Spirit will show you things to come (John 16:13).

Our mandate at Prophecy USA is to help reveal those "secret things"
that the Word of God declares is coming to America. Those "secret
things" revealed in Scripture help us unveil the next three descriptions
of Babylon the Great:

34) (Rev. 2:12–17) (Pergamos believers) She has Christian
(Nicolaitan) leadership that deny hell, sin, and eternal
consequences.
35) (Rev. 2:18–25) (Thyatira believers) She has Christian leadership who promote the Jezebel spirit of immorality (Baal
worship).
36) (Isa. 47:12–13; Rev. 2:14, 20) She has over 3,500 Ashtoreth
poles firmly establishing temples of Baal worship ("high
places") throughout the nation.

CHAPTER EIGHT

LAODICEA BELIEVERS

SCRIPTURE WARNS THAT one of the greatest causes of the end-time apostasy will have to do with an issue that emotionally affects many believers within the church today. That issue is how you handle your money.

Although no sin is necessarily greater than another, the consequences of certain practices do have a greater effect on an individual's life. An example of what is perhaps the most universal sin to challenge believers in the end times can be found in the believers at Laodicea. Within His messages to the seven groups of believers, Jesus specifically spelled out that certain sins tempt some believers more than others. However, there is one sin that every person alive must overcome, because every day of your life, the basis for this sin makes its way into our hands. You cannot eat, you cannot drink, you cannot exist without its power. It is the medium of exchange that we know as money. Everyone owns it, but the question is, does it own you?

For a fuller understanding of the problem affecting the believers in Laodicea as well as Jesus' message to them (and to us), we will first examine His admonition, found in Revelation 3:15–17.

THE SIXTH GROUP: LAODICEA BELIEVERS
(Rev. 3:14–22)

And unto the angel of the church of the Laodiceans write . . .
I know thy works, that thou art neither cold nor hot: I would
thou wert cold or hot. So then because thou art lukewarm, and
neither cold nor hot, I will spue thee out of my mouth.
(Rev. 3:14–16).

On the banks of the Lycus river, between the cities of Hierapolis and Colossae, sat the large and prosperous city of industry, Laodicea. But despite their wealth, the people of Laodicea had one undeniable need—they lacked their own water supply. Meanwhile, Hierapolis, approximately six miles to the north, was known for her therapeutic hot springs, and the city of Colossae, nearly nine miles south, for the cold, refreshing waters that flowed from the snow-topped peak of nearby Mount Cadmus. As you will see, Jesus used these facts in His description of Laodicea's sin. Let's look again:

I know thy works, that thou art neither cold nor hot . . . So then
because thou art lukewarm, and neither cold nor hot, I will spue
thee out of my mouth (Rev. 3:15–16).

As a solution to Laodicea's shortage, water for the population was sourced by aqueduct from the renowned hot springs of Hierapolis. But by the time the water reached Laodicea, it was lukewarm and described as having a nauseating effect. The symbolism Jesus used when describing His disgust would have been abundantly clear to the Laodiceans.

The church of Laodicea sat, in its complacency and wealth,[1] squarely between the therapeutic hot waters to the north and the refreshing and pure waters to the south, yet her believers were neither therapeutic nor refreshing, neither hot nor cold. Despite their wealth and resource, their potential for good, Laodicean believers brought nothing of value to the work of God's kingdom. As a result, their warning from Him is most memorable in its severity.

Now that we understand the meaning behind Jesus' metaphor, let's study to understand where the church at Laodicea went wrong. What turned the believers so lukewarm and useless in the Lord's eyes? We learn the answer to this question by reading further into Jesus' warning.

WEALTH AND PRIDE

The language Jesus used with the church of Laodicea is befittingly harsh. As you will see in verse 17, the rest of his His message does not get any easier to hear:

> *Because thou sayest, I am rich, and increased with goods, and have need of nothing; and knowest not that thou art wretched, and miserable, and poor, and blind, and naked (Rev. 3:17).*

This verse makes clear the root of Laodicea's problem, and it is an issue with something we each deal with daily: money. The problem within the Laodicean church was not money itself, however, but rather how these believers prioritized their money over their relationship with God. For as we read in 1 Timothy 6:10, the concern is not money but rather the *love* of it. Psalm 62:10 also cautions similarly that "if riches increase, set not your heart upon them."

THE HISTORY OF TITHING

In His call for the ancient Hebrew to be "a peculiar people," holy and set apart from the world, we learn of their requirement to tithe of their firstfruits. Deuteronomy 14:22 reads, "Thou shalt truly tithe all the increase of thy seed, that the field bringeth forth year by year." Farmers were likewise commanded to leave a portion of the food in their fields for the poor and widows:

> *And when ye reap the harvest of your land, thou shalt*
> *not make clean riddance of the corners of thy field when*
> *thou reapest, neither shalt thou gather any gleaning of thy*
> *harvest: thou shalt leave them unto the poor, and to the*
> *stranger: I am the LORD your God (Lev. 23:22;*
> *cf. Lev. 19:9–10; Deut. 24:19–22)*

In the earliest days of biblical history, human societies did not have that medium of exchange we refer to as money. Instead, they frequently used the barter system, trading animals, crops, precious stones, metals, or any personal possessions of equivalent value with each other. Still, a man's handling of his substance or accumulated wealth, in whatever form it took, was one way that God evaluated his character or spirit. God also demanded priority of worship among man's material substance: "Thou shalt have no other gods before Me" (Exodus 20:3).

The *New Bible Dictionary* states

> *Before the introduction of coinage in the late 8th century BC*
> *the medium of exchange in commercial transactions was a*
> *modified form of barter. Throughout the ancient Near East*
> *staple commodities, both those which were perishable, such as*
> *wool, barley, wheat and dates, and those which were*
> *non-perishable, including metals, timber, wine, honey and*
> *livestock, served as 'exchangeable goods.' The texts show that*
> *from the earliest times periodic attempts were made to stabilize*
> *the values of these commodities with respect to each other.*

*Thus wealth was measured by possession of cattle (Job 1:3) and
precious metals. Abraham was 'very rich in cattle, in silver, and
in gold' (Gen. 13:2).*[2]

The *Eerdmans Dictionary of the Bible* states:

*Lev. 27:30–33 establishes that all the seeds from the land and
fruits from trees belong to God, and a tenth of all herd and flock
are holy to the Lord. The people were expected to tithe their
grain, wine, oil, and firstlings from the herd and flock (Deut.
14:22–24). An important component of the tithe involved the
bringing of the yield to the designated sanctuary, where the
people would participate together in a meal. If it was not possible
to transport the yield because of distance, then the yield could be
redeemed for cash and the money used for whatever the person
desired. However, if one's yield was redeemed for cash, then a
further fifth of the yield must be added to the sum (Lev. 27:31).*

*The tithe also included a social component to care for the
poor within the society, and every third year the tithe must
be set aside for the Levite, the resident alien, the orphan, and
the widow. Blessings from God are directly connected to this
mandate (Deut. 14:28–29). The worshipper is to make all
offerings, including the tithe, with joy and happiness
(Sir. 35:8–12)*[3]

THE EXAMPLE OF ABRAHAM

We will show through Scripture that the act of tithing holds covenantal
value, and as such, promises a reward from God. Our study of these
things begins with the story of Abram/Abraham.

After defeating his enemies in battle in Genesis 14, Abram—the first man in the Bible to be called a prophet—gave one tenth of his spoils to Melchizedek, king of Salem and priest of the same God in whom Abram worshiped. Immediately following Abram's act of worship, the Lord appeared to him in a vision saying, "Fear not, Abram, I am your shield; your reward shall be very great" (Gen. 15:1 ESV). It was at this time that Abram was promised a son who would be heir to the future patriarchal Jewish race. Only after Abram made it his priority to obey God with the giving of his wealth (Prov. 3:9 substance) did God entrust him as the father of His chosen people, Israel.

Two generations later, Abraham's grandson Jacob chose to participate in his grandfather's covenant with God, declaring: "If God will be with me, and will keep me in this way that I go, and will give me bread to eat, and raiment to put on . . . all that thou shalt give me I will surely give the tenth unto thee" (Gen. 28:20, 22). The covenant blessings God originally promised to Abraham were handed down to each generation following him—as long as they maintained their duties within that covenant. Indeed, God promised Abram in Genesis 12:2–3 (ESV), "I will bless you and make your name great, so that you will be a blessing. I will bless those who bless you, and him who dishonors you I will curse."

Deuteronomy 8:18 says, "But thou shalt remember the LORD thy God: for it is he that giveth thee power to get wealth, that he may establish **his covenant**." Anyone who was to receive God's blessings was required to establish himself in a "preferred position" between God and man so that God could use him to release His blessing to others.

BLESSING AND RIGHTEOUSNESS

The Hebrew word for righteousness is *tsedeq*, which means "righteous deeds"[4] or what we might call acts of loving-kindness. We read in the

New Testament that God, who "supplies seed to the sower and bread for food will supply and multiply your seed for sowing and increase the harvest of your righteousness" (2 Cor. 9:10 ESV). Scripture describes God as "a God of righteousness" over seventy-two times. Jesus, who was God incarnate and "went about doing good and healing all those who were oppressed of the devil" (Acts 10:38 ESV), lived a life anointed by God's acts of loving-kindness. Blessing others, or perhaps what Jesus termed as "doing unto others as you would have them do unto you," (Mat 7:12) best summarizes what God calls righteousness in Hebrew protocol. Being righteous before God is also being righteous toward others—righteous deeds. The litmus test for our righteousness is loving God and how we treat others. We can't be righteous before God unless we're being righteous toward others.

It's fascinating to see that even at the very beginning of human history, Adam received a mandate from God to work and produce substance for his existence (Gen. 3:19). From that first commandment of having "no other gods before you," God performed acts of loving-kindness to offer direction, guidance, and protection to whomever would call upon Him. Psalm 62:11–12 makes clear, "power belongs to God . . . [and] steadfast love. For [He] will render to a man according to his work" (ESV).

Many rabbinical and Christian theologians have concluded that the command to offer a tithe or "firstfruits" of one's wealth was given to the Children of Israel to prevent them from becoming greedy and materialistic, which in turn allowed their acts of loving-kindness to flow to those less fortunate. They were blessed so that they could be a blessing to the world. However, it seems that the believers of Laodicea (and the modern-day believers to which God is speaking through this passage of Revelation) had a problem with the way they prioritized their material blessings.

ABANDONING THE COVENANT BLESSINGS

Earlier we learned that God would make a covenant not only with the nation of Israel, but with any nation or person who wanted to participate in that relationship. This is seen clearly in Paul's letter to the Ephesians, in which he wrote that the "mystery [of Christ] is that the Gentiles are fellow heirs, members of the same body, and partakers of the promise in Christ Jesus through the gospel" (Eph. 3:6 ESV). The basis of the covenant (or promise) was and is man's free will to enter into it and "provoke one another unto love and to good works" (Heb 10:24).

The seven groups of believers that Jesus addressed in Revelation had, of course, become part of that covenant with God. Nevertheless, five of those churches had problems in their relationship with God because of specific sins, ranging from a lack of love toward God and others to idol worship, false teaching, and sexual immorality. Jesus points out exactly where these believers were missing the mark in their lives, calling them to repentance and a change in their lifestyles. In order to follow His commandments and return to the promised covenantal blessings, they needed to make changes—and most of those changes had to do with how they treated others.

Each believer Jesus admonished was impaired by an erroneous view of their own spiritual state. Perhaps the most common temptation within these believers was the one found in the sixth group, who lived in Laodicea. Their sin was tied directly to how they prioritized the use of their money. They were "rich" toward themselves but not "rich" toward God.

The believers of Laodicea had allowed their wealth to create complacency in their hearts, but they appear to have been completely unaware of their sin. They looked at their wealth and felt from it a false sense of security and self-sufficiency.[5] In fact, Roman historian and politician Tacitus wrote that when an earthquake destroyed Laodicea around AD 60–62, the wealthy citizens paid for its rebuilding "without the help of Rome." This is a perfect example of the independent mindset of the population.

While Deuteronomy 8:18 makes it clear that God gives the power to get wealth, the Laodicean believers seem to have thought that their status was owed only to themselves. They had no fear of God, nor did they yearn for Him. They did not work to serve Him or His kingdom. As a result, they were indifferent, and they who thought themselves rich were, in fact, spiritually bankrupt.

In Revelation 3, we read:

> *I know thy works, that thou art neither cold nor hot: I would thou wert cold or hot. So then because thou art lukewarm, and neither cold nor hot, I will spue thee out of my mouth. Because thou sayest, I am rich, and increased with goods, and have need of nothing; and knowest not that thou art wretched, and miserable, and poor, and blind, and naked (Rev. 3:14–17).*

We have explored much of the meaning behind this warning to the Laodicean believers. The message can be further clarified by a parable Jesus told during His ministry. In Luke 12, He tells the parable of the rich fool:

> *The land of a rich man produced plentifully . . . And he said, "I will do this: I will tear down my barns and build larger ones, and there I will store all my grain and my goods. And I will say to my soul, 'Soul, you have ample goods laid up for many years; relax, eat, drink, be merry.'" But God said to him, "Fool! This night your soul is required of you, and the things you have prepared, whose will they be?" So is the one who lays up treasure for himself and is not rich toward God (Luke 12:16–21 ESV).*

In telling this story, Jesus pointed out the contrast between the accumulation of worldly riches and heavenly reward. Similarly, note the difference in the message Jesus gave to the church in Smyrna when He said, "I know thy works, and tribulation, and poverty, (but thou art rich)" (Rev. 2:9).

It is interesting to note that when referring to the rich man in the parable, the Bible uses the Greek word *plousios,* which is defined as "rich" or "wealthy in abundance"—the same word used when the Laodicean believer says "I am rich" in Revelation 3:17. When Scripture uses the word "rich" to refer to God, however, it uses the Greek word *plouteo,* which is defined as "a) to prosper and, b) to be generous."[6] This is the same word the Laodicean believers use when they say, "I have prospered" (Rev. 3:17 ESV), but it also means "I have been generous." Of course, Jesus explains to the Laodiceans that they have been neither!

Perhaps the following story will further explain the difference between these two definitions of the word "rich":

I once heard the story of a German industrialist who before World War II had built a successful manufacturing company. He and his wife decided to use some of their money to buy an organ for the church. Shortly thereafter, World War II broke out, and his factory was bombed; he and his wife were left financially devastated. That Sunday, they visited the small church they had attended years previously. Grief-stricken and almost without words, the husband sat in the pew staring at the organ. Then, after several minutes of silence, he turned to his wife and said: "The only thing we've kept is what we gave away."

GOD'S GENEROSITY

In God's eyes, your financial giving (or lack thereof) establishes Him as Lord of all or not at all.

Being "rich" toward God does not entail any effort on God's part.

Rather, it is an effort on our part that involves being generous with the blessings He has already given us.

In the context of the Laodicean believer, Jesus is talking to believers who seem to be healthy, happy, and financially sound in their own minds. But like the rich ruler (Luke 18:18–23), they are not rich (that is, generous) toward God. They do not acknowledge God, nor do they honor His blessings by using a portion of their firstfruits to bless others. In this situation it appears Jesus is addressing the believers' finances, but it could also mean a portion of their time, their gifts, their talents toward helping others. The adage that "time is money" could be applied to unselfishly giving of one's time for the purpose of releasing "riches" toward God. As Jesus said to his disciples, "Inasmuch as ye have done it unto one of the least of these my brethren, ye have done it unto me" (Matt. 25:40).

Obviously, this group of believers had faith in God's covenant of salvation, but they had not fulfilled the responsibilities that would release that covenant's full benefits. Your time and talents today are usually exchanged for money. However, whatever finances are given to God and His purposes, are also an exchange of your time and talents. When it comes to a believer's approach to God and money, Scripture is clear as to what their priorities should be.

In 3 John 1:2, we read, "Beloved, I wish above all things that thou mayest prosper and be in health, even as thy soul prospereth." This verse emphasizes that the most important asset you have is your soul, not your material assets. Likewise, we read in Deuteronomy 8:18, "But thou shalt remember the LORD thy God: for it is he that giveth thee power to get wealth, that he may establish his covenant." God wants to establish His covenant through all of his children, both Jew and Gentile. But what is that covenant?

Paul teaches us in Romans 11 that through Christ we are grafted into the Jewish family by having our hearts circumcised. He expands on this teaching in Galatians 3:14 (ESV), where he writes, "that in Christ Jesus the blessing of Abraham might come to the Gentiles, so that we might receive the promised Spirit through faith." The first priority of that promise thus concerns our eternal souls, in that God "wishes above all things that we prosper even as our soul prospers" (3 John 1:2).

Scripture tells us that "salvation is of the Jews" (John 4:22), and Paul writes that we who believe in Christ have actually become Jews: "For he is not a Jew, which is one outwardly; neither is that circumcision, which is outward in the flesh: But he is a Jew, which is one inwardly; and circumcision is that of the heart, in the spirit, and not in the letter [of the law]; whose praise is not of men, but of God" (Rom. 2:28–29).

Although tithing in the Old Testament was required by the letter of the Law, the new covenant now rests in the Spirit of the Law. Tithing, in other words, is a voluntary effort on the part of every believer. Those who do not tithe will not participate in the total fullness of God's blessings; conversely, those who tithe will initiate a divine reciprocity—that is, giving and receiving—between themselves and God.

We have just scratched the surface of what Jesus is saying in this letter, specifically what his message is to the modern-day "Laodicean believer." Either a tremendous blessing or a tremendous disappointment awaits end-time believers. The difference clearly lies in the priority one places on his firstfruits' giving of his talents, gifts, and finances. Your God is Lord of all, or not at all.

RICHES IN THE KINGDOM OF GOD

In studying the instructions Jesus gave to those believers, we see that they had serious problems with money, finances, and a total lack of priorities in their relationship with God. In fact, their problems were so severe that with regard to the escape plan for the coming tribulation, Jesus warned, **those who did not prioritize their "riches"** (Rev. 3:17) in being rich [*plouteo*—generous] with their works (time, talents, or finances) toward God's kingdom, would be spued out of His mouth (Rev. 3:16).

We have already learned that when God made His covenant with Abram, He said that He would bless him and "thou shalt be a blessing" to others (Gen. 12:2). In this sense, when you plant your seeds of faith, talents, money, and time in benevolent acts of kindness, those seeds will be multiplied back to you, and in God's eyes, they will become acts of righteousness.

> *He who supplies seed to the sower and bread for food will*
> *supply and multiply your seed for sowing and increase the*
> *harvest of your righteousness [acts of loving-kindness]*
> *(2 Cor. 9:10 ESV).*

WEALTHY, MATERIALISTIC, HIGHLY EDUCATED, AND PROUD AMERICA

According to Scripture, the richest and wisest descendant of Abraham was King Solomon, who reigned between 970 to 931 BC. King Solomon never had a gas furnace, air conditioning, or electricity. He never owned a microwave oven, electric stove, or had hot and cold running water. He never spoke on a cell phone, texted a friend, or surfed the Internet. That technology was all invented within the last one hundred years. In North America today, we have all these things, and yet so many of us complain that we do not have enough. Some even stage protests, demanding that those who have more be taxed so that their wealth can be redistributed to those with less.

While countless others in many regions of the world beg for food, we in North America pay others to help us lose weight. "The majority of Americans are part of the global high-income population that resides almost exclusively in Europe and North America. These two regions accounted for 87% of the global high-income population" in the last decade. What is considered poor here [in the USA] is a level of income still not available to most people globally."[7]

Without a doubt, America is the richest, most technologically advanced region in history. She is number one in space research. She is a world trader, and supplies the globe with many of the products listed in Revelation 18, including flour, wheat, agricultural products, and automobiles. North America has never had a world war on her soil. Her citizens have watched movies, documentaries, and even live footage of world conflicts via satellite, but her cities have been spared invasion by a foreign government. Most of us cannot fathom having bombs explode in our neighborhood. The thought of nuclear weapons unleashed on our land phases few.

The vast majority of North Americans are "given to pleasures," and this generation in particular has "glorified herself and lived deliciously." Let's read again and compare what we find in Scripture with what we see in our nation today:

> *Therefore hear now this, thou that art given to pleasures, that dwellest carelessly, that sayest in thine heart, I am, and none else beside me; I shall not sit as a widow, neither shall I know the loss of children (Isaiah 47:8).*

> *Babylon the great is fallen, is fallen . . . the merchants of the earth are waxed rich through the abundance of her delicacies . . . How much she hath glorified herself, and lived deliciously, so much torment and sorrow give her: for she saith in her heart, I sit a queen, and am no widow, and shall see no sorrow (Revelation 18:2–3, 7).*

America's prosperity is a result of her original foundation of godly principles. "Americans who attend church or synagogue or another form of worship once a week give three times as much to charity as a percentage of their income as do those who rarely attend religious services."[8] However, unless every believer's substance is "sown" or given into other people's lives, it cannot bear acts of loving-kindness or righteousness, as Jesus warned Laodicean believers. The Word of God clearly states that our Creator wants prosperity for His people (3 John 1:2). But the Bible warns that once we take our eyes off the source of our blessings (God), we will fall into trouble.

Pride comes, and then man falls. North America has good reason to be proud of her accomplishments, but have we set ourselves up for a fall? Do you think it's possible that in the last days, the Laodicean believer could be found in the richest country in the history of the world?

We know that this richest country in human history is prophesied to be Babylon the Great, which appears before the New World Order comes into power. Is it possible that the falling away of the church—the "great apostasy" to which the apostle Paul referred—could have something to do with how we use our money? Are the majority of Christians in North America rich in themselves, yet not rich (generous) toward God?

According to an article in *Christianity Today*, "five percent of adults tithe to a church or charitable organization; among born-again Christians, the rate rose to twelve percent."[9] Yet those individuals who do tithe probably underwrite almost 80 percent of church expenses and outreach ministries.[10] Interestingly, the church of Smyrna and the next church we will study, in Philadelphia, are highly commended by Jesus and represent two out of seven types of believers. That is roughly fifteen percent of the total number of believers Jesus pointed to in Revelation. Are eighty-five percent of believers today missing the mark when it comes to the stewardship of their finances? Do they represent the modern-day church of Laodicea?

We know God gives us the power to accumulate wealth in order to establish His covenant. Let's look at more of what is written in Deuteronomy 8 and the wisdom and instruction that might be gained from it:

> When thou hast eaten and art full, then thou shalt bless the LORD thy God for the good land which he hath given thee. Beware that thou forget not the LORD thy God, in not keeping his commandments, and his judgments, and his statutes, which I command thee this day: lest when thou hast eaten and art full, and hast built goodly houses, and dwelt therein; and when thy herds and thy flocks multiply, and thy silver and thy gold is multiplied, and all that thou hast is multiplied; then thine heart be lifted up, and thou forget the LORD thy God . . . and thou say in thine heart, My power and the might of mine hand hath gotten me this wealth. But thou shalt remember the LORD thy God: for it is he that giveth thee power to get wealth, that he may establish his covenant which he sware unto thy fathers, as it is this day (Deut. 8:10–14; 17–18).

JESUS URGES LAODICEA TO REPENT

> Each one's work will become manifest, for the Day will disclose it, because it will be revealed by fire, and the fire will test what sort of work each one has done. If the work that anyone has built on the foundation survives, he will receive a reward. If anyone's work is burned up, he will suffer loss, though he himself will be saved, but only as through fire (1 Cor. 3:13–15 ESV).

Laodicean believers are the only ones to which Jesus gives specific instructions concerning how to repent: "I counsel you to buy from me gold refined by fire, so that you may be rich, and white garments so that you may clothe yourself and the shame of your nakedness may not be seen" (Rev. 3:18 ESV).

The Greek word for "buy" in this passage is *agorazo*, which is sometimes translated "redeem." Paul used this word in 1 Corinthians 6:20 and 7:23 to describe how Christ bought—or redeemed—us through His own blood at Calvary. This same word is also used in Revelation 5:9, where Scripture tells us that Christ was "slain, and hast redeemed [*agorazo*] us to God by thy blood." In Revelation 3:18, Jesus is telling the Laodicean believers to redeem themselves from the sin of greed. Is he actually saying to transfer a portion of their personal wealth into God's kingdom as an act of heartfelt repentance? If so, then only the Holy Spirit can confirm the appropriate amount in a believer's spirit. But based on this interpretation, the only way you can become "rich in God" is by transferring some "hip service" into his kingdom—not just "lip service." As James stated, "be doers of the word and not hearers only" (James 1:22).

Jesus promised that those who obey His commands will be given a white garment and—according to 2 Corinthians 9:10—will increase the fruits of their righteousness (acts of loving-kindness).

Paul explained God's view of our money when he stated in 1 Timothy 6:10, "For the love of money is the root of all evil: which while some coveted after, they have erred from the faith, and pierced themselves through with many sorrows." Paul also described those that covet after money as being "greedy of filthy lucre" (1 Tim. 3:3). When money is used correctly as a medium of exchange, however, it can be a blessing to others: "Even in Thessalonica you sent me help for my needs once and again. Not that I seek the gift, but I seek the fruit that increases to your credit" (Phil. 4:16–17 ESV). Paul calls money that is gained in greed as "filthy lucre," but money used to minister to others "an odour of a sweet smell, a sacrifice acceptable, wellpleasing to God" (Phil. 4:18).

ARE YOU FULFILLING YOUR RESPONSIBILITY?

The principle of tithing is a common thread in Old Testament, running from Genesis to Malachi. Abraham, the father of our faith, set an example by giving ten percent of his firstfruits, demonstrating that our firstfruits also belong to God.

Brian Kluth, founder of Maximum Generosity said, "We're in the midst of a 40-year decline in the percentage that Christians give, and we need to see a generosity movement in America, that Christians re-embrace generosity as a spiritual value, but not for the sake of the church budget, but because of the Bible. Churches have made giving all about the budget, and it's not about the budget, it's all about the Bible."[11]

If you find yourself falling short and committing any of the sins found in Laodicea, I urge you to follow my lead. The only reason you are reading this revelation of America's role in Bible prophecy is because in 1986, I examined myself and decided it was time for me to tithe and get back into covenant (right relationship) with God. You are receiving a revelation on prophecy that no other generation has ever been taught because someone, like Cornelius, gave tithes and offerings to the Lord. Examine your giving. Examine your priorities. In His warning to the Laodicean believers, Jesus gave us this mandate: "I counsel you to buy from me gold refined by fire, so that you may be rich, and white garments so that you may clothe yourself and the shame of your nakedness might not be seen" (Rev. 3:18 ESV).

Ephesians 2:8–9 tells us that eternal salvation is "the gift of God: not of works, lest any man should boast." In other words, His work on the cross is a gift to you, and He gets all the glory for your salvation. However, when it comes to escaping the tribulation coming to earth, there is additional work (obedience) that is required of us to prove our love toward Him: "If you love me you will keep my commandments"

(John 14:15). And in Matthew 25, we read: "'And when did we see you sick or in prison and visit you?' And the King will answer them, 'Truly, I say to you, as you did it to one of the least of these my brothers, you did it to me'" (Matt. 25:39–40 esv).

Remember, you can hear directly from God. You do not need anyone to tell you where you should or should not give tithes and offerings to His kingdom. God will show you where He wants His firstfruits planted. The next time you go to the fridge or sit in your La-Z-Boy chair, or see starving children on TV, or feel a nudge to financially support a worthwhile ministry, ask yourself these questions:

- Have I given to the Lord what is His?
- Have I transferred a portion of my firstfruits, my tangible substance, into God's eternal kingdom?

Whenever a man or woman is called to preach the gospel, go into a missionary field, distribute food to the hungry, or minister to the homeless, it is your financial support that makes their ministry possible. You may not be gifted or called by God to go yourself, but when you send your finances to support His works, in God's eyes it is just as if you were going and doing the works yourself (Matt. 10:40–42).

Scripture reveals that there is a tremendous blessing coming to all covenant believers, and specifically to those who dwell in Babylon the Great. "Come out of her, my people, that ye be not partakers of her sins, and that ye receive not of her plagues" (Rev. 18:4). Jesus also tells us, "Pray that you might be worthy to escape"—but escape what? The answer to that question will be explained in the next chapter.

From the study of Laodicea, we add two more descriptions that point to America:

37) (Rev. 3:14–22) (Laodicea) She has the richest believers in
the history of the world within her.

38) (Rev. 3:18; Mal. 3:8–10) The majority of her believers are
not "tithing" the firstfruits of their substance.

The question remains: What makes a believer's finances "rich toward
God"? The amount they keep or the amount they give? Pray about that!

CHAPTER NINE

THE CHURCH OF PHILADELPHIA

WE HAVE STUDIED thirty-eight biblical descriptions of Babylon the Great so far, and the only country in the history of the world that has met every one is the United States of America. We have also discussed the seven types of believers that Scripture says will be found in the last days. Because Babylon the Great is the last kingdom to appear before the New World Order begins, and because Scripture tells us that God's people are in Babylon (Rev. 18:4), we can easily surmise that these seven types of believers will exist in Babylon.

To identify these seven groups of latter-day believers and discern the category into which we fit, we must look not only at the modern world in general but at America in particular. But why should we care? Because Jesus warned us that certain sins would void a believer's chances of being spared the ordeal of enduring the Great Tribulation. We will look at this in a moment. First, let's review some of what we have already seen.

REVIEW: WHAT BEST DESCRIBES YOU?

Remember there are three types of people reading this book. Atheists (secular humanists), agnostics (not sure God exists) and believers. We have now studied six of the seven groups of believers. The final group we will study, the believers of Philadelphia, is the one community of believers with an incredible blessing from God—a blessing no other generation has ever received.

To review, let's look at the six types of believers we've examined so far and refresh our memories on the "sins that so easily beset" each group.

1) **EPHESUS** (Rev. 2:1–7): Believers were not making God their life's first priority. They had **lost their "first love."**

2) **SARDIS** (Rev. 3:1–6): Believers were doing works for their own benefit rather than allowing God to work through them to serve others in need. Jesus called their efforts "**dead works.**"

3) **SMYRNA** (Rev. 2:8–11): Believers were **suffering persecution**; they were encouraged to stay firm in their faith, for great rewards were awaiting them in heaven.

4) **PERGAMOS** (Rev. 2:12–17): Believers were involved in "**sexually immoral relations**" outside of holy matrimony, including adultery, fornication, and sexual involvement between unmarried men, women, or combination thereof.

5) **THYATIRA** (Rev. 2:18–29): Believers were involved in activities similar to Jezebel, which were rooted in the pagan "**religions of Baal worship,**" which would include pornography, immorality, and child sacrifice from the result of that lifestyle.

6) **LAODICEA** (Rev. 3:14–22): Believers were blessed financially but were acting selfishly by refusing to give God's

kingdom the priority with the "firstfruits" of their finances. In other words, these believers were rich in substance but not generous toward others, which Jesus referred to as "**not being rich toward God**." Many theologians would equate this "firstfruits" portion with prioritizing their finances toward God, just as Abraham gave a tenth of all immediately after his victory in war.

THE SEVENTH GROUP: PHILADELPHIA BELIEVERS (Rev. 3:7–13)

The seventh group of believers, however, avoid all the shortcomings of each of the other six churches, besides Smyrna. In God's eyes, they met all the criteria necessary to be "accounted worthy to escape" the coming tribulation (Luke 21:36). These believers belonged to the church of Philadelphia.

Interestingly, the Greek word for "accounted worthy" in the Luke passage is *kataxioo*. This word is also used in 2 Thessalonians 1:5 as well as in Acts 5:41, in which the disciples rejoice when they are "counted worthy" to suffer shame for the sake of God's kingdom. The emphasis here in Luke 21 is that *our* works, not His, are what lead us to be counted worthy to escape the coming wrath or tribulation. It is by grace that we are eternally saved by His works on the cross (Eph. 2:8). It is by our works, however, that we are counted worthy (*kataxioo*) to be saved from the tribulation. God—and God alone—will determine who is worthy of that honor.

Jesus wrote to the church of Philadelphia in Revelation 3:

I know your works. Behold, I have set before you an open door, which no one is able to shut. I know that you have but little

power, and yet you have kept my word and have not denied my
name. Behold, I will make those of the synagogue of Satan who
say that they are Jews and are not, but lie—behold, I will make
them come and bow down before your feet, and they will learn
that I have loved you. Because you have kept my word about
patient endurance, I will keep you from the hour of trial that
is coming on the whole world, to try those who dwell on the
earth. I am coming soon. Hold fast what you have, so that no
one may seize your crown (Rev. 3:8–11 ESV).

Philadelphia was an agricultural city known well for her wine production, thus her principal deity was Dionysus, the god of wine. She
sat on the Persian Royal Road between Sardis and Susa, making her a
well-trafficked missionary city. Records indicate a large Jewish community in the city where the relatively new Christian church was heavily
persecuted.

According to their letter from Jesus, it appears that the church in
Philadelphia was different from most of the other churches previously
mentioned (with the exception of Smyrna). These believers were not
influenced by worldly views of secular humanism. They had not only
overcome the pitfalls of Babylonian paganism, but they had avoided
the sexual immorality that accompanies it and pagan worship fetishes
such as witchcraft, drug abuse, or the shedding of innocent blood that
is also rampant in modern society. While not specifically stated in the
Scriptures, they were probably wise stewards of God's financial blessings, demonstrating honesty and care toward other people, and in so
doing, put God first in their lives. Through these acts of loving kindness, described in Scripture as righteousness, they had overcome many
of the sins into which most of the other believers had fallen into.

Jesus warned five out of seven groups of believers that unless they
changed their ways, they could lose the blessing of the open door

awaiting the Philadelphian church. And that supernatural blessing would take place within a one-hour time period—it would come and go very suddenly.

THE REWARD PROMISED TO THE PERSECUTED BELIEVERS

Nevertheless, it also appears that the Philadelphian believers suffered some persecution from the "synagogue of Satan" (which, you'll recall, was also mentioned in the commendation to the believers of Smyrna in Revelation 2:9). They were sorely tested, even to the point that Jesus said, "for thou hast little strength" (Rev. 3:8).

As we have previously discussed, following the Word of God in latter-day Babylon the Great could result in being verbally persecuted by the "accuser of [the] brethren" (Rev. 12:10). The *International Standard Bible Encyclopedia* defines "accuser" as "one who speaks in a derogatory way of another (Acts 23:30, 35; 25:16, 18; Rev. 12:10)."[1] In North American society today, following God's Word often results in false accusations from the arsenal of secular humanist progressive *phobia* bombs.

Jesus taught in Matthew 5:

Blessed are you when others revile you and persecute you and utter all kinds of evil against you falsely on my account. Rejoice and be glad, for your reward is great in heaven, for so they persecuted the prophets who were before you (Matt. 5:11–12).

Today's Philadelphian believers do not follow the herd of secular society's groupthink but instead follow God's Word. Because of this, Jesus said they will be rewarded with an "open door" that no man can shut. Specifically, these believers are promised that they will be spared the hour of tribulation that shall come upon the whole world (Rev. 3:10).

It should be noted that the seven groups of believers represent the body of Christ globally, not just in the United States. Anywhere the body of Christ is gathered, any or all of the seven types of believers can probably be found. Each person must overcome the sins by which he or she is tempted. The struggle to overcome temptation is a daily battle, and no believer's life is completely free of sin, "for all have sinned and fall short of the glory of God" (Rom. 3:23 ESV). However, to let a sin go unrepentant, allowing it to become a lifestyle of sin, is what Jesus condemns in His revelation to end time believers.

TO WHOM MUCH IS GIVEN, MUCH IS REQUIRED

"According to the Center for the Study of **Global** Christianity (CSGC) at Gordon-Conwell Theological Seminary, **there** are approximately 41,000 Christian **denominations** and organizations in the **world** today" (April 16, 2020).[2]

The Philadelphian believers do not represent one denomination; rather, this group of believers can be found within every Christian denomination. No single denomination has a perfect membership of believers, but there are believers within each denomination who have pure hearts and are trying to follow God's Word to the best of their knowledge. And it is those individuals who Jesus said would be "counted worthy to escape," based on the condition of their hearts. God will judge you based on what you know and how you put into practice what you have been taught. The more you know, the greater your accountability to obey His Word.

Jesus explained this principle, utilizing the cultural standards at the time, in the parable concerning masters and servants in Luke 12:

And that servant who knew his master's will but did not get ready or act according to his will, will receive a severe beating.

But the one who did not know, and did what deserved a beating,
will receive a light beating. Everyone to whom much was given,
of him much will be required (Luke 12:47–48 ESV).

Did you know that to whom much is given, much is required? What does that mean to us in America—a nation founded upon biblical principles and blessed by God to become the richest nation in the history of the world? We are the most technologically advanced, well-educated civilization in the history of mankind; we dwell in a nation where God's Word is preached daily over internet, radio, television, and multimedia broadcasts. There are nations today where you can be imprisoned simply for owning a Bible, yet in America there are many apps that can read the Bible to us from the palm of our hand. We don't even have to read the Bible ourselves. We have technology that will give us the spoken Word of God, and yet it appears the majority in America have no idea that they are living in the last providential nation on earth before a godless New World Order comes into global power. Why is that?

According to what we have just studied, those who hear the Word of God but fail to act on it will be judged more harshly. However, if you hear and do the Word in these last days, as Jesus prophesied to the Philadelphia believers, a great reward (or open door) awaits you, the likes of which no other generation has ever been given. But what exactly is the open door promised to the Philadelphian believers, and what specifically does that have to do with those of us living in America?

THE OPEN DOOR AND THE HOUR OF TRIBULATION

In Revelation 3:10 (ESV), Jesus said: "Because you have kept my word about patient endurance, I will keep you from the hour of trial that is coming on the whole world, to try those who dwell on the earth." In this verse, we are given a specific correlation between the time of the "open door" and the "hour of tribulation."

As you may remember, we revealed that the Lord warned believers in Babylon the Great, "Come out of her, My people, that ye be not partakers of her sins, and that ye receive not of her plagues" (Rev. 18:4). We are also told in Amos 3:7 (ESV) that "the Lord GOD does nothing without revealing His secret to His servants the prophets." Revelation 3:10 is warning us about something that is coming, something that was shown to John about the end times. On one hand, there will be a great deliverance for the believers of Philadelphia; but on the other hand, a great tribulation will come upon the rest of the earth.

Scripture says that in "one hour" everything on earth will change dramatically. This one-hour time sequence is mentioned several times in the book of Revelation. The angel ties it specifically to the judgment of Babylon the Great in Revelation 14:

> And he said with a loud voice, "Fear God and give Him glory, because the **hour** of His judgment has come" . . . Another angel, a second, followed, saying, "Fallen, fallen is Babylon the great, she who made all nations drink of the wine of the passion of her sexual immorality" (Rev. 14:7–8 ESV).

In Revelation 17, another angel speaks of a ten-nation New World Order coming into power within one hour:

> And the ten horns that you saw are ten kings who have not yet received royal power, but they are to receive authority as kings for **one hour**, together with the beast . . . And the ten horns that you saw, they and the beast will hate the prostitute [Babylon

the Great]. They will make her desolate and naked, and devour
her flesh and burn her up with fire, for God has put it into
*their hearts to **carry out His purpose** by being of one mind and*
*handing over their royal power to the beast, **until** the words of*
God are fulfilled (Rev. 17:12, 16–17 ESV).

Revelation 18 reiterates this:

*For this reason her plagues will come in **a single day**, death and*
*mourning and famine, and she will **be burned up with fire**; for*
mighty is the Lord who Judged her . . . And the kings of the earth
*. . . will weep and wail over her when they see the **smoke of her***
***burning** . . . For in **a single hour** your [Babylon's] judgment*
has come . . . The merchants of these wares, who gained wealth
from her, will stand far off, in fear of her torment, weeping and
*mourning aloud . . . For in **a single hour** all this wealth has been*
laid waste. And all shipmasters and seafaring men, sailors and
all whose trade is on the sea, stood far off and cried out as they
*saw the smoke of her burning . . . For in a **single hour she has***
***been laid waste** (Rev. 18:8, 10, 17, 19 ESV).*

Likewise, Isaiah prophesied:

But these two things shall come to thee [Babylon the Great] in a
*moment in **one day**, the loss of children, and widowhood . . . The*
***fire shall burn them** even thy merchants shall wander every one*
to his quarter; none shall save thee (Isa. 47:9, 14–15).

From these verses, we can infer four specific points the angel has
told us concerning the hour of tribulation:

1) **Rev. 14:7: The hour** of His judgment will be **released by God.**

2) **Rev. 17:12, 16:** In **one hour,** the ten kings will be given power together with the beast (the Antichrist) to form the New World Order, both of whom, we are told, *hate* Babylon the Great.

3) **Rev. 17:16; Revelation 18:9, 18; and Isaiah 47:9–15:** In that same **one hour,** these same ten kings will carry out God's purposes to "burn Babylon the Great with fire."

4) **Rev. 3:8, 10:** In **one hour** God has a plan to deliver His chosen ones, utilizing an "open door to keep thee from the hour of tribulation that shall come upon the earth" (Rev. 3:8, 10).

All these details are written clearly in the Word of God as prophetic utterances from His servants, the prophets, to "go forth and tell." The words were delivered by an angel who spoke directly to John concerning the judgment of Babylon and the **hour** of tribulation that will come upon the earth.

This is not prophetic speculation or a guessing game on the meaning of words. In 750 BC, Isaiah wrote: "I am God, and there is none like Me . . . I have spoken it, and I will bring it to pass; I have purposed, and I will do it" (Isa. 46:9, 11 ESV). God "watches over his word to perform it" (Jer. 1:12). Like many of the other prophecies we have discovered, He has also purposed the hour when the Antichrist and the ten-nation conglomerate will release their **hour of fiery judgment** upon Babylon the Great.

But what exactly is the mystery of the "open door"?

OUR GOOD GOD PROVIDES A WAY OF ESCAPE

We have explored some intensive insights about the **one hour** of tribulation that will come upon not only Babylon the Great, but the entire world. These insights can be extremely sobering, even frightening, when you realize that the Bible does not fool around when it comes to fulfilling prophecy. However, as we well know, the God we serve is a good God. He wishes above all things that we prosper and be in health, even as our souls prosper. He is the same yesterday, today, and forever. In that promise, we can rest assured that what He spoke to Ezekiel 2,500 years ago in historical Babylon is the same as what He speaks to us in Babylon the Great today:

> *As I live, saith the Lord GOD, I have no pleasure in the death of the wicked, but that the wicked turn from his way and live: turn ye, turn ye from your evil ways, for why will ye die (Ezek. 33:11).*

And the words that He spoke to Jeremiah:

> *For I know the thoughts that I think toward you, saith the LORD, thoughts of peace, and not of evil, to give you an expected end (Jer. 29:11).*

And what is that expected end? Jesus, your personal prophet, said in John 14:

> *Let not your heart be troubled: ye believe in God, believe also in Me. In my Father's house are many mansions: if it were not so, I would have told you. I go to prepare a place for you. And if I go and prepare a place for you, I will come again, and receive you unto myself; that where I am, there ye may be also (John 14:1–3).*

From this perspective, it is clear that God has a way of escape for those who choose to obey His ways and will. And the open door in Revelation 3:10 is the mystery through which He will provide your escape, sparing you from the tribulation that is sure to come to Babylon the Great and to the entire world.

God not only has a special place for those who love Him, **He has a supernatural exit plan for those who will go through the open door.** It is a special door, one that only a **chosen generation** will receive; it is a door that defies the laws of nature.

GOD'S SUPERNATURAL EXIT PLAN

But the open door of Revelation 3:8 is a blessing that supersedes God's written Word concerning all other generations of mankind. This supernatural door not only bypasses the *hour* of tribulation, but your appointed time to die as well.

> *But the same day that Lot went out of Sodom it rained fire and brimstone from heaven, and destroyed them all. Even thus shall it be in the day when the Son of man is revealed ... in that night there shall be two men in one bed; the one shall be taken, and the other shall be left. Two women shall be grinding together; the one shall be taken, and the other left. Two men shall be in the field; the one shall be taken, and the other left (Luke 17:29–30, 34–36).*

Notice Jesus said, "one shall be taken, and one shall be left." However, at His second coming, which takes place at the war of Armageddon, "every knee will bow," which is **a gigantic world war climaxed by the second coming of Christ** and which will successfully end the seven-year tribulation period. Within that final event, "the armies which were in heaven followed him upon white horses, clothed in fine linen, white and clean. And out of his mouth goeth a sharp sword, that with it he should smite the nations" (Rev. 19:14, 15). From Paul's account in Philippians (below), we learn that when Christ returns, all will not only see Him but will fully acknowledge who He claims to be: "That at the name of Jesus every knee should bow, of things in heaven, and things in earth, and things under the earth; and that every tongue should confess that Jesus Christ is Lord, to the glory of God the Father" (Phil. 2:10, 11).

In 2 Thessalonians 1:7, Paul brings an identical description of fire being present at the time of Jesus being revealed when he stated:

> And to you who are troubled rest with us, when the Lord Jesus
> shall be **revealed** [**apocalupsis:** *to uncover*] *from heaven with his*
> *mighty angels,* **in flaming fire** *taking vengeance on them that know*
> *not God, and that obey not the gospel of our Lord Jesus Christ.*

In this passage, we are told that fire will come, executing the vengeance that God will bestow on them that "obey not the gospel." The question is, who are "they" who obey not the gospel. Could it be the atheists, agnostics, and groups of unworthy believers Jesus just described, who miss the open-door exit plan and instantly find themselves in "the hour of temptation, which shall come upon all the world, to try them that dwell upon the earth" (Rev. 3:10)?

In this teaching, however, Paul said Jesus will be **revealed** (*apocalypto*: **to reveal oneself**),[3] which would suggest that not everyone is going to *see Him,* nor will everyone be taken. He also compares that day to the day that Lot came out of Sodom and it rained **fire** upon the earth. That was a day of judgment on Sodom. The day Jesus spoke of in Luke 17 will be the same. In other words, it was a **day of judgment** where some were delivered, and others were not.

Matthew 25, Jesus gave us a parable concerning those who will miss His coming. In this parable, ten virgins are waiting for the bridegroom to come. Five have oil in their lamps and five do not have any. When the bridegroom shows up in the middle of the night, the five virgins (brides) without oil leave to buy some more; they ultimately miss the wedding because, as Jesus said, by the time they were ready, the bridegroom was gone.

In 1 Thessalonians 4, the "open door" blessing that comes to certain believers is further explained:

> *For the Lord himself shall descend from heaven with a shout,*
> *with the voice of the archangel, and with the trump of God: and*
> *the dead in Christ shall rise first: Then we which are alive and*
> *remain shall be caught up [rapio/harpazo] together with them*
> *in the clouds, to meet the Lord in the air: and so shall we ever be*
> *with the Lord (1 Thess. 4:16–17).*

The phrase "caught up" in this passage is where we get the term "rapture." Like the term "Trinity," the word "rapture" is not written in Scripture. Its origins are the Latin Vulgate translation *rapio*, meaning to seize or snatch away, and the Greek word *harpazo*, meaning the same.

We also read in 1 Corinthians 15:

> *For the trumpet will sound, and the dead will be raised*
> *imperishable, and we shall be changed. For this perishable body*
> *must put on the imperishable, and this mortal body must put on*
> *immortality. When the perishable puts on the imperishable, and*
> *the mortal puts on immortality, then shall come to pass*
> *the saying that is written:*
> *"**Death** is swallowed up in victory."*
> *"O death, where is **your** victory.*
> *O death, where is your sting?" (1 Cor. 15:52–55 ESV).*

THE SUDDEN HOUR OF ESCAPE

These Philadelphian believers will be just like Elijah (2 Kings 2:11), who was caught up in a chariot and taken to heaven. And just like Enoch, who walked with God and was not (Gen. 5:24), they are the bride of Christ who **never taste death**. This group of believers will heed the warning Jesus gave in Luke 21:36 regarding the rapture—*Watch ye therefore, and pray always, that ye may be accounted **worthy** [kataxioo] to escape all these things that shall come to pass*—and their provided **escape** will take place at the same *one hour* that initiates the seven-year tribulation.

One of the most glaring examples pinpointing the specific time sequence of the rapture happens after the rapture takes place. Keep reading. You don't want to miss this teaching on the specific time sequence that unlocks the mystery of the open door and its direct correlation with the United States of America.

THE HOUR THAT WILL CHANGE THE WORLD FOREVER

We have now studied several verses that describe the hour that will change the world as we know it. To review, we have learned that:

- In **one hour**, ten kings (nations) will form an alliance with the Antichrist and initiate the New World Order.
- In **one hour**, a fiery judgment will be released upon Babylon the Great, allowing that New World Order to begin its seven-year reign.
- In **one hour**, an "open door" will provide an escape route for a chosen generation of believers; in the "twinkling of an eye" (1 Cor. 15:52), they will fulfill one of the greatest mysteries in Scripture by escaping death.

In a moment, in the twinkling of an eye, just as Christ appeared before His disciples instantaneously (John 20:19), those counted worthy will be given the same type of resurrected body. We will be taken off this planet, every atom of our being will be accelerated at the speed of light, caught up in the clouds to meet Christ. Both Paul and John agree that we will be conformed to have the same type of body as Jesus had after He was raised from the dead.

> *For our conversation is in heaven: from whence also we look*
> *for the Savior the Lord Jesus Christ: who shall change our vile*
> *body, that it may be fashioned like unto his glorious body,*
> *according to the working whereby he is able even to subdue all*
> *things unto himself (Phil. 3:20–21).*

> *Beloved, now are we the sons of God, and it doth not yet appear*
> *what we shall be: but we know that, when he shall appear, we*
> *shall be like him; for we shall see him as he is (1 John 3:2).*

Many have theorized about this end-times exodus. Though there are various schools of thought regarding the rapture, most agree on one particular principle. The catching away of believers will mark the number of days remaining for the kingdom of darkness, and it will take place before the seven-year tribulation period.

WHEN WILL THE DOOR OPEN?

After Revelation 18 describes the destruction of Babylon the Great, the following chapter provides evidence that demands a verdict. Revelation 19 tells us:

> *And after these things [the destruction of Babylon] I heard*
> *a great voice of much people in heaven, saying . . . true and*
> *righteous are His judgments: for He hath judged the great*
> *whore, [Babylon the Great] . . . and hath avenged the blood of*
> *His servants at her hand . . . Let us be glad and rejoice, and give*
> *honour to Him, for the marriage of the Lamb has come [begun],*
> *and His wife hath made herself ready (Rev. 19:1–2, 7).*

These verses show that the marriage supper of the Lamb will not take place until *after* Babylon the Great has been judged. Furthermore, this passage shows that her judgment will take place in **one hour**—the same hour of tribulation that will come upon the earth and the same hour when the bride of Christ will escape through the open door, just as Jesus promised the believers of Philadelphia who were counted worthy. It should be noted that this verse also confirms that the *bride* makes *herself* ready.

Remember, in Luke 21, Jesus urged us to pray that we might be counted worthy to escape the coming tribulation. Eternal salvation is a *gift* from God, offered to you freely by the death and resurrection of Jesus—by His works on the cross, not our works, lest any man should boast. However, to be counted *worthy to escape* through the open door and to defy death is a totally different initiative.

Revelation 19:7–8 (ESV) continues: "and His bride has made herself ready; it was granted her to clothe herself with fine linen, bright and pure—for the fine linen [or "white robes" in other translations] is the righteous deeds of the saints."

Remember, only five of the ten brides in Jesus' parable were ready for the bridegroom in Matthew 25. And according to the letters to the seven churches, some of those believers had "lost their first love," some had "dead works, not God's works," some were involved in "sexual immorality and participated in pagan rituals," and others were guilty of "holding back their wealth and not investing into the works of God's kingdom." We should take these verses seriously when we consider our life's priorities. We are living in the last days, in the seventh kingdom of Babylon before the eighth kingdom (the New World Order) takes over. And that event will take place at its appointed time—in *one hour*.

Christine Caine said in an interview, "The lives of Christ's followers should mirror God's work of redemption. In John 17, Jesus prayed, 'Father, I do not ask that you take them out of the world.' Our purpose is to be in the world and have a different value system, a different set of priorities and a different way of thinking."[4]

INSIGHTS FROM HISTORICAL BABYLON

There are various people in the Old Testament whose lifestyle foreshadowed Jesus' lifestyle. Joseph being sold into slavery and Jonah being three days in the belly of a fish that swallowed him foreshadow Jesus' life. However, there is one Old Testament typology that vividly foreshadows the miraculous "open door" described in our modern-day society of Babylon the Great.

From historical Babylon of 600 BC, Daniel 2 tells the story of King Nebuchadnezzar testing three young Hebrew boys because they would not bow to his golden image. Apparently, this king—who ruled in the region of present-day Iraq—had a barbaric, ideological religion that decreed that if people did not worship his god, they were an infidel. Those guilty would suffer death by being burned alive in a fiery furnace made specifically for that purpose.

Shadrach, Meshach, and Abednego were three Jewish believers of the thousands of Jewish people living in Babylon at the time. These three heroic men *would not bow*. King Nebuchadnezzar cast them into a burning fiery furnace to be burned alive, but God miraculously delivered them. According to Daniel 3, a fourth Man appeared in the flames. In utter astonishment, the king said, "Did not we cast three men bound in into the midst of the fire? . . . Lo, I see four men loose, walking in the midst of the fire, and they have no hurt; and the form of the fourth is like the Son of God" (Dan. 3:24–25).

The greatest miracle that ever happened in ancient Babylon could be a prophetic foreshadowing of the rapture of the bride, which will take place in latter-day Babylon and around the world.

Remember, the same spirits that rose during the time of ancient

Babylon are rising again within Babylon the Great today. Just as Nebuchadnezzar was spiritually manipulated to cast Shadrach, Meshach, and Abednego into a burning fiery furnace, so too the spirit of the Antichrist and his ten-nation coalition will be spiritually manipulated to press some buttons and cast certain sections of this planet into a burning fiery furnace (Rev. 7:17). Specifically, targeted will be the United States of America. But just as Shadrach, Meshach, and Abednego were delivered from the flames, God's Word has told us he will miraculously deliver the bride of Christ from the conventional weapons of modern warfare.

The flames "upon whose bodies the fire had no power, nor was an hair of their head singed, neither were their coats changed, nor the smell of fire had passed on them (Dan. 3:27)—for as Paul explained in 1 Corinthians 15, "I show you a mystery, we shall all be changed, instantly, in the twinkling of an eye. Our mortal bodies will put on immortality and our corruptible body will put on incorruptible."

A trumpet will sound; the dead in Christ will rise first, then we who are alive shall behold Him. The fourth Man shall appear again in the fiery furnace of Babylon's destruction, but only *His chosen* will take part at this time in the first resurrection.

THE FIRST RESURRECTION

That first resurrection began over 2,000 years ago. We read in Matthew:

> *Jesus, when he had cried again with a loud voice, yielded up*
> *the ghost. And, behold, the veil of the temple was rent in twain*
> *from the top to the bottom; and the earth did quake, and the*
> *rocks rent; and the graves were opened; and many bodies of the*
> *saints which slept arose, and came out of the graves after*
> *his resurrection, and went into the holy city, and appeared*
> *unto many (Matt. 27:51–53 ESV).*

According to Scripture, the first resurrection is not a one-time event. It is linear, meaning it progresses from one stage to another in a single series of steps. It involves resurrections throughout Scripture that ultimately culminate in the second coming of the Messiah. This progression is explained by Paul, beginning with Adam.

In 1 Corinthians 15:22–23 (ESV), we read, "For as in Adam all die, so also in Christ shall all be made alive. But each **in his own order**: Christ the **firstfruits**, then at His coming those who belong to Christ." From the moment Jesus "yielded up the ghost," the first resurrection began, "and many of the bodies of [some Old Testament) saints arose" (Matt. 27:52). Three days later, at His personal resurrection, the progression continued: "When he ascended up on high, he led captivity captive, and gave gifts unto men. (Now that he ascended, what is it but that he also descended first into the lower parts of the earth? He that descended is the same also that ascended up far above all heavens, that he might fill all things)" (Eph. 4:8–10).

Peter taught that in the three days after His death,[5] Jesus "went and preached unto the spirits in prison" (1 Pet. 3:19), only to rise from the dead, and at that point, lead those spirits out of their waiting place in the bowels of the earth when he "led captivity captive." The Old Testament saints' spirits were taken to heaven, but their bodies are still waiting in the graves, "each in his own order," for their resurrection. That resurrection will take place at the rapture "with the trump of God: and the dead in Christ shall rise first: then we which are alive and remain shall be caught up [*rapio/harpazo*] together with them in the clouds, to meet the Lord in the air" (1 Thess. 4:16–17). This is the resurrection happening in a linear progression.

However, the second coming consists of only two stages: first, the rapture, at which point God selects those worthy of escaping the tribulation through the open door of Philadelphia; and second, when believers who were martyred in the tribulation plus those who survived the tribulation meet Him at the second coming—at which point *every* knee will bow and acknowledge Him as Lord.

So get ready, America. Something good is about to happen to you who believe. Get your house in order. Make Christ first in your life. Give the firstfruits of your financial blessings, your time, and your giftings to those who are in need. Remember:

- When the rain **came down**, Noah's family **went up** (Gen. 9).
- When the fire **came in**, Lot's family **came out** (Gen. 19).
- When the flames **come down** on Babylon the Great, the bride will **go up** (Rev. 19).

For *He* has spoken it, therefore *He* will also do it; *He* has purposed it, and *He* will bring it to pass. So let the poor say, "We are rich," and let the weak say, "We are strong." This battle is already over, and *we win*! **Give glory to the Lamb of God!**

39) (Rev. 3:7–13; 19:1–10) (Philadelphia) The Philadelphian believers are within Babylon praying "to be counted worthy" for the "open door" that will deliver them from the soon coming judgment.

40) (Rev. 18:23; 19:7–9) She has the voice of the bride of Christ inside her before the rapture and subsequent destruction.

Those counted worthy to escape are also referred to as the bride of Christ in both chapter 18 and 19. The different locations of the bride, before and after Babylon's destruction, is the only time sequence in Scripture accurately pinpointing the time of the pretribulation rapture.

However, there are more signs within Babylon that we should look for confirming that the United States of America is the seventh providential in Scripture.

CHAPTER TEN

TWO SIGNS IN SOCIETY

WE HAVE EXPLORED the mysterious "hour" of judgment and deliverance that will come upon Babylon the Great. On one hand, a tremendous fiery judgment will fall on her (Rev. 14:7; 17:16; 18:8, 10, 17, 19; Isa. 47:9–15); on the other hand, God will open a window of deliverance, allowing the bride of Christ to supernaturally escape that judgment (Rev. 3:10; Luke 17:29; 1 Thess. 4:16; 2 Thess. 1:8, 9; 1 Cor. 15:52).

But what are the tipping points or warning signs that Jesus told us to look for within Babylon before this awesome prophecy takes place? We will discuss these signs in this chapter.

REVIEW: THE PROPHETIC HOUR

In previous chapters, we examined the seven types of believers who will be found in the last days. Babylon the Great is the last kingdom to appear before the New World Order begins (Rev. 17:12), and because Scripture tells us that God's people are in Babylon (Rev. 18:4, 24; Isa.

47), we can easily surmise that these seven types of believers are also in Babylon. Of course, God's people are not only in Babylon, but they are scattered throughout the nations of the whole world. However, based on the Scripture's forty descriptions of Babylon the Great thus far, we have concluded that the geographical boundary of the United States of America is the only population center in the history of the world to meet every one of those descriptions.

Our examination of Scripture has further revealed that a one-hour shift will miraculously take place: "Because thou hast kept the word of my patience, I also will keep thee from the hour of temptation, which shall come upon all the world, to try them that dwell upon the earth" (Rev. 3:10).

The Bible foreshadows this miraculous event in its account of historical Babylon of 590 BC (Dan. 3:25), when a fourth Man suddenly reveals Himself and delivers His servants Shadrach, Meshach, and Abednego from Nebuchadnezzar's fiery furnace.

While perhaps other Jewish people in Babylon bent their knees to the dark agenda of the Babylonian government, these three men stood boldly for God's Word. Because of their faith and courage to follow the Word instead of the herd of Babylonian culture, God found them worthy to escape the fiery test that came upon them. This test was imposed by Nebuchadnezzar's law (Dan. 3:4–6), which specifically opposed God's First Commandment to all men: "Thou shalt have no other gods before Me" (Ex. 20:3).

It is important to understand, as Shadrach, Meshach, and Abednego surely did, that Moses did not come down from Mount Horeb with the Ten Negotiating Points; he came down with the Ten Commandments. God did not say, "Let's make a deal." He said, "This is the deal: Walk ye therein." But choosing to obey God is a personal decision.

To this point, Chuck Colson wrote:

Adam and Eve were free either to believe God and obey
his law or to disobey him and suffer the consequences. This
same choice has confronted every person throughout history.
Obedience to God is not just a matter of following rules
arbitrarily imposed by a harsh master. Obedience to God is
a means of entering into real life. A life rich in meaning and
purpose (Deut. 30:15, 19).[1]

KINGDOM CHOICE

Scripture makes it clear that God loves everyone (John 3:16; 2 Pet. 3:9); unfortunately, not everyone loves God in return. Jesus said, "If you love me, you will keep my commandments" (John 14:15 ESV). But God has never forced any person to follow His Word. Instead, He has given us the privilege of free will. In order to take part in God's kingdom, we must choose it. Joshua spoke to the Children of Israel regarding this choice when He said, "choose this day whom you will serve" (Joshua 24:15 ESV). The result of our free will choices can be dramatic blessings or judgments.

The kingdom of darkness offers easy access. All you must do is yield to your basic sin nature. When mankind fell in the garden, he made a choice from the free will that God had given. Mankind chose to operate out of his wants, as Satan enticed him to do. The fruit of that choice still manifests itself in the world today. It is easily recognizable:

Now the works of the flesh are evident: sexual immorality,
impurity, sensuality, idolatry, sorcery, enmity, strife, jealousy,
fits of anger, rivalries, dissensions, divisions, envy, drunkenness,
orgies, and things like these. I warn you, as I warned you

before, that those who do such things will not inherit the
kingdom of God (Galatians 5:19–21 ESV).

As we continue in this chapter to study God's judgment for sin, it is worth remembering the blessings available to those who choose to walk away from their sinful nature and to instead live for God. Some of these blessings are summed up as Galatians continues:

But the fruit [reward] of the Spirit is love, joy, peace, patience,
kindness, goodness, faithfulness, gentleness, self-control
(Gal. 5:22–23 ESV).

There comes a time when each of us must recognize which kingdom we as individuals represent. The fruit of one's lifestyle will often reflect immediately which kingdom is in operation. But it is not only individuals that can form and enter into a spiritual covenant with God. We know from Scripture that nations hold that ability as well (Deut. 28:1–15; Gen. 12:2).

Many of the forty descriptions of Babylon the Great have to do with the benefits or rewards she has reaped from her providential and covenantal beginnings. By reflecting the laws of God in her government legislature, judicial system, and economic policies, the United States of America has reaped the greatest financial blessings of any kingdom in the history of the world. But of course, we know that to whom much is given, much is required (Luke 12:48).

Although historical Babylon's King Nebuchadnezzar acknowledged God as the Most High God and honored Shadrach, Meshach, and Abednego after their great deliverance, the next generation of leaders failed to preserve that legacy. This is not unlike what we are witnessing in America today, and as you will read below, America can gain great wisdom by examining the failures of Nebuchadnezzar's successors.

GOD REMOVES AND ESTABLISHES KINGS

From Daniel, we learned that "He [God] changes times and seasons; he removes kings and sets up kings; he gives wisdom to the wise and knowledge to those who have understanding" (Dan. 2:21 ESV). Nebuchadnezzar was highly favored to see for himself the miraculous power of God in the deliverance of the three Hebrew boys. And although he fully acknowledged the awesome power of the Most High God— "How great are His signs, how mighty His wonders! His kingdom is an everlasting kingdom, and His dominion endures from generation to generation" (Dan. 4:3 ESV)—Nebuchadnezzar's immediate descendants utterly failed to carry on that legacy.

God raised up King Nebuchadnezzar in approximately 605 BC to judge Israel. Nevertheless, in accordance with God's prophetic timing, Babylon's judgment against Israel would only last for seventy years (Jer. 29:10). By 539 BC, Nebuchadnezzar's successor, King Belshazzar, along with his elite leaders, had come to believe in their hearts that Babylon could never fall. And in the middle of a drunken, hedonistic party at the palace, King Belshazzar decided he would mock the Hebrew God (Dan. 5).

At this party, Belshazzar, along with some in his court, drank wine from the "golden vessels that had been taken out of the temple, the house of God in Jerusalem," as they praised other gods. Suddenly, "the fingers of a human hand appeared and wrote on the plaster of the wall of the king's palace . . . and the king saw the hand as it wrote" (Dan. 5:3, 5 ESV). Scripture records that the king was shocked, and that fear overwhelmed him. He called for the wise men and leaders of his Babylonian religions, "the enchanters, the Chaldeans, and the astrologers," to interpret the writing, but none of them could understand what was happening (Dan. 5:6–8 ESV).

Finally, Daniel, the Jewish prophet of the highest God, was called.

He interpreted the handwriting on the wall, saying to the king: "God has numbered the days of your kingdom and brought it to an end . . . you have been weighed in the balances and found wanting" (Dan. 5:26 ESV). Even as Daniel spoke these words, the Medes and Persians were entering the city. Unbeknownst to the king and his drunken, God-mocking leadership, the waters of the Euphrates had been diverted weeks in advance.

In one day—without a major battle, without a huge army—Babylon fell. "The city fell by complete surprise. Half of the metropolis was captured before the rest of it was 'aware' of the fact, according to Herodotus. Cyrus diverted the waters of the Euphrates and by night entered the city through the dried up channel (Dan. 5:30–31)."[2]

THE TIPPING POINT

Historical Babylon was "weighed in the balances and found wanting." In hindsight, we can see there was a watershed moment: a specific time and place when God said, enough is enough, and the kingdom that He prophetically raised up was prophetically laid down. Dr. David Jeremiah wrote, "Is it any wonder that God said, 'Enough is enough. Your number is up!' Belshazzar was not only grossly sacrilegious, he was also stupid."[3]

Sometimes people confuse God's patience with His tolerance. We see evil or we participate in sin and realize nothing is happening. So, we continue in our ways or we continue to let things slip around us in our culture. But we're confusing God's patience with His tolerance. God is patient—He gives us every opportunity to repent (to turn from our sin and coming to Him). But at some point, God's patience runs out, as it did with historical Babylon. He only tolerates sin and sinful behavior for a specific amount of time. He is a holy God. Is He patient with us? Yes. But He doesn't tolerate the sins of people or nations. Speaker and writer Anne Graham Lotz wrote, "God's patience should provoke a deep debt of gratitude in us so that we live our lives for the One who gave His life for us. When we mistake God's patience for tolerance, it is to our own destruction."[4]

The Babylon the Great described in Revelation 17 and 18 is a nation that is prophetically raised up by God, but is also prophesied to be prophetically laid down by God. They will reach the limit of His tolerance. At the **appointed time,** this word will be fulfilled. But what is the tipping point that can bring such a calamity of utter destruction in **one hour?**

By raising America up as a covenant nation, her Founding Fathers invoked the blessings of God. They acknowledged Him in every form of government and in her social structure. Just like Nebuchadnezzar, the Founding Fathers **openly** acknowledged, of their own free will, the God of Israel as the Most High God. Has that legacy continued within the subsequent generations of leaders? Or have we, like Babylon, fallen far from that initial place of humility? Can one generation invoke God's blessing and the next generation—through pride, arrogance, and open defiance of Scripture—provoke God's judgment? Through the lessons we have just learned from the story of Nebuchadnezzar and his successor Belshazzar, it is most certainly possible.

According to Scripture, it will happen to this lady of kingdoms at some point in her future. But does prophecy give us any warning signs or "handwriting on the wall" that can indicate that the "scales have tipped" within Babylon and that judgment is imminent? And as we "weigh ourselves in the balance," should we be able to foresee on the horizon her appointed time, her **one hour** of fiery judgment? The answer to these questions cannot be found in secular humanism, modern science, or pagan Babylonian religions. Instead, it lies in the hidden mystery of God's Word.

John 16:13 (ESV) says, "When the Spirit of truth comes, He will guide you into all the truth, for He shall not speak on His own authority, but whatever He hears, He will speak, and He will declare to you the things that are to come." So let's find out what we can learn from Scripture about these things.

SIGNS OF DARKNESS

Trying to pinpoint the exact timing of the coming hour of Babylon's judgment is absolutely impossible. Even Jesus' own disciples asked that question, and He responded by saying, "But concerning that day and hour no one knows, not even the angels of heaven, nor the Son, but the Father only" (Matt. 24:36 ESV). Jesus did say, however, that believers could watch for signs of this hour. These signs included an increase in knowledge (Dan. 12:4), wars and rumors of wars (Matt. 24:6; Mark 13:7), and the nation of Israel (Isa. 66:8) and her position in world standing (Zech. 2:8–11).

Perhaps one of the greatest future signs of the Lord's coming, though, is the revelation of Babylon's identity. As we've read in previous chapters, it is my opinion and vision that she is the nation that will precede the final New World Order. We have identified her with forty biblical descriptions, all of which point to the United States of America. However, there are more descriptions to come. In fact, some of those descriptions may give us clues of how close we are to Babylon's appointed time of coming judgment. Perhaps the handwriting will be written clearly on the wall for us, just as it was for historical Babylon.

ROMANS 1: A SOCIETY IN DARKNESS

Sit thou silent, and get thee into darkness, O daughter of the Chaldeans [Babylonians]: for thou shalt no more be called, the lady of kingdoms (Isa. 47:5).

We learned in previous chapters that before her destruction, Babylon will fall into spiritual darkness. We are also told in Revelation 18:2, "Babylon the Great is fallen, is fallen, and is become the habitation of devils, and the hold of every foul spirit, and a cage of every unclean and hateful bird." Has North America already become the habitation of devils? What has happened to this God-fearing, Bible-reading, prayer-conscious nation? And what will be the evidence of this darkness? How will it affect her society?

In Romans 1, Paul describes the effects of darkness on a society and how those effects will provoke God's wrath against that society. We will examine this chapter in segments, beginning with verse 18:

. . . .

For the wrath of God is revealed from heaven against all ungodliness and unrighteousness of men, who by their unrighteousness suppress the truth. For although they knew God, they did not honor him as God or give thanks to him, but they became futile in their thinking, and their foolish hearts were darkened (Rom. 1:18, 21 ESV).

- The Greek word used here for "darkened" comes from the word *skotizo*, which means "to be unable to understand" truth.[5]

Isaiah 13 foretells the eventual destruction of the Babylonian Empire. God judged them for their darkness (their sinful ways). As we've seen, God raised up the Medes to conquer Babylon and end the dynasty that was so spiritually dark and unwilling to understand the truth.

Likewise, Paul was concerned about the darkness invading the thinking of the Romans as it had the Babylonians. One commentator wrote, "[Verse 21] confirms the statement that by their unrighteousness these wicked people are constantly attempting to suppress the truth that has been and is continually being revealed to them, and that they are accordingly without excuse.⁶

. . . .

> Wherefore God also gave them up to uncleanness through
> the lusts of their own hearts, to dishonor their own bodies
> between themselves: who changed the truth of God into a lie,
> and worshipped and served the creature more than the Creator
> (Rom. 1:24–25).

- When children are raised thinking they come from monkeys, is it any wonder some grow up to act like animals, with a survival of the fittest attitude that results in school shootings, moral degradation, and the absence of any feelings that would embrace human kindness? This type of reprobate "groupthink" society has totally lost its moral compass.

. . . .

> For this cause God gave them up unto vile affections: for even
> their women did change the natural use into that which is
> against nature (Rom. 1:26).

- The word "vile" in Greek is *atimia*, meaning "a state of dishonor or disrespect."⁷

. . . .

> And likewise also the men, leaving the natural use of the
> woman, burned in their lust one toward another; men with men
> working that which is unseemly (Rom. 1:27).

- The word "lust" in Greek *(epithymeō)* means "to desire earnestly, long for something, lust, covet." It has both negative and positive connotations, but it always describes the inner motivation. The noun form denotes "impulsive, sensual desire," contrary to the will and pleasure of God.[8]

. . . .

And even as they did not like to retain God in their knowledge,
God gave them over to a reprobate mind, to do those things
which are not convenient (Rom. 1:28).

- The word "reprobate" as written in the ancient Greek, is *adokimos*, meaning, "not standing the test, rejected. [The word] was primarily applied to metals (Isa. 1:22). In the above verse, the word applies to a mind of which God cannot approve and must be rejected by Him."[9]

. . . .

Being filled with all unrighteousness, fornication, wickedness,
covetousness, maliciousness; full of envy, murder, debate, deceit,
malignity; whisperers, backbiters, haters of God, despiteful,
proud, boasters, inventors of evil things, disobedient to parents,
without understanding, covenant breakers, without natural
affection, implacable, unmerciful: who knowing the judgment of
God, that they which commit such things are worthy of death,
not only do the same, but have pleasure in them that do them
(Rom. 1:29–32).

- This passage from the first chapter in Romans mentions twenty-three "groupthink" character traits that will appear in a society that will provoke the wrath (or judgment) of

God. Concerning this passage, commentator and Anglican pastor William Barclay wrote:

There is hardly any passage which so clearly shows what happens to a man when he leaves God out of the reckoning. It is not so much that God sends a judgment on a man, as that a man brings a judgment on himself when he gives no place to God in his scheme of things. When a man banishes God from his life he becomes a certain kind of man, and in this passage is one of the most terrible descriptions in literature of the kind of man he becomes.[10]

Isaiah 5:20 says, "Woe unto them that call evil good, and good evil; that put darkness for light, and light for darkness." When a society totally disregards God's moral practices, its members become unhinged, following the mentality of the popular herd instead of God's Word, without even the slightest prophetic insight into the wrath they are about to pull down from heaven. But this is just the proverbial tip of the iceberg. Babylon's moral degradation is falling into darkness, and God is warning to "come out of her my people and partake not in her sins" (Rev. 18:4, paraphrased).

We are in a time of self-examination before God judges Babylon. No man knows the hour or day, but most Christians know that something is happening, especially in America, where the cultural separation is most evident. Paul admonishes this distinction when he says, "For the word of God is quick, and powerful, and sharper than any two edged sword, piercing even to the dividing asunder of soul and spirit, and of the joints and marrow, and is a discerner of the thoughts and intents of the heart" (Heb. 4:12). How can your heart know right from wrong if you don't even know what the Word of God says, let alone care?

"The future and success of America is not in this Constitution, but in the laws of God upon which this Constitution is founded."[11]

You are either for God, Jesus, forgiveness, and peace or you are against God, Jesus, and have unforgiveness and no peace, which results in riots, hatred, and fascist socialism.

The true values of the Church are being tested. If we stand against the darkness, we will be spared the evilest days to come during the seven-year tribulation. There will be persecution before the tribulation begins, yet I believe the worst days will follow, after the exodus of the believers in the rapture. As we will see below, Jesus gave us two specific examples of the type of society to look for before His return.

THE WRITING ON THE WALL: SODOM AND GOMORRAH

We have been searching for the tipping points—the writing on the wall—that would point to the imminent return of Jesus. We learned in the previous chapter that at the time Jesus is revealed in heaven (1 Thess. 4:16, 17; 2 Thess. 1:8; 1 Cor. 15:51, 52), there will be an open door (Rev. 3:10) that miraculously delivers the bride of Christ from Babylon's one hour of judgment. To put it bluntly, when the judgment comes down, the bride will go up.

When asked what the sign of His coming would be, Jesus gave his disciples two examples from specific historical societies in Scripture. We should look for the characteristics of these societies before His imminent return. Luke wrote:

> *Just as it was in the days of Noah, so will it be in the days of the Son of Man. They were eating and drinking and marrying and being given in marriage, until the day when Noah entered the ark, and the flood came and destroyed them all. Likewise, just as it was in the days of Lot—they were eating and drinking, buying and selling, planting and building, but on the day when*

Lot went out from Sodom, fire and sulfur rained from heaven
and destroyed them all—so will it be on the day when the Son of
Man is revealed (Luke 17:26–30 ESV).

We find in this passage that judgment came suddenly upon both societies. One society was the days of Noah, and the other was Sodom and Gomorrah. Do these two examples tie into Paul's explanation of a reprobate society, one gone wild with lust and vile affections? I think they do.

Remember the saying, "those who cannot remember the past are condemned to repeat it"? The two historical societies to which Jesus refers in Luke 17 showcase lifestyles mirrored in our American culture. On one side are political progressives; on the other side are traditional conservatives. Let's look at what the Bible says concerning current lifestyle trends and one of the most controversial issues today: traditional marriage versus gay marriage.

Traditional Christian conservatives gather most of their thinking on this issue from the teachings of Jesus. Matthew 19:4–6 (ESV), for instance, says, "'Have you not read that he who created them from the beginning made them male and female, and said, "Therefore a man shall leave his father and his mother and hold fast to his wife, and the two shall become one flesh"? So they are no longer two but one flesh.'"

We read in Romans 1 that Paul also addressed the issue of men and women and their respective roles in society in Romans 1. However, he also discussed the "darkness" that comes upon society when they turn from God's Word. Recall that Isaiah 47:5 prophesied that before Babylon the Great is judged, she will be driven into "darkness" ("get thee into darkness"). We also read about this darkness in Romans 1:

Their foolish heart was darkened [skotizo]: unable to
understand truth . . . For this cause God gave them up unto vile
affections: for even their women did change the natural use into

that which is against nature: and likewise also the men, leaving the natural use of the woman, burned in their lust one toward another; men with men working that which is unseemly, and receiving in themselves that recompence of their error which was meet. And even as they did not like to retain God in their knowledge, God gave them over to a reprobate mind, to do those things which are not convenient (Rom. 1:21, 26–28).

Jesus' brother, the apostle Jude, traveled with Jesus throughout His ministry. He, too, wrote concerning the example of Sodom and Gomorrah:

And the angels which kept not their first estate, but left their own habitation, he hath reserved in everlasting chains under darkness unto the judgment of the great day. Even as Sodom and Gomorrah, and the cities about them in like manner, giving themselves over to fornication, and going after strange flesh, are set forth for an example (Jude 1:6–7).

But what is this example Jesus and Jude cited in Luke 17 and Jude? What more can we learn about Jesus' return by studying the Old Testament account of Sodom and Gomorrah?

Genesis 19:24–25 describes the destruction of the cities of Sodom and Gomorrah, two cities that most theologians place at the southern end of the Dead Sea at the time of Abraham. The night before Sodom and Gomorrah were destroyed by fire, Abraham's nephew Lot was visited by two angels, who came to his house and warned him of the coming judgment:

But before they [the angels] lay down, the men of the city, the men of Sodom, both young and old, all the people to the last

man, surrounded the house. And they called to Lot, "Where are
the men who came to you tonight? Bring them out to us, that we
may know them" (Gen. 19:4–5 ESV).

Note that the word "know" in Hebrew is the word *yada*. It is the same Hebrew word used in Genesis 4:1, where Scripture says that Adam "knew" Eve, and she conceived. In other words, these men of Sodom did not simply want a meet and greet with the angels. The word *yada* as it was used in Genesis 19:5[12] is a euphemism meaning "carnal knowledge" or sexual intercourse.[13]

The Sodomites tried to force their sexuality on those who did not want it, demanding that Lot hand over the newly arrived guests. Scripture tells us in Genesis 19:7 (ESV) that Lot replied: "I beg you, my brothers, do not act so wickedly." But the men of Sodom responded to Lot by complaining that he was judging them:

> *This fellow [Lot] came to sojourn [or live in our city], and **he has**
> **become the judge!** Now we will deal worse with you than with*
> *them. Then they pressed hard against the man Lot, and drew*
> *near to break the door down. But the men [angels] reached out*
> *their hands and brought Lot into the house with them and shut*
> *the door. And they [the angels] struck with blindness the men*
> *[of Sodom] who were at the entrance of the house, both small*
> *and great, so that they wore themselves out groping for the door*
> *(Gen. 19:9–11 ESV).*

Notice that the Sodomites said to Lot that he had come to live with them, in their city, but was now judging them (v. 9). Lot and the angels did not want to participate in acts of fornication, and in fact, Lot called their proposal wicked. Does this mean, by the terminology so commonly used today, that he was homophobic?

As I live, declares the Lord God, your sister Sodom and her
daughters have not done as you and your daughters have done.
Behold, this was the guilt of your sister Sodom: she and her
*daughters had pride, excess of food, and prosperous ease, **but did***
not aid the poor and needy**. They were **haughty (proud) and did
***an abomination before me**. So I removed them, when I saw it*
(Ezek. 16:48–50 ESV).

Here is what I think: According to the Bible, the last thing God witnessed before Sodom and Gomorrah's destruction was a parade of men who marched down the street accusing Lot of judging them for their lifestyle while at the same time trying to force others to join them in their sexual activities. They were not kind, inclusive, or open to anyone else's opinions. You either agreed with them, even to the point of participating, or you would be verbally and even physically abused.

As the chapter in Genesis continues, we learn that the next morning, at the angels' urging, Lot and his family escaped to the city of Zoar:

Then the Lord rained on Sodom and Gomorrah sulfur and fire
from the Lord out of heaven. And he overthrew those cities, and all
the valley, and all the inhabitants of the cities (Gen. 19:24–25 ESV).

Sodom and Gomorrah met their end in a fiery judgment—exactly like the one hour of fiery judgment prophesied in Revelation 18 will come upon Babylon the Great. But Jesus said in Matthew 24:38 that the coming of the Son of Man will also be like those days before the Flood, when they were "marrying and giving in marriage." How does the example of Sodom and Gomorrah tie into the days of Noah? What is the link between these two civilizations? Additionally, we are aware that every generation, for thousands of years, has married and been given in marriage. So what is the distinction Jesus was pointing to here?

THE WRITING ON THE WALL:
THE DAYS OF NOAH

We have just discussed the culture of Sodom and Gomorrah, one of the signs for which Jesus said we should watch before He returns. But He also mentions another sign: "As it was in the days of Noah, so will it be in the days of the Son of Man" (Luke 17:26 ESV). What, then, is the similarity between Noah's day and Sodom and Gomorrah? Why did Jesus choose these two examples together to describe the state of the world before His return?

In Noah's day, it rained for forty days and forty nights; those who had mocked Noah for the previous 120 years were drowned in that flood. Noah and his family, of course, were spared. But after the flood, God spoke to Noah and gave him a sign "for all future generations":

> And God said, "This is the sign of the covenant that I make
> between me and you and every living creature that is with
> you, for all future generations: I have set my [rain]bow in the
> cloud, and it shall be a sign of the covenant between me and
> the earth . . . I will remember my covenant that is between me
> and you and every living creature of all flesh. And the waters
> shall never again become a flood to destroy all flesh"
> (Gen. 9:12–13, 15 ESV).

However, the story of Noah's life continues, and it's a disappointing account. After the Bible presents to us Noah's three sons and explains how the earth is repopulated, Noah gets drunk, and there is sin. We read:

> Noah began to be a man of the soil, and he planted a vineyard.
> He drank of the wine and became drunk and **lay uncovered** in

his tent. And Ham, the father of Canaan, saw the nakedness of
his father and told his two brothers outside. Then Shem
and Japheth took a garment, laid it on both their shoulders, and
walked backward and covered the nakedness of their father.
Their faces were turned backward, and they did not see their
father's nakedness. When Noah awoke from his wine and
knew what his youngest son had done to him, he said,
"Cursed be Canaan;" (Gen. 9:20–25 ESV)

Why does Noah express such a severe curse for the seemingly minor sin of observing his nakedness?

Theological Wordbook of the Old Testament explains that the "uncovered" in this verse is the Hebrew verb *gālâ*. "It is used most frequently in this stem for designating proscribed sexual activity. The word occurs twenty-four times in Leviticus 18 and 20, in the expression "to uncover the shame," which denotes sexual intercourse in proscribed situations, usually incest, also Deut. 22:30 and 27:20."[14] "Thus, the sin, in the original narrative, is not homosexual sex itself, but forced incest of a son with his father in a situation in which the father has no ability to defend himself; this would explain the harshness of the father's curse."[15]

A rainbow confirmed God's covenant with Noah's descendants, promising He would never judge the earth again by water. However, it was defiled by the forced incestuous act to violate Noah sexually.

Historically, Canaan's (Ham's son) descendants moved to the land of Canaan, which was where the cities of Sodom and Gomorrah eventually emerged. And we just learned that the night before Sodom and Gomorrah were destroyed, the men of Sodom marched militantly down the street, demanding to "know" or sexually violate the angels who came to warn Lot of Sodom's imminent destruction through divine revelation. This is all validated in Scripture.

Today, 4,000 years later,[16] we watch massive citywide parades showcasing rainbow flags, with men and woman marching down the streets, promoting gay pride. Is this the sign within our society that Jesus was referencing when He talked about Noah's day and Sodom and Gomorrah?

America is blindly headed in the same direction as Sodom. As legislation opens the doors to the soul of our nation, Bible prophecy will be fulfilled. Atheists and secular humanists who reject God's moral standards are being spiritually manipulated to fight for the sexual rights of everyone, including children. Those who oppose this ungodly approach are considered homophobic and out of touch with society's needs. Many churches have already been put under pressure to reject their traditional, so-called "regressive" Christian values of morality. In 2012, President Barack Obama lit up the White House in the rainbow colors to celebrate the "progressive" changes to American legislation concerning gay marriage. In 2009 President Obama told CBS, "we do not consider ourselves a Christian nation."[17]

Has our progressive liberal culture really progressed our society, or has it regressed us back to Sodom and the days of Noah? Are secular humanists, who deny the validity of Scripture, promoting a culture that fulfills the very Scriptures they themselves deny?

THE CONSEQUENCES OF LIVING A LIFESTYLE OF DARKNESS

Behold, this was the guilt of your sister Sodom: she and her daughters had pride, excess of food, and prosperous ease, but did not aid the poor and needy. They were haughty and did an abomination before me (Ezek. 16:49–50 ESV).

The United States of America has met forty specific prophetic descriptions of Babylon the Great. Jeremiah prophesied to Babylon the

Great: "Surely I will fill you with men, as many as locusts, and they shall raise the shout of victory over you" (Jer. 51:14 ESV). Meanwhile, in historical Babylon, the prophet Ezekiel is told:

> If I say to the wicked, O wicked one, you shall surely die, and
> you do not speak to warn the wicked to turn from his way, that
> wicked person shall die in his iniquity, but his blood I will require
> at your hand. But if you warn the wicked to turn from his way,
> and he does not turn from his way, that person shall die in his
> iniquity, but you will have delivered your soul (Ezek. 33:8–9 ESV).

The genuine values of the Church are being tested. If we stand against the darkness, we will be spared the evilest days to come during the seven-year tribulation. There will be persecution before the tribulation begins. Yet, I believe the worst days will follow the exodus of the Church. Believers in Christ must stand against the sin, but love the sinner. Endorsing homosexuality is not God's way of delivering people from sin's bondage. Through prayer, counseling, and renewing of the mind with God's Word, the healing power of Christ is available for those seeking change. By coming into obedience to Christ's teachings, deliverance from every dysfunctional lifestyle is possible.

Jesus taught His disciples in Matthew 7: "Judge not, that **ye be not judged**. For with what judgment **ye judge, ye shall be judged**: and with what measure ye mete, it shall be measured to you again" (Matt. 7:1–2). This spiritual principle applies to everyone, not just Jesus' disciples. The Bible does not teach that you can judge others, rather it warns that if you judge others with contempt, it may provoke God to judge you with same malice . In fact, according to many theologians, the wrath poured out on Sodom was a direct result of the hostile, militant actions the men of Sodom directed toward those who came to warn them. "Sodom was not destroyed because it specialized in homosexuality, but because it was a plague center of every kind of depravity, including pride, sensuality, and injustice."[18] Many theologians believe that God's judgment was provoked less by the Sodomites' sexual sins than by the aggressive approach (judging) they took toward those who thought differently than they did.

In today's progressive culture, anyone who voices any disagreement to the sexual promiscuity in our society is met with vile hostility and name-calling. However, when government begins to execute judgment on anyone who follows God's laws, it can provoke God's judgment on that government or the nation it represents. Should pending legislation in Canada be approved, any counselor, clergy, or even common, everyday person attempting to counsel someone concerning changing their sexual desires by means of "conversion therapy"[19] could be legally found guilty of an indictable offense and jailed for up to five years. We'll talk more about this in Chapter Eleven.

Make no mistake though: multiple verses—indeed, whole chapters—in Scripture warn us specifically that fornication, adultery, and incest, are all sexual sins, committed outside the bounds of holy matrimony between a man and a woman. But of course there is no sin that can overcome the forgiveness offered through the shed blood of Jesus Christ (1 Cor. 6:9–11). In Galatians 6:1 (ESV), Paul wrote, "If anyone is caught in any transgression, you who are spiritual should restore him in a spirit of gentleness."

The question that confronts us now is the "tipping point" at which the twenty-three descriptions in Romans 1 of a reprobate society become so provocative in our culture that the wrath of God's judgment is released on Babylon the Great. After all, God still watches over His Word to perform it.

"Sodom was not destroyed because it specialized in homosexuality, but because it was a plague center of every kind of depravity, including pride, sensuality, and injustice."[20] We are told in Ephesians 4:32, "And be ye kind one to another, tenderhearted, forgiving one another, even as God for Christ's sake hath forgiven you." Believers are also told in 2 Corinthians 13:5 (ESV) that they are to "examine yourselves, to see whether you are in the faith. Test yourselves. Or do you not realize this about yourselves, that Jesus Christ is in you?—unless indeed you fail to meet the test!"

If you find yourself participating in a lifestyle of darkness, heed the warning given in Revelation 18:4 (ESV): "Come out of her, my people, lest you take part in her sins, lest you share in her plagues."

Jesus said in Luke 21:

For as a snare shall it come on all them that dwell on the face of the whole earth. Watch ye therefore, and pray always, that ye may be accounted worthy to escape all these things that shall come to pass, and to stand before the Son of man (Luke 21:35–36).

Our team at Prophesy USA has no desire to judge, condemn, or point fingers at any individual group. Jesus confirmed that we are all sinners, and we are to "pray one for another that ye may be healed" (James 5:16), not judge one another in condemnation. It is purely our mandate to repeat the warnings of Jesus that if our society duplicates the sins of Sodom and those in the days of Noah, the return of Jesus could be imminent. And immediately following His brief appearance, a seven-year tribulation period—the likes of which mankind has never experienced—will come.

Babylon appears before the tribulation begins. In order for her to be the nation that appears before the event takes place, America must meet the description of the two signs Jesus gave us:

41) (Luke 17:28–32; Jude 1:7; Gen. 19:1–30) She has a culture similar to the time of Sodom and Gomorrah.
42) (Luke 17:26; Gen. 9) She has a culture similar to the days of Noah.

CHAPTER ELEVEN

THE SIN OF PROVOCATION

IN THE PREVIOUS chapter, we looked at the signs Jesus gave that will point to His return and the fiery hour of judgment. In this chapter, we'll examine in more depth the tipping point, or ultimate provocation, within American society that will guarantee this prophesied event.

A LOOK AT JUDGMENT

In the previous chapter, we determined that the "progressive" secular humanist agenda has not moved our country forward, but instead has regressed our society to the examples of Sodom and the days of Noah that Jesus gave us. The bullying and militant hostility that the men of Sodom directed toward those who refused to participate in their "acceptable" lifestyle helped tip the scale of God's judgment. According to biblical history, this kind of violence toward others helped create societies ripe for God's judgment (Gen. 19; Ezek. 16:49; Rom. 1:29).

These were grim periods of time when God brought judgment to people. Reading the Bible carefully, we also recognize that during those judgments, he saved His people as well. Both Lot and Noah survived the judgments. Why? Because they trusted God and His Word.

Porter Barrington, in his remarkable work *The Christian Life Study Outlines and Notes,* commented, "The Bible is high above all other books as the heavens are above the earth. Some have said, 'Read it to be wise, believe it to be safe, and practice it to be right.'"[1] We need to read and study our Bibles.

In our generation, those who deny the validity of Scripture are fulfilling the very Scriptures they deny. Indeed, only a fool says in his heart that there is no God (Ps. 14:1).

The Bible is abundantly clear that God loves everyone. However, human history has proven that not everyone loves God, wants His presence, or desires for His commandments to rule over their lives. Jesus said, "If ye love me, keep my commandments" (John 14:15). He knew when He first said these words to His disciples that we would break His commandments throughout our lives, so He willingly sacrificed Himself in order that we might have a way back to God. Pastor Charles Williams wrote years ago, "Man, seeking a way back to God, concluded, and rightly, that it should be by sacrifice. He could not, however, discover a sacrifice in which God would or could meet him. So the Lord himself provided a place of reconciliation . . . the sacrifice of Christ is thus a means of approach to God."[2]

John 8:11 tells us that Jesus told the woman who was caught in adultery that she was forgiven, but He then told her to "go, and sin no more." All people, including believers, struggle daily with sin; however, it is another thing altogether to *embrace* a lifestyle of sin—continually choosing sin without remorse or repentance, a decision that carries with it dire eternal consequences. Many of these sins are listed in 1 Cor. 6:9–10; most are based on how we treat others.

But what is it within the free will of man that releases God's judgment on some nations and not on others? Scripture traces a common thread throughout the ages that answers this question. To find that thread, we must examine ancient history and study those who knew God and His ways better than any other people on earth: the nation of Israel.

LESSONS FROM HISTORY

God established His covenant with Abraham so that his descendants would act as ambassadors for God's kingdom establishing His will on earth. This did not make the Jewish people superior to other nations; instead, it gave them more responsibility than any other ancient society. They would have to worship God in very specific ways and live a lifestyle that differed radically from that of other nations. It would be a life dedicated to honoring the Most High God, following His principles, and showcasing His love to humanity. Following God's covenant meant Israel would have to establish godly morals and godly ethics. It meant that their lives would no longer be their own, but their lives would rest in God's plan.

> Now therefore, if ye will obey my voice indeed, and keep my
> covenant, then ye shall be a **peculiar treasure** unto me above all
> people: for all the earth is mine (Ex. 19:5).

God fully intended for Israel to be a peculiar treasure. He wanted them to have a special place in His plan and be a people of great worth because of how they lived and how they impacted the societies that surrounded them.

> For thou art an holy people unto the LORD thy God, and the
> LORD hath chosen thee to be a **peculiar people unto Himself,**
> above all the nations that are upon the earth (Deut. 14:2).

The word "peculiar" in these two verses comes from the Hebrew word *segullah*, meaning "treasured possession" or "personal proper-ty."[3] Is it any wonder that God told Moses in the very first of the Ten Commandments that they were to have no other gods before Him, for He was a jealous God (Ex. 20:5)? The Hebrew word for "jealous" in this Exodus passage is *qanna* (pronounced "kan-naw"). It is used six times in the Hebrew text, and it means something quite different from today's negative interpretation of jealously. *Qanna* is translated as "jealous," "zealous," or "envy." The fundamental meaning relates to a marriage relationship. God is depicted as Israel's husband; He is a jealous God, wanting all our praise for Himself and no one else.[4]

The Jewish people were so beloved by God that they were the apple of God's eye, as the prophet Zechariah stated: "For he who touches you [the Jewish people] touches the apple of His eye" (Zech. 2:8 ESV).

The first four commandments dealt with how the Children of Israel were to embrace their relationship with God; the last six con-cerned how Israel was to live with each other in community. In other words, sixty percent of the Ten Commandments were social morals that regulated Jewish society and culture. Church of Scotland Minister William Barclay wrote, "The Jewish ethic was itself founded on the Ten Commandments. These might well be called the universal foundation, not only for Jewish ethics, but of all ethics. They contain the basic laws of human conduct in society."[5]

Biblical history shows that the Jewish people frequently fell away from their covenant with God, bringing dire consequences to their na-tion. As we read the Old Testament, we find God raising up pagan na-tions to judge or purge His chosen people. For example, the Assyrians marched against the northern kingdom of Israel under Tiglath-pileser (2 Kings 15:29). About twelve years later, under Shalmaneser and Sargon, the area was under siege again. The capital city of Samaria fell after a three-year siege. The result was that over twenty thousand Jews were taken to Assyria as captives. And what was the cause? The Bible answers this question in no uncertain terms:

> *And the king of Assyria did carry away Israel unto Assyria . . .*
> *because they obeyed not the voice of the LORD their God, but*
> *transgressed his covenant, and all that Moses the servant of*
> *the LORD commanded, and would not hear them, nor do them*
> (2 Kings 18:11–12).

But the Bible also tells us that after a time, once they repented, God delivered them from their oppressors and brought them back into covenant with Himself. We see this pattern repeated throughout the Old Testament.

Without any regard for God's commandments, Joseph's eleven brothers sold him into slavery (Gen. 37). Years later, their descendants also found themselves in the bonds of slavery (Ex. 1). Once their time of judgment was over, however, God raised up Moses to deliver them (Ex. 2:11–3:22). And prior to Israel's deliverance, God did to Egypt exactly what Egypt had done to the Children of Israel. The ten plagues or judgments that came upon Egypt were the direct result of Pharaoh's treatment of the Israelites. For example, during Israel's years of captivity, Pharaoh's birth control policy was to drown Hebrew male children in the Nile River as a form of sacrifice to the Egyptian god of the Nile. The tenth plague that God inflicted on the Egyptians was the death of their own firstborn sons. Then, when Egypt chased the Children of Israel across the Red Sea, God drowned the whole Egyptian army in its waters. As Pharaoh learned at the end of his reign: What you do to one of God's chosen people, God will do to you.

Consider this:

In 603 BC: Nebuchadnezzar, King of Babylon, threw Shadrach, Meshach, and Abednego into a burning, fiery furnace. These three faithful Jewish boys were unwilling to break the first commandment and bow to Nebuchadnezzar's idolatrous image. Yet it was only the Babylonian guards who died from the intense heat of the flames meant for the young Jewish boys (Dan. 3:22). The Babylonians had no idea they were touching the apple of God's eye.

In 500 BC: The Persian bureaucrat Haman had a fit of demonic rage when Mordecai[6] refused to bow before him (Est. 3:5). Haman built gallows to hang this Jewish worshipper. However, Queen Esther brought word to the Persian king, resulting in Haman and his whole family being hung on the very gallows they built to exterminate the Jews (Est. 7:9–10). After his defense of the Jewish people, Mordecai's fame became widespread, and the king made him a viceroy.

MODERN HISTORY

But these examples aren't limited to ancient history. Take a look at this example from just this past century:

In AD 1944: During WWII, the demonically influenced maniac Adolf Hitler decided to eradicate God's chosen people. He gassed them, shot them, and burned them in death camps spread across portions of Europe. When the war ended, Hitler voluntarily bit down on a cyanide gas capsule, shot himself in the head, and, to carry out his final wishes, several of his loyal Nazi henchmen burned his body in a futile attempt to destroy the evidence.[7] The same demonic spirits of anti-Semitism eventually did to Hitler exactly what they'd led him to do to the Jews.

It has only been eighty years since the insanity of Nazi Germany and the extreme anti-Semitism that was showcased before and during World War II. Unfortunately, that spirit of hate and rage is still showcased worldwide: rockets from Middle Eastern neighbors are launched toward Israel monthly; protestors promote the Boycott, Divestment, and Sanctions (BDS) movement against Israel on streets and campuses; nations even unite to state in one voice that Israel is an apartheid nation.

But just as Pharaoh of Egypt, King Nebuchadnezzar of Babylon, Haman of Persia, and Adolf Hitler of Germany learned, we too would be wise to acknowledge what history has made so abundantly clear: that those who oppose the apple of God's eye will not escape His judgment. That what you do to a Jew, God will do to you. If you bring them into slavery, God will bring you into slavery; if you try to hang them, God will hang you; if you try to exterminate them, God will exterminate you.

As we learned, there are approximately 14.7 million Jews on the earth, those born through the Jewish bloodline of their parents.

THE EXPANSION OF GOD'S CHOSEN PEOPLE

Today, the world population of Jews by birth is 14.7 million.[8] However, there are hundreds of millions more Jews on the earth, Jews born again through the blood of Jesus Christ. A new breed of Jew, bought through the blood sacrifice of Jesus Christ. Not by physical birth and circumcision of the flesh, but through the spiritual circumcision of the heart (Rom. 2:29), the re-birthing of their spirits (John 4:22), and a renewing of their minds (Rom. 7:25; 8:6; 12:2).

According to apostle Paul, being a Jew does not happen through circumcision of the flesh but rather circumcision of the heart, through personally acknowledging and following the teachings Jesus Christ. Because of what Jesus accomplished on the cross, the ambassadors of God's spiritual kingdom no longer have to enter into His spiritual protocol by physical birth. They can enter simply by recognizing the truth of who Jesus Christ is and why He came.

This expansion of God's chosen people also involves a completely new interpretation of who the apple of God's eye is today. It is still the Jewish people, but it also includes those who have been grafted into God's chosen people by accepting the kingship of the most famous Jew who ever lived, Jesus Christ of Nazareth.

Chinese Christian preacher Witness Lee wrote:

*In Romans 11 Paul goes on to use another illustration—the
grafting of a branch from one tree into another tree . . . as a
result of grafting, the branches from the wild olive tree and
cultivated olive tree grow together organically . . . In the eyes of
God, there are not two trees on earth. There is just one tree.*[9]

Although the way of becoming part of God's chosen people has
changed, the covenant of God watching over His people has not. Genesis
28:15 reminds us of God's promise:

*Behold, I am with you and will keep you wherever you go, and
will bring you back to this land. For I will not leave you until I
have done what I have promised you (ESV).*

Whether we *feel* Him or not, the Lord is with us. We shouldn't let
our feelings or the current anti-God culture separate us from His truth.
We should stand firm as God's chosen and know that He is with us and
He keeps His promises.

What does this tree Paul wrote about in Romans 11, this "one tree"
Witness Lee described, have to do with the United States of America as
a whole? How do these spiritual principles affect us within our society
today?

As I write these words, I am seeing a definite change in our society.
Those who want one nation "under God" to be the guiding principle
in their government structures as well as in their personal lives have
become a minority in our nation. There is an open hostility directed toward those who want to preserve the traditional values laid out by God's
Word and America's Founding Fathers. A hostility toward those who
want to live under God's commandments and be part of His covenant.

This hostility comes directly from those who think it is time to walk away from those values and create a whole new world without God or His commandments.

Here's just one example. The spiritual law of "judge not lest ye be judged" (Matt. 7:1) seemingly is of no concern to the new progressive groupthink. They preach inclusiveness, but only as long as it agrees with their opinions and subsequent worldview. This group deems biblical lessons from the past to be mere fairy tales (Rom. 1). They want government to be god, and they will, of course, create this government based on *their* values, which oppose traditional, scriptural, and moral Judeo-Christian values.

To those who study Bible prophecy, this erosion of biblical values comes as no surprise. God said it would happen, and through the free will of mankind, He watches over His Word to perform it (Jer. 1:12 ESV). Just as it was in the days of Sodom and Noah, today's news media broadcasts the signs Jesus told us to look for, which would point to His imminent return (Luke 17).

We wrote about this in the last chapter, but it's worth mentioning again in this context. Canada recently proposed legislation to amend their criminal code in order to ban the practice of "conversion therapy" and legislate potential penalties of up to five years in jail. This bill passed the house in October of 2020, and this legislation will prohibit speech that dissuades anyone, including children, from adopting the gender orientation that they choose to embrace. In addition, it could possibly restrict counselors from warning against sexual activity outside the scriptural boundaries of holy matrimony between a man and a woman. If such a bill is passed, will it mean that clergy, counselors, or even parents may go to jail for even suggesting that engaging in sexual relations outside of holy matrimony between a man and a woman is sin and should be avoided?

What, then, does this have to do with Bible prophecy? What could this and other laws like it foretell? Let us not forget what history records. That when government leaders such as Pharaoh, Nebuchadnezzar, Haman, and Hitler implemented regulations criminalizing or persecuting God's people, restricting them from practicing His laws, it provoked God's judgment. It was like poking God in the apple of His eye.

JUDGE NOT, LEST YE BE JUDGED

Matthew 7:1–2 says, "Judge not, that ye be not judged. For with what judgment ye judge, ye shall be judged: and with what measure ye mete, it shall be measured to you again." Although this warning was given to followers of Christ, the spiritual principle also applies to those who do not believe in God's laws and who judge Christians.

The Word of God is said to judge us for the purpose of examining and correcting our personal lives (2 Tim. 3:16). The Bible is the only book in the world that while you read it, it reads you. It gives you a checkup from the neck up. However, we are not to judge others outside that book of protocol. Each person must apply Scripture in order to judge themselves (Heb. 4:12). Jesus mandates that it is our job to love others, even those who we think have fallen into sin (John 13:34; Gal. 6:1). The Holy Spirit convicts each of us of our own shortcomings (John 16:8), and it is God's responsibility to judge (Ps. 75:7). Billy Graham summed it up by saying: "It is the Holy Spirit's job to convict, God's job to judge, and my job to love."

A GROWING CULTURE WAR

The United Nations currently has a global agenda for a one world government by the year 2030. Knowing this, we must ask what this means for America and what role current political actors seeking to join that agenda play.

In David Horowitz's book *Dark Agenda,* he argues that progressives in North America want to eradicate the whole concept of "one nation under God."[10] In other words, there is a growing culture war against Christianity, the Bible, prayer in public places, and other public expressions of faith. Many global elites—who have been elected because of progressive groupthink ideology—want a world without borders, both physically and morally. The only way progressives can achieve that goal is though changes to our legislation. Surely it comes as no surprise that the push for those changes is well underway.

SOCIETAL TIPPING POINTS

During our studies of covenant nations, we learned that when a nation's laws embrace God's laws, that nation will invoke God's blessings. However, we also have learned that legislation opposing His laws can provoke His judgment. A nation, especially one raised up in covenant with God, whose laws restrict, prevent, or even punish God's people who follow His laws, will ultimately reap dramatic consequences from the hand of God.

We have discussed Jesus' references to Sodom and Gomorrah and the days of Noah, the two signs He said would precede His imminent return. We also learned that the day He returns—coming as a thief in the night to catch away His bride—will be a day of severe judgment and will initiate the seven-year reign of a New World Order.

Again, what could be the tipping point within a society that would provoke such judgment? The two greatest political and moral controversies in our culture today (nontraditional marriage and abortion) have made it to the courts, and while recent legislation has made both of these legal, they remain controversial. Although modern verbiage and political correctness has coined the term "abortion," biblical terminology describes it throughout the generations as "the shedding of innocent blood."

Our earlier study of Baal worship showed that the Bible warned us of God's disdain for sexual immorality and fornication outside holy matrimony. In ancient Babylon, these practices led to the creation of another god meant to deal with the unwanted children of its immoral society—Baal worship included the sacrifice of children to the god Molech. Children were laid in a huge statue or idol whose belly was a burning cauldron of fire. These children were burned to death in the hopes that Molech would reward the parents with a lifestyle of prosperity.

> *Whoso sheddeth man's blood, by man shall his blood be shed: for in the image of God made He man (Gen. 9:6).*

Revelation 17:4 describes the woman of Babylon as "having a golden cup in her hand full of abominations and filthiness of her fornication." What is this filth of her fornication? Revelation 17:6 continues, "And I saw the woman drunken with the blood of the saints, and with the blood of the martyrs of Jesus." The Greek word for "blood" in this passage is *haima*. It is the same word used in Mark 5 to refer to the woman who touched the hem of Jesus' garment and was healed from an "issue of blood." It is generally understood that this was some sort of vaginal bleeding. We can glean from this that the blood mentioned in Revelation 17:6 includes blood from the womb.

Additionally, the descriptive term "saints" from Revelation 17:6 is the Greek word *hagios*, meaning "people of God"[11] or "a believer in Christ,"[12] and "in Revelation, it is a frequent term for the Christian martyrs."[13] God said of the prophet Jeremiah, "Before I formed you in the womb I knew you, and before you were born I consecrated you; I appointed you a prophet to the nations" (Jer. 1:5 ESV). Knowing this truth, how many of the over 60 million children who have been aborted in America[14] would have grown up to become apostles, prophets, teachers, evangelists, and pastors. How many of those murders, performed in a nation whose currency reads "In God We Trust," resulted in the death of His saints?

GOD'S HISTORICAL RESPONSE TO THE SHEDDING OF INNOCENT BLOOD

Let's look at several responses from Scripture concerning shedding innocent blood:

- **Genesis 4:10**: [After Cain killed Abel, God said to him] "What hast thou done? The voice of thy brother's blood crieth unto me from the ground."
- **Numbers 35:33**: "So ye shall not pollute the land wherein ye are: for blood it **defileth** the land: and the land cannot be cleansed of the blood that is shed therein, but by the blood of him that shed it."
- **Numbers 35:34**: "**Defile** not therefore the land which ye shall inhabit, wherein I dwell: for I the LORD dwell among the Children of Israel."
- **Leviticus 18:21**: (ESV): "You shall not give any of your children to offer them to Molech, and so profane the name of your God: I am the LORD."

According to Jeremiah 32:35 (ESV), King Manasseh had "built the high places of Baal in the Valley of the Son of Hinnom, to offer up their sons and daughters to Molech." Before Judah, the southern kingdom of Israel, was judged in 605 BC by the invading armies of Babylon, King Josiah read God's commandments and removed all the Ashtoreth (Asherah) poles and temples of Molech that King Manasseh, his grandfather, had built. For the next forty years, Josiah's righteous actions staved off God's judgment (2 Kings 22–23; 2 Chronicles 34–35). However, after his death, King Zedekiah returned to Manasseh's ways. Once this regression occurred, God's judgment was quickly enacted.

We read in 2 Kings 24:3–4 that King Manasseh "filled Jerusalem with innocent blood; which the LORD would not pardon." We do not know how many children King Manasseh sacrificed in Jerusalem before historical Babylon judged her. However, we do know that after Manasseh's death and several years of discontinued rituals, Zedekiah reintroduced Baal worship, and was warned by the prophet Jeremiah to stop the abomination of child sacrifice.

Another prophet by the name of Hananiah contradicted Jeremiah's warnings. He took the yoke Jeremiah had been carrying around his neck and broke it off. He then prophesied that God had broken the yoke of Babylon from off the nation of Judah. Many laughed and mocked Jeremiah's words, and Jeremiah took this up with the Lord. The Lord responded quickly saying, "I have not sent these prophets, yet they ran: I have not spoken to them, yet they prophesied. But if they had stood in my counsel, and had caused my people to hear my words, then they should have turned them from their evil way, and from the evil of their doings" (Jer. 23:21–22). Interestingly, the verse before says "in the latter days ye shall consider it perfectly" (verse 20). Eight weeks after this, Hananiah dropped dead, exactly as Jeremiah prophesied he would.

In the ninth year of Zedekiah's reign, nobody was laughing when Babylon captured Jerusalem and forced King Zedekiah to watch his own family being slaughtered. Zedekiah then had his eyes burned out and was led away to Babylon blind, naked, and totally humiliated before his own people. Many who laugh at the message contained in this book will also stop laughing in a single day, as they stand in muted silence, spectators of their own defiance of God's eternal laws.

The documented number of innocent children slain in the abortion clinics of the US and Canada is a staggering figure . . . and it does not include those whose deaths were not recorded. The primary reason for abortion in North America is the financial burden of raising a child. This is the very same reason that children were sacrificed to Molech in ancient times: their parents were seeking financial blessings.

Manasseh filled Jerusalem with the shedding of innocent blood, just as the woman who rules over the beast has a cup filled with innocent blood. Jesus warned modern-day believers of Thyatira—those who follow after Jezebel, who teaches and seduces God's servants to commit fornication and to practice the things of Baal—saying, "I will cast her into a bed, and them that commit adultery with her into great tribulation, except they repent of their deeds. And I will kill her children with death" (Rev. 2:20–23).

In all we have studied these last chapters, it has become clear *what* the tipping point will be. Only one question remains: *When* will we reach this "tipping point"?

Babylon is promised swift judgment when her final day in Bible prophecy, her "appointed time," comes. Jesus warns us to stay far away from her sins, and He reminds us that "If you have done this to least of My brethren you have done it unto Me."

This brings us to the next descriptions of Babylon:

43) (Rev. 17:6) She has temples of Molech to sacrifice her children.

44) (Rev. 17:4–6; Rev. 2:20–23) She sacrifices children (saints) to Baal for the purpose of financial gain.

45) (Isa. 47:6) She "shows no mercy" to God's people: "You have heavily laid your yoke" (paraphrased).

46) (Num. 35:33; Rev. 2:23) The land is defiled: "You shed His blood, He will shed yours" (paraphrased).

47) (Rev. 18:4) She has warnings written to her in Scripture not to partake in the sin.

48) (Rev. 18:4; Jer. 51:14) She has verbal (*rhema*) warnings not to partake in her plagues.
49) (Rev. 18:24; Jer. 51:14) She has prophets within her before her destruction.
50) (Rev. 17:6; 18:24; Jer. 51:14) She persecutes those who "raise up a shout."

GOD'S SOLUTION TO THE SIN OF PROVOCATION

The Bible says that God knows every detail about every person, down to the number of hairs on their head (Luke 12:7) and their appointed time to die (Heb. 9:27). In Jeremiah's case, God said, "Before I formed you in the womb I knew you, and before you were born . . . I appointed you a prophet to the nations" (Jer. 1:5 ESV).

We at Prophecy USA want you to know that when God releases a prophetic warning to a nation, it is never sent to put you down—it only comes to set you free. The Bible assures us that He has "no pleasure in the death of the wicked, but that the wicked turn from his way and live (Ezek. 33:11).

God knows the name of every child that has been aborted in this nation. He knows the name of every desperate mother who made that decision and the name of every delinquent father who abandoned that desperate mother. He knows the names of every doctor and nurse who performed those procedures and the name of every person who was involved in selling body parts for financial gain. He knows the name of every politician who voted that procedure into legislation and the name of every voter who empowered those politicians by "strengthening the hand of evil doers" (Jer. 23:14). Through that legislation, this nation has opened the floodgates for the shedding of innocent blood. These laws have defiled the land and, according to Scripture, this land will most assuredly be judged.

Suppose your name has been associated in the process of this travesty. In that case, even if you have shed the innocent blood of your child, I have good news for you: You cannot change the past, but you can drastically alter your future.

Two thousand years ago, Jesus shed innocent blood for you. There is a name that is above every name given among men, and it can forgive you of any sin known to man. This name has the power to wash your past as white as snow and cleanse you from all unrighteousness (1 John 1:9).

Several months ago, I made a phone call to a cousin of mine. Johnny and I grew up together, but we had since chosen vastly different lifestyles. At the age of eighteen, I decided to go to Oral Roberts University to study the Bible and seek God's direction. Johnny chose a lifestyle of partying, drinking, smoking dope, and riding his motorcycle.

Before I made the phone call, I had just learned that Johnny received a report from the hospital that he was full of cancer and had only six months to live. He was ecstatic that I had called, and asked me to visit him because he had questions about the Bible. The next day, I saw Johnny, and he began our conversation with a tirade of incredulous exclamations, asking: "Why is God doing this to me? I'm not even sixty years old. I haven't yet retired. Now He gives me cancer, and I'm going to die."

I knew there was no fooling around with this type of attitude. I thought I might as well go for the jugular and let Johnny have the news plain and clear. I said, "Johnny, let me get this right. For the last forty-five years, you chose to party like a drunk sailor on steroids, smoke like a chimney, fill your body with every toxin known to mankind, and now, at the end of your life, it's all God's fault that you have cancer?"

Johnny looked at me with utter surprise and then burst into laughter.

"Yeah, you're right," he said. "I guess I just wish I had longer to live. But I *am* going to heaven, right? I mean, I've been a good father to my son, and I've supported my wife and family with a stable job."

"Have you ever lied? Have you ever cursed God's name? Have you ever had sexual intercourse before you were married?" I asked him.

Johnny laughed. "Of course I have—but so has everybody else."

"Well, in God's eyes, you are a lying, blaspheming fornicator, and according to 1 Corinthians 6:9, you will not be allowed into heaven."

Johnny's jaw dropped. Fear washed over his face. He knew I wouldn't lie to him. I let that sink in for several seconds, then said, "But there is a way; there is a way you can get into heaven. Do you remember the movie *The Passion*?"

Johnny acknowledged that he did.

"Do you remember when Jesus was getting whipped, and how the blood flowed from His back, and then suddenly He fell to his knees because He was in such agonizing pain? Do you remember how He slowly got back up so they could finish the flogging of forty stripes?"

"Yes, I remember."

"Well, when He got up, He stood up in *your place*, Johnny. Two thousand years ago, He knew that without the shedding of innocent blood, the sins of mankind could not be forgiven. That blood was pre-destined for "such a time as this." It was for you, right now. The key to your salvation is on the tip of your tongue. It's a name that is above all names given among men."

When Johnny was ready, I led him in the following prayer. Read along and pray the prayer that Johnny prayed:

Dear Jesus, I call on Your name and repent of my sins. I ask You to wash me in Your blood, to set me free from the past, and to take my hand and lead me into the future. In the name of Jesus Christ of Nazareth I pray. Amen.

Johnny wept as he prayed, but there was a brightness in his eyes that I had never seen there before. "I feel as light as a feather!" he said. "What is happening to me?"

"The burden of your sins has been removed. Jesus is now carrying the load. God is looking at you through a bloodstained lens—and you, my friend, are as white as snow."

Three months later, my cousin died, but I do not doubt that someday I will see him again.

Our team at Prophecy USA believes that God's prophetic time clock is the same for our nation as it was for Johnny that day. It is saying loud and clear: "Come back to Me, America, and all my people in her, because ready or not, I am coming back for you."

CHAPTER TWELVE

THE HOUR THAT CHANGES EVERYTHING

THE PROPHET ISAIAH asked the question, "Can a nation be birthed in a day?" (Isa. 66:8). US President Harry S. Truman answered that question in the affirmative on May 14, 1948. On that day, he made the United States the first country in the world to recognize Israel as a nation, following David Ben-Gurion's declaration of her independence.[1]

But when it comes to the providential nation of Babylon, we must ask a different question: Can a nation be destroyed in an hour? As we learned in Chapter Ten and from the story of Sodom and Gomorrah, the answer to that question is undoubtedly yes. God watches over His Word to perform it, and we have learned that God will judge Babylon because of the many sins she has committed. Specifically, as we highlighted in the prior chapter, the "shedding of innocent blood" is the sin that will tip the scale and provoke the final judgment, which will come by fire.

IS BABYLON THE ONLY NATION JUDGED?

In Chapter Two, we learned of eight providential nations that were unveiled in Nebuchadnezzar's image, Daniel's dream, and John's two visions. Some of those nations existed in the past. One (Rome), was present at that time, while others were still to come. Yet these are not the only world powers that will be active in the last days. The Bible lists geographical regions that will be present during the time of the great Babylon's appearance. Historically, these regions are the direct offspring of Noah's descendants, who are listed in Genesis 10. These families moved to different geographical locations on the earth; locations that have become great population centers today.

TERRITORIAL SPIRITS

In approximately 2400 BC, just after the Flood, Noah's three sons, Ham, Shem, and Japeth, began to repopulate the earth. Eventually, several of Noah's grandsons decided to move their families to different geographical locations.

In earlier chapters, we determined that mankind does not wrestle with "flesh and blood" (Eph. 6:12), but with spiritual entities who try to control not only individuals, but entire groups of peoples and nations. According to God's Word, the controlling demonic entity who dominated various areas of Europe where Japeth's sons settled is called "Gog." Gog was there when Japeth's sons Mesheck and Tubal established their cities,[2] and he is still there today, ruling and reigning, according to the orders from his commander-in-chief, Satan.

In his book *Spiritual Warfare*, Dean Sherman explains this type of spiritual entity: "Within demonic hierarchy is that of 'principalities,' often referred to as 'territorial spirits.' Principalities are simply beings with broad areas of influence in Satan's kingdom. A 'prince' is a leader with the title; the suffix 'pality' has to do with both geography and demography."[3] Other spirits of this category were exposed by Daniel, who referred to the "Prince of Persia" and the "Prince of Grecia" (Dan. 10:13, 20). In these verses, we see that Daniel did battle with the archangel Michael against these principalities.

In 587 BC the prophet Ezekiel was captive in Babylon. He prophesied into the spirit realm against the ruling territorial spirit called Gog:

> *And the word of the LORD came unto me, saying, Son of man,*
> *set your face toward Gog, of the land of Magog, the chief prince*
> *of Meshech and Tubal, and prophesy against him*
> *(Ezek. 38:1–2 ESV).*

> *And you, son of man, prophesy against Gog and say, Thus says*
> *the Lord GOD: Behold, I am against you, O Gog, chief prince of*
> *Meshech and Tubal (Ezek. 39:1 ESV).*

THE WAR THAT BEGINS THE TRIBULATION

According to the prophet Ezekiel prophesying from historical Babylon in 550 BC, there will come a time in history when an evil thought will enter into the mind of Gog (Ezek. 38:10ff), the chief prince of Meshech and Tubal. This spirit will decide to manipulate the people living under Gog's authority to come against Israel.

> *[Ezekiel's] prophecy begins with a word of warning to Gog and*
> *Magog. The word, Gog, simply means "ruler." Who is the ruler*
> *of the land of Magog? In 500 BC, Greek historian, Herodotus,*
> *identified the land of Magog as that of the Scythians, ancestors*
> *of the Russians. Roman historian, Flavius Josephus, who lived*

shortly after the time of Christ, identified Magog as the land we know today as Russia. Throughout the centuries, scholars have identified Magog as Russia, due north of Israel.[4]

It is important to remember that we are not dealing with flesh and blood here, but with principalities, powers, and rulers of darkness in high places (Eph. 6). The ultimate desire of these powers is to steal, kill, and destroy. They hate mankind, and especially Israel. As chief prince of Meshech and Tubal, Gog represents a spirit ruling over a nation located in the area where two of Noah's offspring, Meshech and Tubal, eventually settled. It is my belief that this is the area known today as Russia.[5]

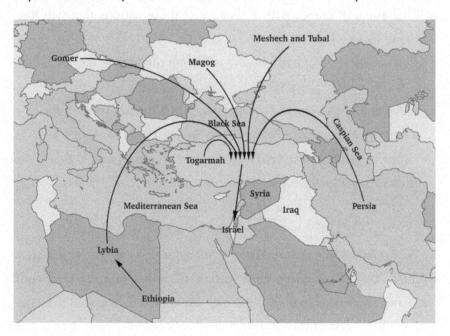

When Gog and Russia come against Israel, they will be accompanied by several other nations:

> *Thus saith the Lord GOD; Behold, I am against thee, O **Gog**, the chief prince of **Meshech** and **Tubal** . . . **Persia**, **Ethiopia**, and **Libya** with them; all them with shield and helmet: **Gomer**, and*

*all his bands; the house of **Togarmah** of the north quarters, and all his bands: and many people with thee (Ezek. 38:3, 5–6).*

At the time of Ezekiel's prophecy, **Persia** was a "country laying just to the east of Mesopotamia (modern Iraq) and covering virtually the same territory as present-day Iran. It was known in ancient times by various forms of Fars or Pars, which came down to us as Persia. It continued to be known as Persia until 1935, when its name was changed to Iran."[6] **Ethiopia**'s name remains the same; **Libya**'s name and borders, likewise, are unchanged. **Gomer** refers to Eastern Europe, specifically the Germanic peoples. **Togarmah** refers to modern-day Turkey. Turkey will fall and will march with Russia.[7] It is these nations that will join Russia in its attack on Israel.

We are also told of nations who will align themselves *against* Gog:

__Sheba__, and __Dedan__, and the merchants of __Tarshish__, with __all the young lions thereof__, shall say unto thee, Art thou come to take a spoil? hast thou gathered thy company to take a prey? to carry away silver and gold, to take away cattle and goods, to take a great spoil? (Ezek. 38:13).

Sheba and Dedan were Ham's sons, who was one of Noah's sons (Gen. 10:6–7); they generally represent the inhabitants of the Saudi Arabian Peninsula. Tarshish, meaning "land of tin," is believed to be the land farthest west of the Middle East. The word "Britain" also means land of tin. According to Scofield and other scholars, Tarshish is made up of Britain, France, Spain, and Italy. We assume "**all the young lions thereof**" represents Britain's offspring, or colonies, which would include the United States and Canada.

In this war that is prophesied to come, **Gog**—Russia, Iran and Iraq, Ethiopia, Libya, Germany, and Turkey—will rise up against the nation of Israel and her allies. Saudi Arabia, Egypt, Britain, Spain, Italy, France, Canada, and the United States will stand together with Israel against Gog.

EZEKIEL'S PROPHECY FOR WORLD WAR III (EZEKIEL 38:3–6)

AGGRESSORS:	ALLIES:
Iraq and Iran	Israel
Russia (Magog, Meshach, Tubal)	Saudi Arabia (Sheba, Dedan)
Germany (Gomer)	France, Italy, Spain, Britain (Tarshish)
Turkey (Togamar)	United States, Canada (young lions)
Ethiopia (Ethiopia)	
Libia (Libya)	

RESULTS OF THIS WAR

These passages in Ezekiel lay out God's "sure word" of prophecy in detail. Ezekiel 38 and 39 describes not only the war itself, but its end result as well. Ezekiel records how God will judge these aggressors for coming against His chosen people who dwell in Israel. This judgment will come by fire.

God will burn five-sixths of the aggressors' forces (Ezek. 39:1–2) from their position in the northern mountains of Israel known as the Golan Heights—the same disputed territory that American policy has just recently declared belongs to Israel. However, another nation will be burned with fire as well. This nation "dwells carelessly in the isles [or coastlands]," according to the prophet Ezekiel: "And I will send a fire on Magog, and among them that dwell carelessly in the isles [coastlands]: and they shall know that I am the LORD" (Ezek. 39:6).

Only one nation dwells carelessly among the isles (coastlands) at the time of the Gog-Magog War in Scripture. Her name is Babylon the

Great, which now has fifty descriptions, all pointing to the United States of America. This is the nation "that sitteth upon many waters," where the "merchants of the earth," where "every shipmaster, and all the company in ships, and sailors, as many as trade by sea . . . were made rich" as they traded at her coastland ports (Rev. 17:1; 18:11, 17, 19).

Most people in North America believe they are far, far away from the Mideast turmoil—or so they think. "Carelessly" in this passage is the Hebrew word *betah*, meaning "confident and unsuspecting." *Nelson's Expository Dictionary of the Old Testament* explains that "*betah* emphasizes the status of a city which was certain of not being attacked (Gen. 34:25). Thus the city was unsuspecting regarding the impending attack."[8] The ESV uses the word "securely" when translating *betah*. It is the word used to describe the seventh nation, who is deposed before the New World Order comes into power:

> *Now therefore hear this, you lover of pleasures, who sits **securely**,*
> *who says in your heart, I am and there is no one beside me:*
> *I shall not sit as a widow or know the loss of children*
> *(Isa. 47:8 ESV).*

> *Therefore shall evil come upon thee, thou shalt not know from*
> *whence it riseth: and mischief shall fall upon thee . . . and*
> *desolation shall come upon thee suddenly, **which thou shalt***
> ***not know** (Isa. 47:11).*

As these verses show, Babylon's destruction (Rev. 17:6) will be at the same time as the Gog-Magog destruction. In modern-day terminology, it will come in the form of a sudden, pre-emptive, fiery strike ("thou shall not know from whence it riseth . . ." Isa. 47:11) in an attempt to take out America—which Iran calls "Big Satan"—before trying to take out Israel (which Iran calls "Little Satan").[9]

A PROPHET SPEAKS

Ironically, another insight into this attack comes from the same prophet who prophesied the destruction of Jerusalem to King Zedekiah in historical Babylon of 605 BC. Jeremiah was laughed at, mocked, scoffed at, and eventually thrown into a cistern for his word of prophecy toward Israel. False prophets refused to acknowledge the sins of Baal worship and child sacrifice in their nation. They prophesied peace, but Jeremiah was determined to deliver the word the Lord had spoken to him instead of the candy-coated fluff the people wanted to hear.

Jeremiah's frustration with these false prophets is fully explained by God in Jeremiah 23:9–40; this in turn gave him courage to prophesy the following warnings:

> Blow the trumpet among the nations, prepare the nations against her, call together against her the kingdoms of **Ararat, Minni**, and **Ashchenaz** . . . Prepare against her the nations with the kings of the **Medes**, the captains thereof, and all the rulers thereof, and all the land of his dominion. And the land shall tremble and sorrow: for every **purpose of the LORD** shall be performed against Babylon, to make the land of Babylon a **desolation** without an inhabitant. (Jer. 51:27–29).

Ararat was "a country located in eastern Asia Minor which flourished from the 9th to the 6th centuries BC. Its center was near Lake Van and its boundaries (uncertain at times and places) extended into modern Iran, Iraq, Russia, and Turkey."[10]

The **Minni** were "a people and a state of Armenia in the area south of Lake Urmia and east of the Zagros Mountains, in what is present-day Iran. The Minni are mentioned only once in the Bible. The prophet Jeremiah called on them to make war against Babylonia (Jer. 51:27)."[11]

The **Medes**, "an Indo-Iranian people who inhabited the plateau of northern Iran, around the area of modern Hamadan (ancient Ecbatana), and enjoyed a degree of military prominence during the 7th and 6th centuries BC."[12]

The Expositor's Bible Commentary states: "It has troubled some scholars that Chapters 50–51 predict the violent destruction of Babylon, whereas its defeat by Cyrus in 539 BC took place without a battle and with no damage to the city. But as with other predictive prophecies, if a fulfillment does not occur in one period, it is to be sought for in another and future one."[13]

However, Jeremiah states, "As God overthrew Sodom and Gomorrah and the neighbour cities thereof, saith the LORD; so shall no man abide there, neither shall any son of man dwell therein" (Jer. 50:40).

One hundred years earlier, Isaiah confirmed this by prophesying: "And Babylon, the glory of kingdoms, the beauty of the Chaldees' excellency, shall be as when God overthrew Sodom and Gomorrah. It shall never be inhabited, neither shall it be dwelt in from generation to generation" (Isa. 13:19–20).

As mentioned in an earlier chapter, the night historical Babylon of 539 BC fell, the Persians had diverted the waters of the Euphrates river, lowering them so that they could secretly enter the city under the gates of the waterways. At the same time, in fact the very same night that Daniel interpreted God's handwriting on the wall to the king and his party of drunken Babylonian diplomats, the Persians came into the palace and slayed the king and every leader of the Babylonian government. They did not destroy Babylon. They captured her without any battle or any destruction and then occupied her right up to the time Alexander the Great conquered Persia 270 years later.

The Jeremiah prophecy (50:5) is dual in nature: it refers to both historical Babylon and latter-day Babylon the Great. So we now have Turkey, Iran, and the lands bordering Russia, as prophesied 2,650 years ago ("then and there"), being used to burn latter-day Babylon the Great with fire ("here and now"). These nations are part of the coalition of aggressors involved in Ezekiel's Gog-Magog war against Israel. Remember, five-sixths of their armies will be burned with fire on the Golan Heights.

According to Ezekiel, it will be God who ultimately sends "a fire on Magog, and among them that dwell carelessly in the isles: and they shall know that I am the LORD (Ezek. 39:6). From this perspective, God simultaneously uses fire to judge both Babylon and the nations attacking Israel. That fire will be the result of the free will of men, utilizing weapons of mass destruction as they march toward the Holy City thinking "an evil thought" to "take a spoil" (Ezek. 38:10, 12).

Sobering events of February 2019 witnessed the leaders of Russia, Turkey, and Iran forming the very "not so close-knit" alliance that was prophesied by Jeremiah 2,650 years ago. Two of these nations, Russia and Turkey, have more nuclear warheads than America.[14] Iranians, meanwhile, are desperately spinning weapons-grade plutonium, even as the US enhances more global sanctions against them. "Iran is preparing for the Biden presidency by acting out, in hopes the new administration will rush to appease it."[15] Oddly enough, those in congress who want to oblige Iran also want God, prayer, and the Ten Commandments evacuated from all government properties. This is all taking place while Iran continues to call America "The Great Satan."

THE JUDGMENT: A REVIEW

This coming war is not to be confused with the Battle of Armageddon. This war, World War III, will end by fire, whereas the Battle of Armageddon will end with the second coming of Christ. World War III will take place at the beginning of a seven-year tribulation period. Armageddon will take place at the *end* of that tribulation period.

But the same day that Lot went out of Sodom it rained fire and
brimstone from heaven, and destroyed them all. Even thus shall
it be in the day when the Son of man is revealed. . . . I tell you,
in that night there shall be two men in one bed; the one shall be
taken, and the other shall be left. Two women shall be grinding
together; the one shall be taken, and the other left. Two men
shall be in the field; the one shall be taken, and the other left.
And they answered and said unto him, Where, Lord? And he
said unto them, Wheresoever the body is, thither will the eagles
be gathered together (Luke 17:29–30, 34–37).

The disciples were perplexed at Jesus' statement and asked Him
where these people would go when they were taken away. Jesus told
them that their bodies would be taken up into heavenly places where
the eagles fly. It would happen instantaneously on a day when it rained
fire and brimstone. Sudden and unexpected destruction would come as
a complete shock to those who had been speaking "peace and safety."

For yourselves know perfectly that the day of the Lord so cometh
as a thief in the night. For when they shall say, Peace and safety;
then sudden destruction cometh upon them, as travail upon a
woman with child; and they shall not escape (1 Thess. 5:2–3).

HOW LONG WILL THE PRE-EMPTIVE STRIKE TAKE?
John gives us multiple verses to answer this question:

They [the merchants] will stand far off, in the fear of her
torment, and say, "Alas! Alas! You great city, you mighty city,
*Babylon! For in a **single hour** your judgment [punishment]*
has come" (Rev. 18:10 ESV).

And he said with a loud voice, "Fear God and give Him glory,
*because the **hour of His judgment** has come, and worship Him*
who made heaven and earth, the sea and the springs of water"
(Rev. 14:7 ESV).

WHO WILL ADMINISTER THE JUDGMENT?

And the ten horns that you saw are ten kings who have not yet
received royal power, but they are to receive authority as kings
for one hour, together with the beast. . . . And the ten horns that
you saw, they and the beast will hate the prostitute. They will
make her desolate and naked, and devour her flesh and burn
her up with fire, for God has put it into their hearts to carry out
His purpose by being of one mind and handing over their royal
power to the beast, until the words of God are fulfilled
(Rev. 17:12, 16–17 ESV).

With these prophecies, coupled with Jeremiah 51:27, it is our conclusion that regions of Iran, Turkey, and Russia will be part of the coalition of kings, or the ten geographical regions of the earth who will come
into agreement with the Antichrist and join the New World Order.
From these verses (and others), we can discover that the judgment of
Babylon will take **one hour**. We can also see that this seventh providential nation—Babylon the Great—is deposed by the eighth providential
nation, the New World Order, represented by the Beast.

God shows us in perfect detail who administers the judgment, the
time it will take, and what method will be used to carry it out. The
Antichrist and his ten nations perform the judgment in perfect fulfillment of God's purposes, for they "carry out his purpose by being
of one mind and handing over their royal power to the beast" (Rev.
17:17 ESV).

WHERE IS THE BRIDE OF CHRIST AT THE TIME OF JUDGMENT?

As we have already studied, the Philadelphian believers have made themselves ready and are "counted worthy to escape" through the "open door" that awaits them. They are the body of Christ who, like the wise virgins, have oil in their lamps (Matt. 25). They have overcome the sins that Jesus unveiled within the other five churches. By staying away from immorality and dead works, by putting God first in their life, by following the eternal Word and not the progressive herd, and by prioritizing their finances with firstfruits offerings, this group of believers has been placed into a "preferred position."

God alone will determine who is worthy to escape the hour of tribulation that shall come upon the earth. Scripture is abundantly clear in its warnings to God's people in Babylon to "come out of her, my people, that ye be not partakers of her sins, and that ye receive not of her plagues (Rev. 18:4 ESV).

THE OPEN DOOR

To the church of Philadelphia, God promised:

> *I know your works. Behold, I have set before you an **open door**, which no one is able to shut. I know that you have but little power, and yet you have kept my **word** and have not **denied** My name. . . . Because you have kept my word about patient endurance, I will **keep you from the hour of trial** that is coming on the whole world, to try those who dwell on the earth (Rev. 3:8, 10).*

We at Prophecy USA believe this promise is the only time sequence in Scripture that hints of the pre-tribulation rapture, which will begin the seven-year period in heaven known as the marriage supper of the Lamb. God specifically warns us to "come out of her, my people, and that ye be not partakers of her sins" (Rev. 18:4). That spiritual separation is rewarded when, after Babylon is judged, "and the light of a candle shall shine no more at all in thee; and the voice of the bridegroom and of the bride shall be heard no more at all in thee" (Rev. 18:23).

Scripture states that "the spirit of man is the candle of the LORD, searching all the inward parts of the belly" (Prov. 20:27). However, the light from man's candle can only come from "God, who commanded the light to shine out of darkness, [and] hath shined in our hearts, to give the light of the knowledge of the glory of God in the face of Jesus Christ" (2 Cor. 4:6).

The angel told John that included in this exodus, "the voice of harpers, and musicians, and of pipers, and trumpeters, shall be heard no more at all in thee" (Rev. 18:22). These are the same instruments of worship used when Solomon and the priests "lifted up their voice with the trumpets and cymbals and instruments of musick, and praised the LORD, saying, For he is good; for his mercy endureth for ever" (2 Chron. 5:13), and they entered into God's glory.

Like the glory found at the temple celebration, the worshippers on earth and the bride have departed at this point. So it is the voice of the Bridegroom, who "bringeth forth the wind out of his treasures (Jer. 51:16), and who lifts up a shout of warning against Babylon (Jer. 51:14). So where did the worshippers and the bride go?

We now find the bride and a great voice of worshippers rejoicing in heaven, giving praise for the "open door" that just delivered them from the hour of tribulation that has come upon the earth:

And after these things I heard a great voice of much people in heaven, saying, Alleluia; Salvation, and glory, and honour, and power, unto the Lord our God: for true and righteous are his judgments: for he hath judged the great whore, which did corrupt the earth with her fornication, and hath avenged the blood of his servants at her hand. . . . Let us be glad and rejoice, and give honour to him: for the marriage of the Lamb is come, and his wife hath made herself ready. . . . Blessed are they which **are called** unto the marriage supper of the Lamb (Rev. 19:1–2, 7, 9).

At this point in the sequence of events, we can see that the bride of Christ is neither on the earth nor in Babylon. She is at the marriage supper of the Lamb, immediately after Babylon is judged.

THE TIME TO COME

Proponents of the worldwide progressive movement—those who do not want God, the Ten Commandments, public prayer, Bibles in schools, or Judeo-Christian moral protocols within our culture—will finally get their way. They will live in a world without God or His believers, a world without His provision, protection, or guidance. It will be a godless society, governed by a godless leadership—but it will be the biggest mess the world has ever seen, because in **one hour**, everything will change. But before that hour comes, the following descriptions—the final three—will be evident in Babylon the Great:

51) (Rev.17:16) She will be hated by the antichrist spirit and the ten nations before they are empowered.
52) (Rev.17:6, 16; Rev. 18:24) She will have believers within her who will be persecuted and hated by the antichrist spirit dwelling both in her and outside of her.
53) (Ezek. 38:13) She will be a supporter and stand up for Israel as a "young lion" of Tarshish.

The prophets Isaiah (750 BC), Jeremiah (630 BC), Ezekiel (550 BC), and the Apostle John (AD 70) gave us many descriptions of this powerful, wealthy population center "dwelling carelessly" and "securely" in the coastlands, and every description points to the **United States of America.**

WHERE ARE WE NOW?

It is very possible that believers are about to enter a time of the testing of our faith just before the rapture takes place. But we are not alone. We have the Holy Spirit and His gifts. We have the whole armor of God (Ephesians 6). We have many coming news events already written for us in the Word of God. This will be an "open book" test. All we have to do is obey God's Word. He will be faithful and just to keep His promises and deliver us from the evil to come.

So, are you ready? Are you at peace with God? Has the Holy Spirit shown you anything in your life that needs to be changed?

The Bible is the only book in the world that, while you read it, it reads you. Jesus sits at the door of your heart and knocks. If any man hears His voice and opens the door to his heart, His Holy Spirit will come in and sup with you and you with Him. The key to total peace lies on the very tip of your tongue. Like my cousin Johnny, pray this prayer with me:

Dear Jesus, forgive me for my sins. Come into my heart and lead me, guide me, and direct me. Help me be more like You so the life of Christ might be made manifest in my mortal flesh. In Jesus name, amen.

If you have prayed that prayer, please let us know. Our team at Prophecy USA are praying for you and believing that the best things in your life are yet to come. God loves you, we love you, and Jesus loves you.

But what should you expect if you miss the rapture? What is waiting for those who refuse to believe, who refuse to seek God's face on this side of the open door? Scripture warns us:

If any man worship the beast and his image, and receive his mark in his forehead, or in his hand, the same shall drink of the wine of the wrath of God (Rev. 14:9).

And it was given unto him [the Antichrist] to make war with the saints, and to overcome them (Rev. 13:7).

The only choice for Christians is found in Revelation 12:10–11:

*For the accuser of our brethren [the Antichrist] is cast down, which accused them before our God day and night. And they overcame him by the blood of the Lamb, and by the word of their testimony; and **they loved not their lives unto the death.***

And I heard a voice from heaven saying unto me, Write, Blessed are the dead which die in the Lord from henceforth: Yea, saith the Spirit, that they may rest from their labours; and their works do follow them (Rev. 14:13).

However, it is not God's will that you go through the tribulation period. His ultimate desire is that through your free will, you walk clean before Him and seek the "open door" promised you to escape the wrath that is to come. "For God hath not appointed us to wrath, but to obtain salvation by our Lord Jesus Christ" (1 Thess. 5:9).

The divine mandate that we at Prophecy USA live under is found in Ezekiel 33:6:

But if the watchman see the sword come, and blow not the trumpet, and the people be not warned; if the sword come, and take any person from among them, he is taken away in his iniquity; but his blood will I require at the watchman's hand.

God sends his watchmen for a reason, to warn you, not to scare you or condemn you. He desires that everyone should escape the wrath to come. However, your free will can always void the promises of God. But His desire for you is abundantly clear in Scripture: "As I live, saith the Lord GOD, I have no pleasure in the death of the wicked; but that the wicked turn from his way and live: turn ye, turn ye from your evil ways; for why will ye die" (Ezek. 33:11).

WHAT YOU DO TO A JEW, GOD WILL DO TO YOU

On Jan 10, 2021, the US big tech industry, together with global elites demanding progressive change, banned thousands of conservatives from social media. Instantly, conservatives, many of whom held Judeo-Christian values, could not hear, could not speak, could not communicate. But God was watching. When He says, **"Reward her even as she rewarded you, and double unto her double according to her works"** (Rev. 18:6), He means it.

There is coming a day in America very soon when all bullying, when all lying, will end. When God will instantly judge all corruption to the highest levels of government. The government will silence every technical device. Communications will cease, and all forms of social media will come to a halt in the twinkling of an eye. The same things done to Christians in this nation will unexpectedly come upon those who inflicted that pain. It will come swiftly, suddenly, and without warning. It will begin what the Bible calls the wrath of God.

But what exactly is the wrath of God? And how will it affect the eighth kingdom's role during its seven-year reign?

CHAPTER THIRTEEN

THE FOUR HORSEMEN AND BABYLON'S DESTRUCTION

JESUS CHRIST IN heaven initiates the beginning of the tribulation period by opening the first four seals released upon the earth (Rev. 6:1–6). These events have not happened. We wait for their appointed time. But what exactly are the first four seals, and how do they align with the hidden mystery of America's role in Bible prophecy?

THE ALIGNING OF NATIONS

The main purpose in this chapter is to show the parallel between the Four Horsemen of the Apocalypse and the destruction of Babylon, which God has specifically "time sequenced" at the beginning, not the end, of the tribulation period.

In Chapter Three, "Timing is Everything," we confirmed that the Book of Revelation, like many other parts of the Bible, was not written in chronological order. The time sequence of Revelation 17 and 18 is a description of events that take place before the seven-year tribulation, when the beast and ten kings have not yet received authority

(Rev. 17:12). We also confirmed that the destruction of Babylon was an event that preceded the tribulation period. Jesus initiates that tribulation period when He opens what the Bible calls the seven seals, seven trumpets, and seven bowls or vials (Rev. 6–16). This chapter will further confirm that time sequence.

We are currently witnessing the global elites of the United Nations, the World Health Organization, the World Economic Forum, and the high-tech social media billionaires position their progressive operatives and influence within sovereign nations. One of their goals is an attempt to create their world without borders. Democratic governments around the world, and especially in America, have had massive amounts of money from outside the country funneled to radical left-wing politicians and even to Democratic presidential candidates "during the first three months of the year on the 2020 election."[1] Their intended goals extend beyond governments, as even parenting your children is being disrupted, as their mantra states, "It takes a village to raise a child."[2] This attitude is assuming authority even when the child's parents disagree with the "village" educating them.

The Agenda 2030 is now the "Decade of Action." This agenda is being accelerated by the COVID–19 pandemic and, as Rex Murphy stated in Canada's national post, "the very last people we want 're-imagining' how the world should be arranged are the over-ardent, unaccountable global warming preachers."[3]

On Aug 13, 2020 the Abraham Accords Peace Agreement brought "the government of the United Arab Emirates and the government of the State of Israel . . . *Aspiring* to realize the vision of a Middle East region that is stable, peaceful and prosperous, for the benefit of all States and peoples in the region."[4] However, while this agreement calls for peace in the region, Russian, Iran, and Turkey are still in alignment against it.

Russia's latest military base in Tartus Syria "is an important military facility. Russia also maintains Humaymim airbase in Syria. It thus has strongholds in the region where the interests of global powers clash."[5] According to French based *Naval News* magazine, the Russian "frigates, corvettes and submarines armed with Kalibr missiles can target the Mediterranean area and the Middle East."[6]

Turkey and Russia have over 50% of the nuclear weapons on earth[7] while Iran defies UN sanctions and chants "death to America" (Great Satan)[8] and "death to Israel" (Little Satan).[9] All this is happening while the chief prince of Gog, a demonic stronghold over the region of Meshech and Tubal, waits for his moment in infamy to fulfill God's Word.

As we watch this shifting and the attempts at new alignments happen in real-time, God is also watching. He knows precisely what events are coming. God knows what man will do when they reject His governance. He knew what they would do to Jesus, and gave us three hundred prophecies in advance to prove it. God knows what the free will of man under Satan's influence will do to the bride of Christ. He knows the number of hairs on your head, the day you were born, and the day you will die. And He also knows the choices you will make in the future. He has given all of us "free will" to believe His Word or reject it. He has given you free will to obey His voice, walk in His covenant, or walk away from His covenant. In this sense, He is in full control of everything, but His sovereign observance will not make you, nor progressive ideologues, obey His voice. Those who refuse to heed his warnings, who create a world without God, will reap the rewards of their efforts, fulfilling the very prophecies that they themselves deny.

TOUCH NOT MY ANOINTED

Many times throughout history, the persecution of God's saints has activated God's supernatural hand and produced "signs and wonders." God's hand unleashed Moses's rod and released ten major signs on an

Egyptian government that persecuted God's people. God knew this would happen "that I may lay my hand upon Egypt, and bring forth mine armies, and my people the Children of Israel, out of the land of Egypt by great judgments. And the Egyptians shall know that I am the LORD, when I stretch forth mine hand upon Egypt" (Ex. 7:4–5).

For eighty years, the people of the northern kingdom of Israel, people who had inherited the land of Israel, followed God, but were now serving Canaanite gods, especially Queen Jezebel's favorite god, Baal. It was time for action. Elijah called down fire, consuming the altar and then slew 450 priests of Baal (1 Kings 18:40). Persecution of God's people has always moved the hand of God.

In the New Testament, eleven of the twelve disciples were martyred.[10] Many historians believe that before their glorious entrance into heaven, they were persecuted (Matt. 5:10). However, that persecution released power from on high. Such was the case in Iconium:

> But the unbelieving Jews stirred up the Gentiles, and made their minds evil affected against the brethren. Long time therefore abode they speaking boldly in the Lord, which gave testimony unto the word of his grace, and **granted signs and wonders to be done by their hands**. But the multitude of the city was divided: and part held with the Jews, and part with the apostles
> (Acts 14:2–4).

The final descriptions of Babylon the Great before her destruction point to a great division within her culture. There will be total opposition to her once Judeo-Christian culture. What once was a nation birthed by covenant with God, will become so aggressively opposed to that covenant, her antichrist government will begin to persecute God's people within her. The prophet Isaiah, in his description of the humiliation of Babylon, wrote:

Sit thou silent, and get thee into darkness, O daughter of
the Chaldeans: for thou shalt no more be called, the lady of
kingdoms. I was wroth with my people, I have polluted mine
inheritance, and given them into thine hand: thou didst shew
them no mercy; upon the ancient hast thou very heavily
laid thy yoke (Isa. 47:5–6).

In Isaiah's description, we find God angry and handing His people over to Babylon, presumably to her leadership. Babylon shows them no mercy, perhaps referring to persecution. In this passage, God seems to be testing His people within the lady of kingdoms.

We see this pattern also in the Promised Land, with the Children of Israel, who had inherited the land from the previous generation but had fallen away from covenant with God. Judges 2:20–23 reads:

And the anger of the LORD was hot against Israel; and he said,
Because that this people hath transgressed my covenant which
I commanded their fathers, and have not hearkened unto my
voice; I also will not henceforth drive out any from before them
*of the nations which Joshua left when he died: **that through***
***them I may prove Israel**, whether they will keep the way of*
the LORD to walk therein, as their fathers did keep it, or not.
Therefore the LORD left those nations, without driving them out
hastily; neither delivered he them into the hand of Joshua.

In the past, God used pagan nations to "prove" his people with testing. It is hard to believe that this testing by persecution could happen in America and to what extent it might be. But we need to remember, within Babylon is not only believers, but the bride of Christ. This remnant of believers has "made herself ready," and God has set before them an open door, "and no man can shut it: for thou hast a little strength, and hast kept my word, and hast not denied my name. . . . Because thou hast kept the word of my patience, I also will keep thee from the hour of temptation, which shall come upon all the world, to try them that dwell upon the earth" (Rev. 3:8, 10).

The deliverance of the bride will be initiated by something that triggers God's hand. It is an appointed time in the future that will release the most significant move of His hand, not only upon Babylon the Great, but upon the whole planet. We have already established that at Gog's appointed time, "things come into thy [Gog's] mind, and thou shalt think an evil thought" (Ezek. 38:10). to attack Israel. At that point, God "will send a fire on Magog, and among them that dwell carelessly in the isles" (Ezek. 39:6). According to the time sequences we have revealed, when that judgment comes down in Babylon, the bride will rise.

We need to remember that God has a special place for His anointed. While persecution may happen, God is always there. 2 Tim. 3:12 reminds us that God's people can expect persecution. When Jesus was reviled, He didn't seek revenge, nor did He run. He trusted the outcome to His Father. He knew His Father loved Him and had a plan for Him. The same is true for us, as God loves His anointed and works out all things, including persecution, for their good.

THE SOUND OF HOOFBEATS

Where exactly is the transition from today and into the first day of the tribulation period? Prophecy teachers, seminaries, and even denominational institutions who tell you that America is nowhere to be found in Scripture also cannot tell you how America's transition into the tribulation will take place. However, as we've shown in this book, Scripture blatantly states that the destruction of Babylon the Great will come suddenly, in **one hour**, and in **one day**, everything will change (Rev. 3:10; 17:12, 16; 18:8, 10, 17, 19; Isa. 47:9–11, 14).

The Book of Revelation uses many metaphors and pictorial narrations to communicate its apocalyptic descriptions. But according to the *Nave's New Topical Bible*, horses in Scripture represent strength (Job 39:19–25), swiftness (Jer. 4:13), and war (Ex. 14:9; 15:19; 1 Kings 22:4; 2 Kings 18:23; Jer. 47:3; 51:21).[11]

We find an example in Job 39:19–25 (ESV):

> *Do you give the horse his might? Do you clothe his neck with*
> *a mane? Do you make him leap like the locust? His majestic*
> *snorting is terrifying. He paws in the valley and exults in his*
> *strength; he goes out to meet the weapons. He laughs at fear and*
> *is not dismayed; he does not turn back from the sword. Upon*
> *him rattle the quiver, the flashing spear, and the javelin. With*
> *fierceness and rage he swallows the ground; he cannot stand still*
> *at the sound of the trumpet. When the trumpet sounds,*
> *he says 'Aha!' He smells the battle from afar, the thunder of*
> *the captains, and the shouting.*

When discussing the hour that will change the world, is it not surprising that the first four seals released in the tribulation period are what theologians have labeled "**the Four Horsemen of the Apocalypse.**" But what does this have to do with America's role in Bible prophecy? The answer is **everything**! According to Scripture, the four horsemen are not only riding into the world; before they circle the globe, those hoofbeats will be heard first—and loud and clear—in the United States of America.

The *Concise Oxford English Dictionary* states that "apocalypse" is "an event involving destruction or damage on a catastrophic scale."[12] As we shall see, by reason of this definition, the four riders of the Apocalypse are in essence the four riders (horsemen) of "an event involving destruction or damage on a catastrophic scale." That event will only begin at God's appointed time in history.

GOD'S APPOINTED TIME

John wrote in Rev. 5:5 (ESV), "And one of the elders said to me, 'Weep no more; behold, the Lion of the tribe of Judah, the Root of David, has conquered, so that he can open the scroll and its seven seals.'" At God's appointed time within his prophetic time clock, Jesus of Nazareth will open the first seal. And the wrath of God will be poured out on this planet. The story continues in Revelation 6:1:

1. THE WHITE HORSE

And I saw when the Lamb opened one of the seals, and I heard,
as it were the noise of thunder, one of the four beasts saying,
Come and see. And I saw, and behold a white horse: and he that
sat on him had a bow; and a crown was given unto him: and he
went forth conquering, and to conquer (Rev. 6:1–2).

The Greek word for "conquer" in this passage is *nikao*, denoting "subdued, defeated" or "to overcome or gain dominion over by force of arms" or "bring one to one's knees."[13] In other words, certain nations will willingly or unwillingly be conquered, defeated, won over, and brought to their knees to join the Antichrist. It would appear that this paradigm shift of sovereign nations is already happening. The shift utilizes the mantras of climate change, a world without borders, redistribution of wealth, and a call to global governance within the global elite. The shift to global governance is not here yet, but the Bible boldly declares that someday, globalists will achieve it.

We have already learned that the angel who carried John away said, "Come, and I will me show you the destruction of Babylon The Great" (Rev. 17:1 paraphrased). We will now see that the description of Babylon's destruction matches perfectly with the release of the first four seals.

In previous chapters, we learned that the ten-nation New World Order must agree to be under the Antichrist's submission for him to rule the earth.

Remember, horses represent **strength**, war, and **swiftness**. Immediately after the first seal is opened, another seal is released. It is the second rider.

2. THE RED HORSE

*And when he had opened the second seal, I heard the second beast say, Come and see. And there went out another horse that was red: and power was given to him that sat thereon to take peace from the earth, and that they should kill one another: and there was given unto him a **great sword** (Rev. 6:3–4).*

The parallel Scripture of Babylon's destruction at the beginning of the tribulation states:

And the ten horns that you saw, they and the beast will hate the prostitute. They will make her desolate and naked, and devour her flesh and burn her up with fire (Rev. 17:16 ESV).

In this passage, we see that immediately after the white horse's rider conquers or convinces other nations to join him, the red horse's rider takes peace away from the earth with a war, utilizing a **great sword** that he carries. Notice that it's not just a sword; it is a *great* sword. The Greek word for "great" here is *megas*. It depicts a weapon with "intensity considerably above average."[14] So how will the Antichrist and his ten-nation conglomerate pull this off?

Revelation 17:17 (ESV) gives us a clue. John wrote, "For God has put it into their hearts to carry out his purpose by being of one mind and handing over their royal power to the beast, until the words of God are fulfilled."

Remember that horses in Scripture represent strength, war, and swiftness. Once the first seal is completed, Jesus immediately opens the second seal, and the second horseman swiftly releases his weapon of mass destruction that takes peace from the earth (Rev. 6:4). Just as Jezebel's priests of Baal watched Elijah call down a fire in 850 BC, the rider on the red horse, authorized by God's purpose, releases his sword and calls down fire on modern-day Babylon. Baal worshippers who have been seduced by the antichrist spirit and have been opposing the bride of Christ within Babylon and around the world will "stand afar off for the fear of her torment" (Rev. 18:15).

This second horseman alone will fulfill Jesus' warnings. His warnings point us to the days of Noah, and specifically to Sodom and Gomorrah, when "the same day that Lot went out of Sodom it rained fire and brimstone from heaven, and destroyed them all. Even thus shall it be in the day when the Son of man is revealed (Luke 17:29–30).

In our previous chapters, multiple verses were shown to confirm Babylon's providential covenant, wealth, military might, her falling in darkness, and even the seven types of believers that would be found within her. It took over two hundred years for America to fulfill these fifty-three descriptions. However, her fifty-fourth description of fiery judgment will come swiftly, in one hour, as confirmed by multiple Scriptures (Isa. 47:5–12; Rev. 14:7; Rev. 18:8, 10, 17, 19).

That same swift, one-hour transition is linked directly to the coming Gog-Magog War, as Babylon "dwell[s] carelessly in the isles" (Ezek. 39:6), while saying, "I sit a queen . . . and shall see no sorrow" (Rev. 18:7). Our eyes need to be centered on Israel, and specifically Jerusalem, for there lies the powder keg soon to be lit that will change the world forever as we know it.

The hook will soon be set, and the nations who hate Israel, Babylon (the United States), and the Judaeo-Christian value system will be drawn to the northern mountains of Israel, like sheep to the slaughter.

Many speculate that America will never be judged so severely, and that if she is judged, it will probably be a stock market collapse. It appears that many believe that *we sit a queen and will see no sorrow* (Rev. 18:7 paraphrased).

Many traditional prophecy teachers tell you that America is not in the Bible. "Church fathers like Lactantius, Tertullian, Irenaeus, and Jerome believed that Rome was the Babylon mentioned in Revelation 17–18 [Rhodes, 2019]."[15] Those same early theological scholars also did not know what electricity, cell phones, nuclear weapons, satellite technology, cars, or even airplanes were. They never knew that America even existed because it didn't exist when they wrote their theories on who Babylon the Great was. And yet many modern-day teachers and pastors still follow these prophetic speculations. Unfortunately, traditional theology has made God's Word of little or no effect for millions of believers worldwide.

To traditional prophecy teachers, the thought of God judging America, a covenant nation, as described in the preceding chapters is unbelievable. It is as if in their minds they think, "Who does God think He is to judge America? Does He think He's God?"

So how will America lose its global financial position, and how will the **New World Order** finally achieve global governance of everyone's finances. Scripture answers this question immediately after we see the second (red) horseman fulfill His God-given purpose to depose America, and at the same time, defend Israel.

3. THE BLACK HORSE

When the third seal is swiftly opened, we see how quickly things will change when the black horse makes his appearance.

And when he had opened the third seal, I heard the third beast
say, Come and see. And I beheld, and lo a black horse; and he
that sat on him had a pair of balances in his hand. And I heard
a voice in the midst of the four beasts say, A measure of wheat
for a penny, and three measures of barley for a penny; and see
thou hurt not the oil and the wine (Rev. 6:5–6).

The word translated "balances" in this verse is "a type of scale commonly used to measure currency and commodities in the ancient world."[16] Emphasizing that fact, the angel uses the four common commodities from John's time, wheat, barely, oil and wine,

After the red horse of war is released upon Babylon the Great, who because of, "the merchants of the earth [grew] rich from the power of her luxurious living" (Rev. 18:3 ESV), she is in one hour, financially deposed.

Revelation 18:17 (ESV) reminds us, "For in a **single hour** all this **wealth** has been laid waste."

The Greek word used for "wealth" in this verse is *ploutos*, which means a "sign of God's blessing and approval."[17] The God-given power and authority the US has had through her covenant with God, together with her riches "becomes totally useless after her judgment takes place." And with such devastation "a country goes bankrupt; the most basic systems and institutions disappear. Power companies stop their operations, gas stations close, grocery stores run out of food, banks close their doors, and the government is unable to pay salaries to its civil servants."[18]

Of course, when such an event occurs to the nation whose currency is the global standard, it makes sense that the whole world would be dramatically affected.

However, it appears that the Antichrist and his ten-nation conglomerate have been planning for such an event. According to Scripture, the third seal, once opened, releases a black horse, whose rider swiftly receives God-given authority to control the global economy. This new global currency is the direct result of the ten kings who originally pre-planned and authorized Babylon the Great's destruction.

Babylon the Great is the woman who they have hated for years, and whose covenant with God made her the strongest, most powerful nation in the world, as she repeatedly resisted the agenda of the global elites. She's also a woman who, over the years, has fallen away from her covenant with God. Her hedge of protection is gone. Due to her shedding of innocent blood, she has filled her cup, by her own free will, to fulfill her role in Bible prophecy and receive her judgment. For "whoever sheds the blood of man, by man shall his blood be shed" (Gen. 9:6 ESV).

To the believers of Thyatira, who have followed the teachings of Jezebel, God promises that He "will kill her children with death; and all the churches shall know that I am he which searcheth the reins and hearts: and I will give unto every one of you according to your works (Rev. 2:23).

The transition from one world currency to another will be a well-planned initiative by the Antichrist's ten-nation conglomerate. Just as we watched COVID-19 paralyze the world in fear, the release of the red horseman's great sword will pave the way for one of the most provocative symbols that prophecy teachers have talked about for decades. Seemingly overnight, the current US currency will be disposed of, as the black horseman swiftly and methodically institutes a global census for those who survive the war. These plans are already in place:

> *Senior economist Marion Laboure believes that once a*
> *regulatory framework is in place in key regions of the world*
> *and the government-backed move towards cashless societies*
> *continues, cryptocurrencies* **have the potential to replace**
> **cash by 2030** *(emphasis mine).*[19]

For those who do not understand this modern technological development already being used among nations, "cryptocurrency (or "crypto") is a digital currency that can be used to buy goods and services but uses an online ledger with strong cryptography to secure online transactions."[20]

European lecturer and trend watcher Richard Ban Hooijdonk writes, "An RFID (short-range radio frequency identification) implant can hold all the information we usually carry in our wallets. It can transmit our identity information as we walk through a security checkpoint, enable us to use public transport and make long lines at the supermarket checkout a thing of the past. The future of microchipping is exciting, with many interesting potential applications. Chips like the ones we now use in our pets could become commonplace in the next decade."[21]

The greatest hinderance to the use of the new cryptocurrency is the paper currency from Babylon the Great. But once the red horseman executes his judgment, the black horseman of the Apocalypse will easily fulfill the written word of God, which says:

> And he causeth all, both small and great, rich and poor, free and
> bond, to receive a mark in their right hand, or in their foreheads:
> And that no man might buy or sell, save he that had the mark,
> or the name of the beast, or the number of his name. Here is
> wisdom. Let him that hath understanding count the number of
> the beast: for it is the number of a man; and his number is Six
> hundred threescore and six [666] (Rev. 13:16–18).

> If any man worship the beast and his image, and receive his
> mark in his forehead, or in his hand, the same shall drink of the
> wine of the wrath of God, which is poured out without mixture
> into the cup of his indignation; and he shall be tormented with

fire and brimstone . . . and the smoke of their torment ascendeth
up for ever and ever (Rev. 14:9–11).

The penalty for taking the mark of the beast is extremely sobering. And to think that today, 85 percent of the body of Christ, the believers of Laodicea, get outright hostile when you even mention the principle of tithing their money for the work of God's kingdom. Believers who do not have faith to tithe somehow think they will supernaturally resist taking the mark of the beast. Without the mark, you will not be able to purchase food at the local market, fuel for your car, or pay the bank for your mortgage payment. Without utilizing the new digital currency, the government will turn off your heat and water. And there will be nowhere to run and hide. You will have nothing to eat unless you take that mark. Sound far-fetched? Just look how swiftly the COVID-19 corona bug altered your lifestyle. And COVID is a cakewalk compared to what Scripture says is coming.

Of course, the last horse of the Apocalypse is the direct result of the actions of the first three horses.

4. THE PALE HORSE
And when he had opened the fourth seal, I heard the voice of
the fourth beast say, Come and see. And I looked, and behold a
pale horse: and his name that sat on him was Death, and Hell
followed with him. And power was given unto them over the
fourth part of the earth, to kill with sword, and with hunger, and
with death, and with the beasts of the earth (Rev. 6:7–8).

The tremendous destruction that comes upon Babylon will come swiftly, as on September 11, 2001, when the world watched the World Trade Center fall to the ground. In March 2020, the fear released by the COVID-19 pandemic kept people quarantined in their homes for months. But the massive destruction and subsequent nuclear fallout emanating from Babylon the Great will be the catalyst for most people to accept any vaccines, any digital implants (mark of the beast), and any new cryptocurrency that will be swiftly forced upon them. Those who mocked Bible prophecy, refused to listen, or just outright rebelled and became non-compliant will be consumed by incredible fear.

Even now, as you read this book, the technology is ready to go, the microchips are easily processed, and the distribution network is already intact.[22] All the New World Order needs is for God's **appointed time** to fulfill every agenda they are planning, and every **purpose** God has spoken (Isaiah 46:7). Technology has finally caught up to the prophecies of biblical forth-telling. However, these prophecies are global and not restricted to the Middle East and Europe.

We do not believe that commercial Babylon the Great is a little city in Italy sitting on seven hills. Nowhere in Scripture does it say that Babylon the Great is going to be built by the Antichrist in some far east country. Nowhere in Scripture does it say he will rule from Babylon. Babylon is not judged at the end or the middle of the Great Tribulation. She is judged at the beginning, as time sequenced by the deposing of the seventh kingdom (United States), in order for the eighth kingdom (New World Order) to rise and take authority (Rev. 17:16).

For millions of believers around the world, 500 year old traditional theology has made the Word of God of no effect (Mark 7:13). God's Word is the final authority for judging Bible prophecy. You will not be judged by what others say or teach. You will be judged by what the Holy Spirit says directly to you. What is He saying to you right now? Can you see that the dots are not only lining up, but they are becoming a line in the sand for you to choose this day whom you will serve (Josh. 24:15)? God will not be mocked. "The fierce anger of the LORD will not turn back until he has executed and accomplished the intentions of his mind. In the latter days you will understand this" (Jer. 30:24 ESV).

Babylon is alive and well before the Antichrist arrives (Rev. 17:12). She is the seventh of eight providential nations (Rev. 17:10), and its time we in North America wake up and smell the coffee. God's fifty-three biblical descriptions of Babylon the Great do not lie. America meets every description. Within this lady of kingdoms "having a golden cup in her hand full of abominations" (Rev. 17:4) has now become the measuring cup for God to "reward her even as she rewarded you, and double unto her double according to her works: in the cup which she hath filled fill to her double" (Rev. 18:6).

Since the 1973 Roe v. Wade decision, over sixty million deaths through the shedding of innocent blood (abortion) have taken place.[23] Now Babylon's judgment will render to her double according to her works, resulting in one hundred million deaths, equalling close to one-third of her population center. And it will only take one-hour, compliments of the great sword of the red horseman.

However, the death of one third of Babylon the Great's population is just the forerunner of things to come. After the pale horse is released, the seals, trumpets, and plagues will cover the earth for the next seven years. Those who have taken the mark of the beast will break out in sores (Rev. 16:2). Climate change will become a man-made problem. Nuclear fallout from "the smoke of her burning" (Rev. 18:9) will leave the world paralyzed in fear. The rapture of the bride, together with the decimation of a third of Babylon's population, will be the poster child of what the nuclear fallout will do. Prophetic Scripture is very detailed. Over the subsequent seven years, the Pale Horse plagues will destroy:

- The third part of trees was burnt up, and all green grass was burnt up (Rev. 8:7).
- The third part of the sea became blood (Rev. 8:8).
- The third part of the creatures that were in the sea and had life, died (Rev. 8:9).

- The third part of the ships were destroyed (Rev. 8:9).
- The third part of the sun was smitten.
- The third part of the moon, and the third part of the stars; so as the third part of them was darkened . . .
- the day shone not for a third part of it, and the night likewise (Rev. 8:12).

At their appointed time, Jesus Christ will release the Four Horsemen of the Apocalypse. They will circle the globe and initiate the most extraordinary catastrophic events in the history of the world. But when they appear, they won't be coming to Jerusalem, Rome, or any other European country. The United States will hear first the four horses' hoofbeats, and when they arrive, they will change the world forever.

Are you ready? Is it time to come out of her and be not partakers of her sins and receive not her plagues (Rev. 18:4)? Have you asked Jesus Christ into your life? Or are you like the fools that God said would mock and laugh at His warnings until the time of His appearance? We hope that is not the case, and reiterate what Paul spoke to those in Thessalonica:

> And to you who are troubled rest with us, when the Lord Jesus
> shall be revealed from heaven with his mighty angels, In flaming
> fire taking vengeance on them that know not God, and that obey
> not the gospel of our Lord Jesus Christ (2 Thess. 1:7–8).

Friends, don't let this message scare you. Remember, "no weapon that is formed against thee shall prosper" (Isa. 54:17) . . . not even the great sword coming with the second rider of the Apocalypse.

The fourth Man in Shadrach, Meshack and Abednego's fiery furnace has never lost His power to **deliver**, and for those of you who believe, remember this promise from the prophet Malachi:

Then they that feared the LORD spake often one to another: and the LORD hearkened, and heard it, and a book of remembrance was written before him for them that feared the LORD, and that thought upon his name. And they shall be mine, saith the LORD of hosts, in that day when I make up my jewels; and I will spare them, as a man spareth his own son that serveth him (Mal. 3:16, 17).

For, behold, the day cometh, that shall burn as an oven; and all the proud, yea, and all that do wickedly, shall be stubble: and the day that cometh shall burn them up, saith the LORD of hosts, that it shall leave them neither root nor branch. But unto you that fear my name shall the Sun of righteousness arise with healing in his wings; and ye shall go forth, and grow up as calves of the stall. And ye shall tread down the wicked; for they shall be ashes under the soles of your feet in the day that I shall do this, saith the LORD of hosts (Mal. 4:1–3).

The apostle John wrote this about the blessing that awaits those of us who are the bride of Christ:

Praise our God, all ye his servants, and ye that fear him, both small and great. . . . Let us be glad and rejoice, and give honour to him: for the marriage of the Lamb is come, and his wife hath made herself ready. And to her was granted that she should be arrayed in fine linen, clean and white: for the fine linen is the righteousness of saints. And he saith unto me, Write, Blessed are they which are called unto the marriage supper of the Lamb (Rev. 19:5, 7-9).

So when will these prophecies be fulfilled? Nobody knows. But our loving heavenly Father has promised us:

I am the Lord. I have spoken; it shall come to pass; I will do it. I will not go back (Ezek. 24:14 ESV).

And it will come within . . .

THE HOUR

THAT CHANGES EVERYTHING!

ENDNOTES

INTRODUCTION

1 https://onecampus.oru.edu/p/holy-spirit-in-the-now.

2 Paul J. Achtemeier, *Harper & Row and Society of Biblical Literature, Harper's Bible Dictionary* (San Francisco: Harper & Row, 1985), 1132.

3 We'll spend more time later in the book discussing secular humanism. For now, it's a philosophy of life that is based on human reason.

4 The isle of Patmos is located in the Aegean Sea off the coast of Asia Minor. It is the location of the Apostle John's banishment and where he recorded the book of Revelation.

CHAPTER ONE: THE STILL, SMALL VOICE

1 Oral Roberts, *The Daily Guide to Miracles*, (New York, Revell, 1977), 264.

2 Genesis introduces the longer name [Abraham] as part of the covenant God made with Abram, so the new name confirmed God's control and marked a stage in the Patriarch's career (No other person in the Old Testament bears the names "Abram" or "Abraham" (or "Isaac" or "Jacob"); they were names which held a special place in Hebrew tradition (like the names "David" and "Solomon"). David Noel Freedman, Editor-in-Chief, *The Anchor Bible Dictionary, Vol. 1*, (New York, Doubleday, 1992), 38.

3 Soanes, Catherine and Angus Stevenson, *Concise Oxford English Dictionary*, (Oxford, Oxford University Press, 2004), 1150.

4 Warren Wiersbe, *Be Reverent*, (Colorado Springs, CO: Cook Communications), 205, Logos Software Edition.

5 Merrill F. Unger, William White, Jr, *Nelson's Expository Dictionary of the Old Testament*, (Nashville, TN: Thomas Nelson Publishers, 1985), 93.

6 W.E. Vine, *An Expository Dictionary of New Testament Words*, (Nashville, TN: Thomas Nelson Publishers, 1985), 532.

7 Abraham Heschel, *The Prophets*, (New York, HarperCollins, 2001), 14.

8   Unger, White, Jr., *Nelson's Expository Dictionary of the Old Testament*, 139.

9   Dates in this section are from J.E. Smith, *Old Testament Survey Series*, Logos Research Edition.

10 Philip Comfort, Walter A.Elwell, *The Complete Book of Who's Who in the Bible*, (Chicago, Tyndale House Publishers, 2004), 238.

11 A midrash is an interpretation of the Bible by ancient Jewish scholars who closely examined the meaning of words, especially in the first five books of the Old Testament (commonly referred to as the books of Moses or, in Judaism, the Torah.

12 "The Gemara expands on the events surrounding Isaiah's death: Rava said: Manasseh judged him as a false witness for issuing statements contradicting the Torah and only then killed him." Yevamot 49b:7 William Davidson Edition, *The William Davidson Talmud*.

13 Walter A. Elwell and Barry J. Beitzel, "Jeremiah (Person)," *Baker Encyclopedia of the Bible* (Grand Rapids, MI: Baker Book House, 1988), 1110.

14 Edited material from: https://www.chabad.org/library/article_cdo /aid/3630049/jewish/Daniel-the-Prophet-of-the-Bible-His-Life-and -Accomplishments.htm#Stature.

15 M. G. Easton, *Easton's Bible Dictionary* (New York: Harper & Brothers, 1893).

16 Janet Meyer Everts, "Dreams in the New Testament and Greco-Roman Literature," ed. David Noel Freedman, *The Anchor Yale Bible Dictionary* (New York: Doubleday, 1992), 231.

17 Examples of visions in the Bible include Abraham's vision in Genesis 15; the visions of Isaiah in Isaiah 6, Daniel is Daniel 4, and the visions of Ezekiel throughout his book.

18 Both Joseph (Genesis 40:12, 13, 18-19, 41:25–32) and Daniel (Daniel 2:16–23, 28–39 and 4) had the unique ability not merely to have dreams but interpret them as well.

19 John F. MacArthur Jr., *Galatians, MacArthur New Testament Commentary* (Chicago: Moody Press, 1983), 24.

20 David Abell, *Common Sense Apologetics: One God, One Book, One Way*, (Nashville: WestBow Press, 2010), 124.

21 Robert D. Prescott-Ezickson, *God Has a Plan for You: 52 Bible Study Lessons*, (Lima, OH, CSS Publishing Co, 2001), 95.

22 In the mid-1950's Westmont College's Professor Peter Stoner worked with six hundred students to come up with their best estimate of the mathematical probability of just eight prophecies being fulfilled. Stoner calculated the odds at one chance in a hundred million billion. Excerpted from: Ravi Zacharias and Norman Geisler, *Who Made God and Answers*

to over 100 Other Tough Questions, (Grand Rapids, MI, Zondervan, 2003), 95.

23 Wayne Grudem, *The First Epistle of Peter: An Introduction and Commentary,* (Grand Rapids, MI: Wm. B. Eerdmans Publishing Company, 1988), 101.

CHAPTER TWO: PROVIDENTIAL NATIONS

1   Kenneth Boa and William Kruidenier, *Romans, vol. 6, Holman New Testament Commentary* (Nashville, TN: Broadman & Holman Publishers, 2000), 135.

2   As expected the agreements to divide Alexander's kingdom were not maintained. Soon after his death, power struggles and wars (War of the Successors) occurred for control and rule of his empire.

3   Mystical [or religious] Babylon is described in the Book of Revelation chapter seventeen. Most theologians agree that this chapter refers to a world religion (or religions) that will appear in the last days. It will be a mixture of the same religions that were practiced by ancient Babylon.

4   www.cio.com › governance-what-does-governance-mean.

5   https://www.cfr.org/backgrounder/group-twenty.

6   https://www.cfr.org/backgrounder/g7-and-future-multilateralism.

7   https://www.independent.co.uk/news/world/politics/un-human -rights-council-members-saudi-arabia-china-venezuela-abusers -violators-a7958271.html.

8   https://www.foxnews.com/opinion/say-what-un-human-rights-council -declares-israel-worlds-no-1-human-rights-violator.

9   https://www.cnn.com/2020/04/15/world/trump-who-funding-explainer -intl-hnk/index.html

10 https://www.bbc.com/news/world-us-canada-52289056.

11 This book is written before the final outcome of the United States' 2020 election. The U.S. policies toward Israel may change based on who is confirmed as president for the next four years.

12 According to sustainabledevelopment.un.org, this agenda is for people, planet, and prosperity. There are seventeen Sustainable Development Goals seeking to realize human rights of all and achieve gender equality and empowerment for women and girls. The Goals target people, planet, prosperity, peace, and partnership. All nations voted to accept the Sustainable Development platform.

13 https://nationalpost.com/opinion/rex-murphy-the-great-reset-no-one -asked-for.

14 Ibid.

15 Ibid.

16 https://www.un.org/sustainabledevelopment/decade-of-action/.

17 Ibid.

18 https://www.cluboforme.org/impact-hubs/rethinking-finance/.

19 https://www.bibliotecapleyades.net/sociopolitica/esp_sociopol
_clubrome10.htm.

20 https://uwspace.uwaterloo.ca/bitstream/handle/10012/747/jlchurch2006
.pdf?sequence=1&isAllowed=y.

21 https://altamontenterprise.com/09252019/elitists-have-created-myth
-climate-change-eliminate-national-sovereignty.

22 https://altamontenterprise.com/09252019/elitists-have-created-myth
-climate-change-eliminate-national-sovereignty.

23 https://www.cluboforme.org/about-us/history/.

24 Warren W. Wiersbe, *The Bible Exposition Commentary, vol. 2* (Wheaton, IL: Victor Books, 1996), 604.

25 *Oral Roberts Bible Commentary, King James Version, Oral Roberts Edition*, (Tulsa, OK, Oral Roberts Evangelistic Association Inc.), 181.

26 Some works translate Luther to have written "The papacy is indeed nothing but the kingdom of Babylon and of the true Antichrist." Eckhard Schnabel, Benjamin, Merkle, Series Editor, *40 Questions about End Times*, (Grand Rapids, MI: Kregel Academic & Professional, 2011), 205.

27 Martin Luther, *The Babylonian Captivity of the Church, 1520, The Annotated Luther Study Edition*, Erik H. Herrmann and Paul W. Robinson, Ed., (Minneapolis, MN, Fortress Press, 2016), 15.

28 *The HarperCollins Bible Dictionary*, Paul J. Achtemeier General Editor, (New York: HarperCollins, 1985, 1996), 171-172.

29 "Seven Hills of Rome, group of hills on or about which the ancient city of Rome was built. The original city of Romulus was built upon Palatine Hill(Latin: Mons Palatinus). The other hills are the Capitoline, Quirinal, Viminal, Esquiline, Caelian, and Aventine (known respectively in Latin as the Mons Capitolinus, Mons Quirinalis, Mons Viminalis, Mons Esquilinus, Mons Caelius, and Mons Aventinus)." https://www.britannica.com/place/Seven-Hills-of-Rome

30 Paul J. Achtemeier, Harper & Row and Society of Biblical Literature, *Harper's Bible Dictionary* (San Francisco: Harper & Row, 1985), 660.

31 Spiros Zodhiates, *The Complete Word Study Dictionary: New Testament* (Chattanooga, TN, AMG Publishers, 1992), e-Sword Electronic Edition.

32 Matt. 11:15; 13:9; 13:43; Mark 4:9; 4:23; 8:18; Luke 8:8; 14:35; Rev. 2:7; 2:11; 2:17; 2:29; 3:6; 3:13; 3:22; 13:9.

CHAPTER THREE: TIMING IS EVERYTHING

1 Kittel, Bromiley, and Friedrich, *Vol 2, Theological Dictionary of the New*

Testament, (Grand Rapids, MI: Eerdmans, 1964, Logos Software Edition.

2   Robert G. Bratcher and Howard Hatton, *A Handbook on the Revelation to John, UBS Handbook Series* (New York: United Bible Societies, 1993), 239.

3   Johannes P, Louwk and Eugene Albert Nida, *vol 1, Greek-English Lexicon of the New Testament,* Logos Software Edition.

4   Joseph H. Thayer, D.D., *A Greek-English Lexicon of the New Testament,* (New York: American Book Company, 1889), 420.

5   https://bible.org/seriespage/23-babylon-seen-scripture-introduction -rev-17-18.

6   See Gen. 10 for a genealogy of the children of Noah.

7   Derek Kidner, *Genesis: An Introduction and Commentary, vol. 1, Tyndale Old Testament Commentaries* (Downers Grove, IL: InterVarsity Press, 1967), 119.

8   James Montgomery Boice, Daniel: *An Expositional Commentary* (Grand Rapids, MI: Baker Books, 2003), 83.

9   https://biblearchaeologyreport.com/tag/east-india-house-inscription/.

10 Daniel 3:27.

11 Daniel L. Dreisbach, Mark D. Hall, Jeffry H. Morrison, Editors, *The Founders on God and Government,* (Lanham, Maryland, Rowman & Littlefield Publishers, Inc, 2004), 5.

12 Michael A. Shea, *In God We Trust: George Washington and the Spiritual Destiny of the United States of America,* (Derry, NH, Liberty Quest, LLC, 2012), 344–345.

13 George Grant, *The Courage and Character of Theodore Roosevelt: A Hero Among Leaders,* (Nashville, TN: Cumberland House Publishing, Inc., 2005), 168.

14 Frank E. Grizzard, Jr. George Washington: *A Biographical Companion,* (Santa Barbara, CA, ABC-CLIO, 2002), 272.

15 George E. Mendenhall and Gary A. Herion, "Covenant," ed. David Noel Freedman, *The Anchor Yale Bible Dictionary* (New York: Doubleday, 1992), 1179.

16 Warren W. Wiersbe, *Be Equipped,* "Be" Commentary Series (Colorado Springs, CO: Chariot Victor Pub., 1999), 167.

17 https://worldpopulationreview.com/countries/countries-by-gdp.

18 Kay Dee Lilley, *God's Country, America's Heart Cry,* (Xulon Press, 2010), 61.

19 www.globaltrademag.com/usports and exportvirginia.org.

20 https://www.bbc.com/news/magazine-17604991.

21 https://www.deseret.com/2017/2/10/20605880/when-president-abraham -lincoln-derived-strength-from-the-scriptures#abraham-lincoln-statue -in-the-lincoln-memorial-at-the-national-mall-in-washington-d-c-on -friday-sept-23-2016.

22 www.ncjrs.gov › ovc_archives › ncvrw.

23 https://www.investopedia.com/terms/b/brettonwoodsagreement.asp.

24 https://www.investopedia.com/terms/b/brettonwoodsagreement.asp.

CHAPTER FOUR: WHAT POPULATION CENTER IS LIKE THIS GREAT CITY?

1 Edward F. Murphy, *Handbook for Spiritual Warfare* (Nashville: Thomas Nelson, 1996), Logos Bible Software Edition.

2 Hamilton, Victor P. "Satan." Edited by David Noel Freedman. *The Anchor Yale Bible Dictionary*. New York: Doubleday, 1992.

3 "One of three major Jewish feasts also called the Feast of Weeks. The name "Pentecost" is derived from the Greek word meaning "fifty." Pentecost occurs in the [Jewish calendar] month of Sivan (May/June), 50 days after Passover, and celebrates the end of the grain harvest. The Pentecost that followed Jesus' death and resurrection was the occasion on which the Holy Spirit was given to believers in Jerusalem [Acts 2:2]." Chad Brand, Charles Draper, Archie England, *Holman Illustrated Bible Dictionary*, (Nashville, Holman Reference, 2003), Logos Bible Software Edition.

4 C. Wagner and F. Pennoyer, *Wrestling with Dark Angels: Toward a Deeper Understanding of the Supernatural Forces in Spiritual Warfare* (Gospel Light, 1990), 50.

5 https://www.healthline.com/health/different-genders#why-it-matters.

6 https://altamontenterprise.com/09252019/elitists-have-created-myth -climate-change-eliminate-national-sovereignty.

7 Jonathan and Amanda Witt, *Effective Stewardship: Doing What Matters Most Participant's Guide* (Grand Rapids, MI, Zondervan, 2009), 57.

8 https://seanmcdowell.org/blog/was-paul-beheaded-in-rome.

9 Stephen McDowell, *The Economy from a Biblical Perspective* (Charlottesville, VA, Providence Foundation Biblical Worldview University, 2009), 14.

10 https://sciencevibe.com/2019/11/13/which-evil-dictator-killed-the-most -people/.

11 U.S. military spending 2019 | Statista www.statista.com › Society › Politics & Government.

12 www.nationalpriorities.org › campaigns › us-military-spending.

13 https://www.politico.com/magazine/story/2015/06/us-military-bases -around-the-world-119321

14 https://www.pgpf.org/chart-archive/0053_defense-comparison.

15 https://www.businessinsider.com/military-aircraft-strength-of-every -country-2016-5.

16 www.naval-technology.com › features › china-boasts-worlds-largest-navy.

17 www.cfr.org › backgrounder › sea-power-us-navy-and-foreign-policy.

18 https://www.globalfirepower.com/aircraft-total.asp.

19 https://www.flightglobal.com/us-carrier-gap-could-see-naval-air-power
-dip-in-gulf-region/117560.article.

20 https://www.weforum.org/agenda/2019/03/chart-of-the-day-the
-countries-with-the-most-satellites-in-space/.

21 https://www.weforum.org/agenda/2019/03/chart-of-the-day-the
-countries-with-the-most-satellites-in-space/.

22 http://www.unoosa.org/oosa/en/ourwork/topics/long-term-sustainability
-of-outer-space-activities.html.

23 airandspace.si.edu › wright-brothers › online › fly.

24 Unless specifically noted most of the dates of these inventions were found
here: https://blog.talk.edu/culture-exchange/american-inventions
-changed-nation/.

25 sites.cs.ucsb.edu › ~almeroth › classes › Alaa-Gharbawi.

26 www.geotaBCom › blog › gps-satellites.

27 https://www.inc.com/kevin-j-ryan/greatest-inventions-decade-2010-2019
.html.

28 Ibid.

29 https://www.ucsusa.org/resources/satellite-database.

30 William Barclay, *The New Daily Study Bible, The Revelation of John, Vol. II*,
(Louisville, KY, Westminster John Knox Press, 1976, 2004), Logos Bible
Software Edition.

31 J. Alec Motyer, Isaiah: *An Introduction and Commentary, vol. 20, Tyndale
Old Testament Commentaries* (Downers Grove, IL: InterVarsity Press,
1999), 337.

32 Rambam, Mishneh, *Torah, Repentance 5:3*. Translated by Simon Glazer,
1927.

33 Joseph Henry Thayer, D.D., *A Greek-English Lexicon of the New Testament*,
(New York, American Book Company, 1886), e-Sword Bible Software
Edition.

CHAPTER FIVE: FALLEN, FALLEN, BABYLON HAS FALLEN

1 Charles Colson, *Kingdoms in Conflict: An Insider's Challenging View
of Politics, Power, and the Pulpit* (Grand Rapids, MI, Zondervan, a
copublication of William Morrow and Zondervan Publishing House,
1987), 44.

2 Colson, *Kingdoms in Conflict*, 43.

3 Wendell Willis, "Darkness," ed. David Noel Freedman, Allen C. Myers,
and Astrid B. Beck, *Eerdmans Dictionary of the Bible* (Grand Rapids, MI:
W.B. Eerdmans, 2000), 317.

4 W. E. Vine, Merrill F. Unger, and William White Jr., *Vine's Complete*

Expository Dictionary of Old and New Testament Words (Nashville, TN: T. Nelson, 1996), 290.

5 James Strong, *Enhanced Strong's Lexicon* (Woodside Bible Fellowship, 1995).

6 James Strong, *Enhanced Strong's Lexicon* (Woodside Bible Fellowship, 1995).

7 James Strong, *Enhanced Strong's Lexicon* (Woodside Bible Fellowship, 1995).

8 https://www.lexico.com/definition/whence.

9 Francis Brown, S. R. Driver, and Charles Briggs, *The Abridged Brown-Driver-Briggs Hebrew-English Lexicon of the Old Testament,* (New York, Houghton Mifflin and Company), Logos Bible Software Edition.

10 Francis Brown, S. R. Driver, and Charles Briggs, *Brown-Driver-Briggs' Hebrew Definitions,* 1906; public domain, E-sword Editon.

11 Brown, Driver, and Briggs, *Brown-Driver-Briggs' Hebrew Definitions.*

12 *Brown-Driver-Briggs' Hebrew Definitions.*

13 https://www.psychologytoday.com/us/blog/the-secular-life/202002/what -is-secular-humanism.

14 Matthew Henry, *Matthew Henry's Commentary on the Whole Bible: Complete and Unabridged in One Volume* (Peabody, MA: Hendrickson, 1994), 569.

15 George Santayana, *The Life of Reason: Or the Phases of Human Progress,* (New York, Charles Scribner's Sons, 1920), 284.

16 David Horowitz, *Dark Agenda: The War to Destroy Christian America,* (West Palm Beach, FL: Humanix Books, 2018), 11.

17 Allen C. Myers, *The Eerdmans Bible Dictionary* (Grand Rapids, MI: Eerdmans, 1987), 261.

18 M. G. Easton, *Easton's Bible Dictionary* (New York: Harper & Brothers, 1893).

19 M. G. Easton, *Easton's Bible Dictionary,* (New York: Harper & Brothers, 1893).

20 University of Southern California. "American drug overdose death rates the highest among wealthy nations." *ScienceDaily.* www.sciencedaily.com /releases/2019/02/190221083419.htm (accessed September 30, 2020).

21 James Montgomery Boice, *The Minor Prophets: An Expositional Commentary* (Grand Rapids, MI: Baker Books, 2002), 43.

22 Joseph Thayer, *Thayer's Greek-English Lexicon of the New Testament,* e-Sword edition.

23 Chad Brand et al., eds., "Reprobate," *Holman Illustrated Bible Dictionary* (Nashville, TN: Holman Bible Publishers, 2003), 1378.

24 https://www.canadianbusiness.com/blogs-and-comment/u-s-leads-the -way-in-porn-production-but-falls-behind-in-profits/.

25 https://pando.com/2013/08/05/infographic-what-countries-host-the -most-porn/.

26 https://www.webroot.com/ca/en/resources/tips-articles/internet
-pornography-by-the-numbers.

CHAPTER SIX: THE WORLD VERSUS THE WORD

1 W. E. Vine, *An Expository Dictionary of New Testament Words*, (Nashville TN: Thomas Nelson Publishers, 1985), 349.

2 W. E. Vine, *An Expository Dictionary of New Testament Words*, 17.

3 Lewis A. Drummond, *The Canvas Cathedral* (Nashville, TN: W Pub. Group, 2001), 263.

4 John F. MacArthur Jr., *Revelation 12–22, MacArthur New Testament Commentary* (Chicago: Moody Press, 2000), 180.

5 https://www.worldatlas.com/articles/which-countries-have-the-most
-christians-around-the-world.html.

6 Leon Morris, *Revelation: An Introduction and Commentary, vol. 20, Tyndale New Testament Commentaries* (Downers Grove, IL: InterVarsity Press, 1987), 68.

7 https://www.worldatlas.com/articles/which-countries-have-the-most
-christians-around-the-world.html.

8 Civitas: Institute for the Study of Civil Society, London.

9 In his book, *Christianophobia: A Faith Under Attack* (Rider 2012), Shortt quotes figures from both the Pew Foundation and the World Evangelical Alliance. He estimates that "200 million Christians are socially disadvantaged, harassed or actively oppressed for their beliefs."

10 Kelly James Clark, "The Most Persecuted Religion in the World," Huffington Post, January 4, 2013, updated March 6, 2013.

11 Remarks by Vice President Pence at the United Nations Event on Religious Freedom, New York, September 23, 2019: https://www
.whitehouse.gov/briefings-statements/remarks-vice-president-pence
-united-nations-event-religious-freedom-new-york-ny/.

12 https://thebridgehead.ca/2017/09/20/the-agony-of-north-koreas-christians/.

13 Remarks by Vice President Pence at the 2nd Annual Religious Freedom Ministerial, July 18, 2019: https://www.whitehouse.gov/briefings
-statements/remarks-vice-president-pence-2nd-annual-religious
-freedom-ministerial/.

14 Linda Lowry, "215 Million Believers Face Persecution for Their Faith in Christ," January 10, 2018, https://www.opendoorsusa.org/christian
-persecution/stories/215-million-believers-persecution-for-their-faith
-in-christ/.

15 Eliza Griswold, "Is This the End of Christianity in the Middle East? July

22, 2015: https://www.nytimes.com/2015/07/26/magazine/is-this-the
-end-of-christianity-in-the-middle-east.html.

16 A phobia is a fear of something that does not necessarily exist. Just because you don't agree with a person's religion or sexual agenda does not make you afraid of them or hate them.

17 David Horowitz, *Dark Agenda: The War to Destroy Christian America*, (West Palm Beach, FL, Humanix Books, 2018), eBook edition.

18 Walter A. Elwell, *Baker Encyclopedia of the Bible*, Vol. 1 & 2, (Grand Rapids, MI: Baker Book House Company, 1988), Logos Bible Software Edition.

19 Horowitz, *Dark Agenda*, eBook edition.

20 Saul D. Alinsky, *Rules for Radicals: A Pragmatic Primer for Realistic Radicals*, (New York, Vintage Books, a Division of Random House, 1971), IX.

21 Alinsky, *Rules for Radicals*, 75.

CHAPTER SEVEN: THE BELIEVERS OF PERGAMOS AND THYATIRA

1 Stelman Smith and Judson Cornwall, *The Exhaustive Dictionary of Bible Names* (North Brunswick, NJ: Bridge-Logos, 1998), 177.

2 Later in the biblical narrative is the book of Ruth featuring a Moabitess who marries a Jewish man (Boaz). This is an important union of Jew and Gentile because from their children came King David and later Jesus, Messiah. Among the lessons from Ruth and Boaz is how the Kingdom of God will include both Jew and Gentile.

3 John MacArthur, Jr., *The MacArthur New Testament Commentary: Revelation 12–22*, (Chicago, Moody Press, 2000), 308.

4 The Gnostics believed that what was done in the body had no bearing on the soul.

5 https://www.christianity.com/wiki/people/who-were-the-nicolaitans-in
-revelation-why-did-god-hate-their-practices-so-much.html.

6 Inc Merriam-Webster, *Merriam-Webster's Collegiate Dictionary*. (Springfield, MA: Merriam-Webster, Inc., 2003).

7 John F. Walvoord, "Revelation," in *The Bible Knowledge Commentary: An Exposition of the Scriptures*, ed. J. F. Walvoord and R. B. Zuck, vol. 2 (Wheaton, IL: Victor Books, 1985), 970.

8 https://www.ibidworld.com/united-states/market-research-reports/strip
-clubs-industry/.

9 https://www.psychologytoday.com/ca/blog/all-about-sex/201611/dueling
-statistics-how-much-the-internet-is-porn.

10 https://fightthenewdrug.org/by-the-numbers-see-how-many-people-are

-watching-porn-today/.

11 https://www.webroot.com/ca/en/resources/tips-articles/internet
-pornography-by-the-numbers.

CHAPTER EIGHT: LAODICEA BELIEVERS

1 Laodicea was noted for its strategic geographic position, and textile products, the local wool was said to be softer and a black color that was rare and popular. It also was purported to be a chief medical center of the area. The people were materially affluent and self-sufficient. Excerpts taken from: *The Anchor Bible Dictionary*, David N. Freedman Editor-in-Chief, (New York, Doubleday, 1992), Logos Bible Software edition.

2 D. J. Wiseman, "In the Old Testament," ed. D. R. W. Wood et al., *New Bible Dictionary* (Leicester, England; Downers Grove, IL: InterVarsity Press, 1996), 779.

3 Hemchand Gossai, "Tithe," ed. David Noel Freedman, Allen C. Myers, and Astrid B. Beck, *Eerdmans Dictionary of the Bible* (Grand Rapids, MI: W.B. Eerdmans, 2000), 1315.

4 Robert L. Thomas, *New American Standard Hebrew-Aramaic and Greek Dictionaries : Updated Edition* (Anaheim: Foundation Publications, Inc., 1998).

5 Tacitus, Annals 14:27.

6 James Swanson, *Dictionary of Biblical Languages with Semantic Domains: Greek* (New Testament) (Oak Harbor: Logos Research Systems, Inc., 1997).

7 https://www.pewresearch.org/fact-tank/2015/07/09/how-americans
-compare-with-the-global-middle-class/.

8 https://www.philanthropyroundtable.org/the-generosity-of-america.

9 https://www.christianitytoday.com/news/2017/september/your-split
-tithe-doesnt-have-to-go-to-church-ministries.html.

10 https://church-development.com/what-percentage-of-church-members
-tithe/.

11 Jeff Schapiro, "Study: Christians Who Tithe Have Healthier Finances Than Those Who Don't," *Christian Post Register*, May 15, 2013, https://www.christianpost.com/news/study-christians-who-tithe-have
-healthier-finances-than-those-who-dont.html.

CHAPTER NINE: THE CHURCH OF PHILADELPHIA

1 W. W. Davies, "Accuser," ed. James Orr et al., *The International Standard Bible Encyclopedia* (Chicago: The Howard-Severance Company, 1915), 35.

2 https://www.learnreligions.com/christianity-statistics
-700533#:~:text=Number%20of%20Christian%20

Denominations,organizations%20in%20the%20world%20today.

3 James Swanson, *Dictionary of Biblical Languages with Semantic Domains: Greek* (New Testament) (Oak Harbor: Logos Research Systems, Inc., 1997).

4 Rebecca van Noord, Jessi Strong; John D. Barry, *The Bible in the Real World: 31 Inspiring Interviews*, (Bellingham WA, Lexham Press, 2014), Logos Software Edition.

5 Many commentators believe Peter is referencing to the descent of Jesus' Spirit into Hades between His death and resurrection to offer people who lived before the Flood a second chance of salvation.

CHAPTER TEN: TWO SIGNS IN SOCIETY

1 Chuck Colson and Nancy Pearcey, *How Now Shall We Live*, (Carol Springs, IL: Tyndale House Publishers 1999), eBook edition.

2 Merrill F. Unger, *Unger's Commentary on the Old Testament* (Chattanooga, TN: AMG Publishers, 2002), Jer. 50:23.

3 Dr. David Jeremiah with C.C. Carlson, *The Handwriting on the Wall: Secrets from the Prophecies of Daniel*, (Nashville, TN: W Publishing Group an imprint of Thomas Nelson, 2019), 95.

4 Anne Graham Lotz, *The Vision of His Glory*, (Nashville, TN: Thomas Nelson Publishers, 1996, 1997, 2009), 113.

5 James Swanson, *Dictionary of Biblical Languages with Semantic Domains: Greek* (New Testament) (Oak Harbor: Logos Research Systems, Inc., 1997).

6 William Hendriksen and Simon J. Kistemaker, *Exposition of Paul's Epistle to the Romans, vol. 12–13, New Testament Commentary* (Grand Rapids: Baker Book House, 1953–2001), 71.

7 William D. Mounce, General Editor, *Mounce's Complete Expository Dictionary of Old & New Testament Words*, (Grand Rapids, MI: Zondervan, 2006), Logos Bible Software Edition.

8 William D. Mounce, *Mounce's Complete Expository Dictionary of Old & New Testament Words* (Grand Rapids, MI: Zondervan, 2006), Logos Bible Software Edition.

9 Vine, Ungar, White, *Vine's Complete Expository Dictionary of Old and New Testament Words*, (Nashville, TN: Thomas Nelson Publishers, 1985), 527.

10 William Barclay, ed., *The Letter to the Romans, The Daily Study Bible Series* (Philadelphia: The Westminster John Knox Press, 1975), 33.

11 https://www.christianheadlines.com/contributors/scott-slayton/inspiring -quotes-about-faith-and-the-bible-from-us-presidents.html.

12 *Yada* is used in this context in several verses: Genesis 24:16; 38:26; 1 Sam. 1:19; Judges 19:25; and Judges 11:39 to cite a few.

13 https://www.biblehuBCom/hebrew/3045.htm.

14 Bruce K. Waltke, "350 הָלַל," ed. R. Laird Harris, Gleason L. Archer Jr., and Bruce K. Waltke, *Theological Wordbook of the Old Testament* (Chicago: Moody Press, 1999), 161.

15 Dr. Rabbi David Frankel. https://www.thetorah.com/article/noah-ham-and-the-curse-of-canaan-who -did-what-to-whom-in-the-tent.

16 https://biblearchaeology.org/research/patriarchal-era/2364-the-discovery -of-the-sin-cities-of-sodom-and-gomorrah.

17 https://thenewamerican.com/obama-america-not-a-christian-nation/.

18 James Montgomery Boice, *Genesis: An Expositional Commentary* (Grand Rapids, MI: Baker Books, 1998), 623.

19 The phrases "conversion therapy" and "reparative therapy" refer to discredited psychotherapy methods that aim to change a person's sexual orientation or gender identity. https://www.nytimes.com/2016/11/30/us /politics/mike-pence-and-conversion-therapy-a-history.html.

20 Boice, *Genesis: An Expositional Commentary*, 623.

CHAPTER ELEVEN: THE SIN OF PROVOCATION

1 Porter Barrington, "The Christian Life Study Outlines and Notes", *The Open Bible*, (Nashville, TN: Thomas Nelson NASB Edition, 1976, 1978), 903.

2 Charles Williams, *The Sacrifice of Christ: An Inquiring into the Fact and the Doctrine of Christian Atonement*, (London: Simpkin, Marshall & Co., 1858), 180.

3 Merrill F. Unger, William White, Jr. *Nelson's Expository Dictionary of the Old Testament*, (Nashville, TN: Thomas Nelson Publishers, 1985), 182.

4 https://blogs.blueletterbible.org/blb/2012/08/28/the-names-of-god-qanna/

5 William Barclay, *The Ten Commandments: Pocket Guide*, (Louisville, KY: Westminster John Knox Press, 2001), 4.

6 Mordecai was a cousin of Esther, whom he adopted as his daughter.

7 James Cross Giblin, *The Life and Death of Adolph Hitler*, (New York: Clarion Books, 2002), 213.

8 https://www.jewishvirtuallibrary.org/jewish-population-of-the-world

9 Witness Lee, *Life Study: Colossians*, (Anaheim, CA: Living Stream Ministry, 2011), eBook edition.

10 Summarized from: David Horowitz, *Dark Agenda: The War to Destroy Christian America*, (West Palm Beach, FL: Humanix Books, 2018), various pages.

11 Allison A. Trites, "Saints," ed. David Noel Freedman, Allen C. Myers, and Astrid B. Beck, *Eerdmans Dictionary of the Bible* (Grand Rapids, MI: W.B. Eerdmans, 2000), 1151–1152.

12 M. G. Easton, *Easton's Bible Dictionary* (New York: Harper & Brothers,

1893).

13 Paul J. Achtemeier, Harper & Row and Society of Biblical Literature, *Harper's Bible Dictionary* (San Francisco: Harper & Row, 1985), 892.

14 https://www.lifenews.com/2020/01/10/61628584-babies-have-been -killed-in-abortions-since-roe-v-wade-in-1973/.

CHAPTER TWELVE: THE HOUR THAT CHANGES EVERYTHING

1 https://www.jewishpress.com/indepth/opinions/why-harry-s-truman -recognized-the-state-of-israel/2020/03/10/.

2 Henry M. Morris, *The Revelation Record: A Scientific and Devotional Commentary on the Prophetic book of the End Times*, (Co-published by Tyndale House Publishers (Wheaton, IL),and Creation-Life Publishers (San Diego, CA), 1983), 109.

3 Dean Sherman, with Bill Payne.

4 Jon Courson, *Jon Courson's Application Commentary: Volume Two: Psalms-Malachi* (Nashville, TN: Thomas Nelson, 2006), 675.

5 Commentators differ on the precise location of these offspring of Noah. "Dr. Jack Van Impe believes [as did C.I. Schofield and Mark Hitchcock] that each of these names can be located within present-day Russia. Meshech is referred as Moscow and Tubal located within present-day Russia. . . Joel Richardson states that he believes they are all in Asia Minor or modern day Turkey." Canes Iclophat, Before the Final Judgment, (Xlibris Corp.), eBook edition.

6 Walter A. Elwell and Barry J. Beitzel, "Persia, Persians," *Baker Encyclopedia of the Bible* (Grand Rapids, MI: Baker Book House, 1988), 1648–1649.

7 Courson, *Jon Courson's Application Commentary: Volume Two: Psalms-Malachi*, 675.

8 Merrill F. Unger, William White, Jr. *Nelson's Expository Dictionary of the Old Testament*, (Nashville, TN: 1985), 218.

9 Dennis Ross and David Makovsky, *Myths, Illusions, and Peace: Finding a New Direction for America in the Middle East*, (New York: Viking, Published by the Penguin Group, 2009), eBook edition.

10 Lloyd R. Bailey, "Ararat (Place)," ed. David Noel Freedman, *The Anchor Yale Bible Dictionary* (New York: Doubleday, 1992), 351.

11 Ronald F. Youngblood, F. F. Bruce, and R. K. Harrison, Thomas Nelson Publishers, eds., *Nelson's New Illustrated Bible Dictionary* (Nashville, TN: Thomas Nelson, Inc., 1995). Logos Bible Software Edition.

12 Gerald M. Bilkes, "Medes, Media," ed. David Noel Freedman, Allen C. Myers, and Astrid B. Beck, *Eerdmans Dictionary of the Bible* (Grand Rapids, MI: W.B. Eerdmans, 2000), 877.

13 https://bible.ucg.org/bible-commentary/Jeremiah/Prophecy-against
-Babylon/.

14 https://www.cnbc.com/2018/12/05/here-is-how-many-nuclear-weapons
-us-and-russia-have.html.

15 https://nypost.com/2021/01/09/iran-is-pushing-for-more-appeasement
-from-joe-biden/.

CHAPTER THIRTEEN

1 https://www.politico.com/news/2020/04/10/soros-pumps-28-million
-democratic-groups-2020-179367.

2 https://www.amazon.ca/Takes-Village-Hillary-Rodham-Clinton
/dp/1416540644.

3 https://nationalpost.com/opinion/rex-murphy-the-great-reset-no-one
-asked-for.

4 https://www.whitehouse.gov/briefings-statements/abraham-accords
-peace-agreement-treaty-of-peace-diplomatic-relations-and-full
-normalization-between-the-united-arab-emir.

5 https://www.navalnews.com/naval-news/2020/05/russia-builds-up
-mediterranean-naval-force/.

6 https://www.navalnews.com/naval-news/2020/05/russia-builds-up
-mediterranean-naval-force/.

7 https://worldpopulationreview.com/country-rankings/countries-with
-nuclear-weapons.

8 "In a speech given at the outbreak of the Islamic Revolution in Iran in
1979, Ayatollah Khomeini referred to the United States as the 'Great Satan'
and to Israel as the 'Little Satan.'" Excerpted from: https://www.jerusalem
-herald.com/single-post/2017/07/06/great-satan-little-satan-if-the-shoe
-fits.

9 https://www.jpost.com/breaking-news/netanyahu-for-irans-mullahs
-israel-is-the-small-satan-and-american-is-the-great-satan-407742.

10 John is the only one of the apostles generally thought to have died a
natural death from old age.

11 James Swanson and Orville Nave, *New Nave's Topical Bible* (Oak Harbor:
Logos Research Systems, 1994).

12 Catherine Soanes and Angus Stevenson, eds., *Concise Oxford English
Dictionary* (Oxford: Oxford University Press, 2004).

13 *Merriam-Webster, Merriam-Webster's Collegiate Thesaurus* (Springfield,
MA: Merriam-Webster, 1996).

14 Catherine Soanes and Angus Stevenson, eds., *Concise Oxford English
Dictionary* (Oxford: Oxford University Press, 2004).

15 https://www.cs.ubc.ca/~knorr/public/comparison_of_eschat_models.pdf.

16 John D. Barry et al., eds., "Balance," *The Lexham Bible Dictionary* (Bellingham, WA: Lexham Press, 2016).

17 Eugene E. Carpenter and Philip W. Comfort, *Holman Treasury of Key Bible Words: 200 Greek and 200 Hebrew Words Defined and Explained* (Nashville, TN: Broadman & Holman Publishers, 2000), 382.

18 https://www.dailysabah.com/economy/2015/06/28/83-countries-went -bankrupt-in-200-years.

19 https://medium.com/the-capital/could-digital-currencies-replace-cash -in-the-future-a5fe32e5c4fb.

20 https://www.nerdwallet.com/article/investing/cryptocurrency-7-things -to-know.

21 https://www.richardvanhooijdonk.com/blog/en/human-microchipping -the-benefits-and-downsides/.

22 https://www.thomasnet.com/insights/the-future-of-microchip-implants -in-humans/.

23 https://www.nrlc.org/uploads/communications/stateofabortion2018.pdf.

ProphecyUSA.org